THE GAMESMASTER

FLINT DILLE

THE GAMESMASTER

ALMOST FAMOUS IN THE GEEK '80s

Rare Bird Books
Los Angeles, Calif.

THIS IS A GENUINE RARE BIRD BOOK

Rare Bird Books
453 South Spring Street, Suite 302
Los Angeles, CA 90013
rarebirdbooks.com

FIRST HARDCOVER EDITION

Set in Dante
Printed in the United States

10 9 8 7 6 5 4 3 2 1

Library of Congress Cataloging-in-Publication Data

Names: Dille, Flint, author.
Title: The Gamesmaster: Almost Famous in '80s Geek World / Flint Dille.
Description: Los Angeles, CA : Rare Bird Books, 2020. |
Includes bibliographical references.
Identifiers: LCCN 2019051700 | ISBN 9781644280126 (hardback)
Subjects: LCSH: Dille, Flint. | Video games—Design. | Motion pictures—
United State—20th century—Anecdotes. | Video game designers—
United States—Biography. | Screenwriters—United States—Biography.
Classification: LCC GV1469.3 D54 2020 | DDC 794.8--dc23
LC record available at https://lccn.loc.gov/2019051700

A Fascinating Collision in Geek Culture History

IT WAS SOMETIME IN the spring of 1985. Steve Gerber sat across the table from me in the conference room at the Sunbow office in Westwood. We'd been there long enough to stop noticing the traffic outside. We both smoked cigarettes and had scripts in front of us. Mine still had the perforation stubs on the side because it was printed on my daisy wheel printer. His was Xeroxed. We were working on the central scene of what would become *Transformers: The Movie*. Namely, we were trying to figure out how to kill Optimus Prime, mortally wound Megatron, and leave Hot Rod a little bit responsible for the death.

Prime, of course, couldn't lose. Megatron had to kill him through treachery. The bones of the scene were there and had been since the beginning. This was all about fitting together the nuances, the details.

Steve wasn't really on *Transformers*, he was on *G.I. Joe*, but we all helped out in a pinch. He was arguably the best story editor in the business, and animation writing was his second career. He'd already had an epic comic career, creating Howard the Duck and writing God knows how many comics before coming to LA and getting into animation. He and Joe Ruby had created *Thundarr the Barbarian*. He didn't have a lot of time. A friend of his from New York who'd just moved to LA was coming for lunch.

So we were reading the scene, imitating bad actor voices for the characters. I'd sketched the geography of the scene in stick figures because I was the only person in the animation business who couldn't draw—except for maybe Steve. We were laughing, having fun. Neither of us had any idea that the scene we'd been working on would scar a generation of kids, or that thirty years later I'd be doing an interview for the Blu-Ray disk edition of *Transformers: The Movie*.

Hildy Mesnik stepped into the room. "Your lunch meeting is here…"

"Send him in," Steve said. "Flint should meet him."

A minute later, a guy with an ammo bag came walking in. He had long hair, but he didn't seem like a hippie. He was something different. Intense. Focused. He reminded me of John Lennon. We told him what we were working on, and it turned out he had a problem too. He was working on a Batman graphic novel. I wasn't really sure what a graphic novel was. Unlike Steve or Marty Pasko or Buzz Dixon or Roger Slifer, I wasn't really a comic book guy. I'd read the usual comics when I was a kid and took the DC side of the Marvel vs. DC argument of the late sixties, but I'd stopped reading comics sometime around junior high, and except for occasionally wandering into the comic shop near UC Berkeley, I hadn't thought about comics again until I met these guys.

His problem was a fight between Batman and Superman. Didn't seem like much of a problem to me. Unless Batman had some kryptonite, it was game over. It was probably game over even if he did have kryptonite, as Superman could fly really fast and turn back time, or he had freeze breath or heat vision or could punch Batman all the way to Mars if he wanted to. World's Finest didn't make any sense to me. Batman was smarter, arguably, but sometimes Superman had a super brain, too, so even that wasn't certain.

They were patient with me, explaining that Superman was more like the Fleisher Superman (I only vaguely knew what that was) or like George Reeves in the TV show, not like Christopher Reeve in the movies. I could sort of see that, though George Reeves versus Adam West still didn't seem like much of a fight. But I just listened. After all, I was writing a scene in which a robotic Walther PPK was fighting a semi-trailer truck and they were the same size in the scene, so it wasn't like I had the logical high ground.

Anyway, we worked out an elaborate scene. Batman had prepped the battlefield. He'd rigged bombs in a building. I didn't think bombs would hurt Superman, but I was told, "They'll keep him busy."

It was a good enough answer.

We moved over to our scene. I said I wanted Optimus's death to feel like Davy Crockett's death in the John Wayne version of *The Alamo*. I'd seen that movie when I was five, and it became the centerpiece of my early childhood.

Steve's friend hadn't seen *The Alamo*. Instead, the movie that inspired him the same way when he was a kid was called *The 300 Spartans*. And by now you've probably figured out that the guy was Frank Miller and that the Batman comic book he was talking about was the fourth installment of *The Dark Knight Returns*.

I've told this story a lot of times to a lot of people for a wide variety of reasons. Transformers fans love hearing about how *Transformers: The Movie* was created. I talk about it in lectures at the USC film school, because that scene is about something a lot bigger than Frank or Steve or I, or even Transformers and Batman. To me, it's about the incredible burst of creativity that happened in the eighties and in other golden (okay, or silver, or platinum) ages.

Introduction

THIS IS A STORY about being in the right place at the right time. It was the mid-eighties, one of those golden eras in my life that violated probability. A magical period when there are so many coincidences, serendipitous events, and unique and improbable people that the normal rules of life seem to have been suspended.

For me, it was having an all-access pass to the geek eighties and working with an amazing collection of people who laid the foundations for what would be popular culture decades later.

So, yeah, it's a memoir—but it's also about something a lot bigger than I.

It will never be 1985 again, but it would sure be great if we could drag some of 1985 into the 2020s. Lord knows we could use the fun. So somewhere in here is a piece about a golden age, and how—hopefully—to inspire another one.

While I believe everything in this book is the truth, the reality is that I function more like a fictional character in this book than an actual person. It even feels fictional as I write it down, but everything you'll read here would pass a polygraph, and most of it has corroborating witnesses.

As this is being written as a memoir and delivered in the linear form of a book, it is almost impossible for me not to turn chaotic, random events into a narrative. That is how the brain works, and it's also why memory is tricky. Because we all know that the real world is not linear. It is non-linear, chaotic, uncoupled and coupled at the same time, and at best all we are working with is a very limited data set. Some of it has been forgotten, some of it is unknowable, and some of it is hidden. That's how life works.

We make narratives and tell ourselves stories, literally, to make sense of the world.

So, on one level, this book is one big wild adventure.

On another level, though, it is about the process of going from being a complete noob to being a seasoned writer headed for the next challenge. It's about learning the tricks of the trade from masters, and then having to use those tricks all alone in front of a blank page. It's about success and failure—I mean really big, embarrassing failure. And then more success and even worse failure. Rinse and repeat. It even ends with simultaneous triumph and disaster—Kipling's old impostors. But they sure feel real when they're happening to you.

When asked, we all work out a narrative, an "elevator pitch" as to how it happened, but that's just a story. It is always more complex than that, and this book is about some of that complexity. It is wins and losses and respawns and power-ups in the great game of life. There's good luck and bad luck. To some extent, it's what you do with the wins and losses. For me, it started with *Mister T*, went to *Droids* and Lucasfilm, then to *G.I. Joe, Transformers, Bigfoot and the Muscle Machines, Inhumanoids, Agent 13, Visionaries, Sagard*, and literally ended in the trash can with *Garbage Pail Kids*. Then, suddenly and unexpectedly, a whole new era began. Interestingly, as I started this book, writing from a Google Doc I'd compiled of various interviews— three decades and several eras later—I was creative lead at a company called Niantic Labs, and we were a startup about to release a make-or-break new game called *Pokémon Go*.

The curious thing about this journey is that it more or less follows what Joseph Campbell called "the hero's journey." It's been parsed a hundred different ways, and I'll give you one more. But when I refer to it, this is what I'm referencing.

The Joseph Campbell Heroic Template

1. Heroes are introduced in the ORDINARY WORLD, where
2. they receive a CALL TO ADVENTURE.
3. They are RELUCTANT at first or REFUSE THE CALL but
4. are ENCOURAGED BY A MENTOR to

5. CROSS THE FIRST THRESHOLD and enter the Special World where

6. they encounter TESTS, ALLIES, and ENEMIES and find their Hidden Lair (Sanctus Sanctorum).

7. They approach the INMOST CAVE (Belly of the Beast), crossing a SECOND THRESHOLD

8. where they endure an ORDEAL.

9. They take possession of their REWARD and

10. are PURSUED on THE ROAD BACK to the Ordinary World.

11. They cross a THIRD THRESHOLD, experience a RESURRECTION, and are transformed by their experience.

12. They RETURN WITH THE ELIXIR, a boon or treasure to benefit the Ordinary World.

You can decide whether I ended up a triumphant hero or a pile of bones, but all of the elements are there. And that whole concept is very fitting for this particular material because, near the dead center of this story, the real George Lucas handed me a copy of *The Hero with a Thousand Faces* (along with *The Uses of Enchantment: The Meaning and Importance of Fairy Tales* by Bruno Bettelheim). There are thresholds and guardians, allies and enemies, temptresses, goddesses, a road of trials, a few inmost caves, and the bellies of a few beasts.

The book is really about the elixir, which doesn't exactly come in a bottle so much as in the form of incredible life lessons from the extraordinary people I traveled this road with over thirty years ago. And while this is marketed as my story, it really isn't. I'm more a Zelig, or like Virgil in *The Inferno*, except we weren't in Hell.

Far from it.

This was a golden age, distant in some ways and present in others.

The world isn't much like it was in 1985, but even in 2019, *Transformers* and superhero movies rule the big screen, *Dungeons & Dragons* and paper RPGs are having a huge comeback, and, in fact, I'd argue that in many ways, the late teens of the twenty-first century are getting to look more and more like a reflection of the mid-eighties. As Mick Jagger said when he played the Hollywood Bowl for the first time since 1966, "Everything has changed except the playlist."

So, like any good myth, we'll start in the place where I was living when this whole adventure started—the "ordinary world," as Campbell would call it.

Hollywood As It Was When I Got Here

(Summer 1976–1982)

MY FIRST REAL EXPOSURE to Hollywood came after my junior year at Berkeley, in the summer of 1976, when I drove down to Los Angeles for six weeks for the USC/Universal Summer Cinema Program. I was heading into my senior year and had no idea what I wanted to do with my life. In high school, I'd figured I was going into the movie business, but when I chose Berkeley over USC, I put that on hold. After all, USC had the *best* film department, and Berkeley had *no* film department.

Anyway, the USC/Universal Summer Cinema Program ended up as something of a bust for me. I got a sinus infection and didn't initially take to LA. I made two terrible films, showed no talent, and secured zero contacts in the industry. In fact, I remember almost nobody from the experience, and none of them resurfaced in my life ever again.

That said, it did condition me for what was to come and give me a great base of Hollywood knowledge. What was great about it was that we spent a third of our day in production, a third of our day in criticism classes, and the other third at Universal Studios. It all added up to an almost perfect view of Hollywood as it was, right on the eve of everything changing forever.

At Universal Studios, we met with a range of industry characters. Henry Bumstead, the legendary production designer, came and talked to us. Their veteran sound guy (whose name I've forgotten) gave one of the best illustrations of the use of music in films that I've ever seen. He projected a sequence with a guy pulling up to a house in his car. He played suspenseful music, and it seemed like a murder was about to happen. He played floozie music, and we figured the woman was of low repute, and then he played romantic music, and it felt like a romance. I never undervalued soundtrack after that.

One executive told us a story about when MCA bought Universal Studios. He was at MCA, and Universal apparently believed it was really a merger. This guy's job was to let the Universal guy know it was a takeover, and so he sent a construction crew over to the office area where the Universal executive was and started jackhammering the steps to his office. Somehow that ended the power struggle. MCA was in charge. I'm butchering that story, but that's the gist—in the end, some bold tactical maneuver answered a deep corporate question.

It was also a story about how the world worked in the last of the Wild West days of Hollywood. Don't like your opponent? Bulldoze his office. Today you'd probably be cited for not doing an environmental impact report and run into fifty other problems, but in the old days, boldness paid off. Or maybe it was just a literal example of "move fast and break things."

Even though the story seems profoundly "anus-esque," it was also pretty amusing. I left with the impression that the industry was a whole lot of fun back then if you knew how the game worked and were willing to play.

On a lighter note, Edith Head came and talked to us. She didn't have any good demolition stories, but she talked about costuming Doris Day and how "that was really all her." I took that as a reference to Doris Day's figure but wasn't sure. Doris Day was somebody I remembered from my childhood. It seemed like an old reference; it added to that creaky feeling of the movie industry. It didn't seem to be about what was happening right now.

Hollywood had gone through one major shift a decade earlier. After *Easy Rider*, nobody wanted to see an old-style Hollywood movie again. Everything changes after a paradigm shift. As one executive said, "Every young guy with a beard got to direct." This of course meant Francis Coppola, Martin Scorsese, Steven Spielberg, George Lucas, John Milius, and on and on and on. New people arrive and the old are gornished.

That summer, Universal screened upcoming movies for us. There are few better feelings in the world than sitting in a studio screening room and seeing a movie before it was released. We even saw some before they were final, which really made us feel like Hollywood insiders long before there was a show with that name. There's no way to overstate how cool and special people felt when they got a peek at the fame and glamour of Hollywood in the seventies. Stars and directors had a real mystique back then due to rare public exposure and carefully manicured images. They were larger than life and extremely exotic, only seen at red carpet events or iconic appearances, and, of course, on celluloid.

That summer we saw *The Hindenburg*, *Family Plot* (Alfred Hitchcock's final film), *Car Wash*, *Midway*, and *Swashbuckler*, among others. Look at that list again. These were the products of an industry that didn't know what to do, or one that perhaps thought movies had hit "design exhaustion."[1] I'll leave it to film historians to decide whether *The Hindenburg* destroyed the disaster film, but despite a big cast and big special effects, the movie tanked. (I suspect that slow dirigibles are hard to pull off on film, but that's a different discussion.) The point is, if you look at the movie slate from 1976, it's the kind of slate you have when you're waiting for the next big thing to happen.

And it would.

Star Wars would come out less than a year later. And that's relevant, because you can't understand the eighties without understanding *Star Wars*. This time it was Alan Ladd Jr. and Fox. It seems they put the last quarter in the slot machine and came up with a jackpot. And, just to put a button on Universal, George Lucas had pitched *Star Wars* to them and they'd rejected it. The legend is that Frank Price told George Lucas to take his robots and split.

So that was the Joseph Campbell "Ordinary World." And even though *Star Wars* would change everything a year later, the world doesn't morph that fast. Much of the old world would still be hanging around by the time I got to LA to obtain my master's degree in film at USC between 1979 and 1981.

Kid Dropped in from the Twenty-Fifth Century

FROM AN EARLY AGE, I had a very interesting relationship with the worlds of fantasy and science fiction. I grew up in a suburb of Chicago in a house that

---

1   Anthropological term for when you can go no further. For instance, a heel on a shoe can only be so high before it is no longer a heel and nobody can walk on it.

looked like a smaller Wayne Manor and a dad who collected antique cars and whose own father was the originator of Buck Rogers. This fact is going to become very relevant to this story from here on out. For those of you who don't know, Buck Rogers began as a comic strip in 1929. It was based on a novella or short story called "Armageddon 2419." My grandfather owned a newspaper syndicate called the John F. Dille company (you'll find those words in the corner of every early Buck Rogers comic strip). We had various Buck Rogers artifacts around the house, ranging from old rocket ships to ray guns to solar maps and stand-ups. My dad still owned the newspaper syndicate, which owned the rights to Buck Rogers, and every now and again people would try to make it into a television show.

The extrinsics of my life can pretty much be described in sixties sitcom terms. My father reminded me of Dick Van Dyke in *The Dick Van Dyke Show*. My mother was more Donna Reed than Laura Petrie. My sister was seven years older than me. My grandfather reminded me of James Arness in *Gunsmoke*, and my grandmother was a small jewel of a woman. We were the opposite of a dysfunctional family.

Dad had a Lincoln Continental Town Car that looked like both the Batmobile and the Black Beauty if you caught it from the right angle. He had a Silver Cloud I that looked exactly like Amos Burke's Rolls in *Burke's Law* and a Bentley R Type the same color and model as the one on the front of Delaney & Bonnie's *On Tour with Eric Clapton*. Dad's office building was in the Civic Opera Building, which looked exactly like the building I imagined Thomas and Martha Wayne visited before they were killed in Crime Alley. We went to a lot of car shows, and thus none of the cars I'd see in James Bond movies or *The Great Race* were particularly alien to me.

But all of this gives a much more lavish and outsized version of my childhood than it should. We were what was known as "comfortable." The town I grew up in was called Glenview, and it bore a great similarity to every Riverdale from *Archie*, with bits and pieces of the Hardy Boys and later *Risky Business*, along with just about any John Hughes film. It was Chicago. We played baseball in the summer, football in the fall. We threw snowballs in the Siberian winter and could really feel the first day of spring.

For what it matters, I was an undersized dyslexic kid with mixed dominance (neither side of my brain was dominant) who had to be in a special "Gillingham method" reading class with Mrs. Kratz at North Shore Country Day School in Winnetka, Illinois. I knew there was something wrong from all the whispers and poorly veiled euphemisms, but I couldn't quite figure out whether I was "retarded," like my friend Skipper down the street, or whether it was more of a minor glitch.

Other than various learning difficulties, I functioned more or less normally. I was good at games. In fact, the only reason I was able to watch the first generation of *Star Trek* and *Batman* in color was that Andy Baldwin, our neighborhood "brain," would call me up to play chess, and I'd drag the games out in order to watch the shows. So I figured I wasn't stupid—not if I could play chess with Andy Baldwin. I planned it so I'd win just over half the time. If he won too much, I'd be boring. If I won too much, I'd be frustrating. It was my first experience in life with "play balance."

The two most influential movies of my childhood were John Wayne's *The Alamo*, which I saw when I was almost five, and *Goldfinger*, which came out when I was nine. Those two, and films like them, would have a profound impact on the work I did, especially early on.

So I had a semi-normal Midwestern childhood. Unlike most of my friends and colleagues from the Sunbow era, there was little about my childhood that suggested I'd spend most of my adult life in sci-fi or fantasy (leave Buck Rogers out of this for a moment). I read the normal amount of comic books and loved *Mad Magazine*. Because of my reading problems, my parents would buy me just about anything if they thought I'd read it.

When I was in sixth grade, the big fight was over whether Marvel or DC was better. We'd have endless debates about Batman versus Spider-Man, or Aquaman versus Namor, or Thor versus Superman. I was conflicted. I sided in almost all cases with Batman and thought Peter Parker was a wiener, but at the same time I never voluntarily missed an episode of the *Spider-Man* cartoon, and the DC animated shows seemed lame to me. My favorite animated shows were probably the really early Marvel ones, which almost weren't animated at all.

Sixth grade was my ultimate year for kid geekdom. Friday night in 1966 might also have been the best night ever for television. It started with *The Green Hornet*. The parting kissers. The Black Beauty, which really looked like it might be able to patrol the slicked back-lot streets, the sting. The trench coat. I loved the feel of it. More than anything, I think I loved what the show could have been more than what it really was. Oh, yeah, and "The Flight of the Bumblebee." And the drone that came out of the back of the Black Beauty. The cars spinning around in the garage. The buzz of the Hornet Sting. It felt like there really could be a superhero, or at least a vigilante, in that world. After *The Green Hornet* came *The Time Tunnel*, then *The Man from U.N.C.L.E.* or *The Wild Wild West*, then *T.H.E. Cat*.

After sixth grade, my mother sent me to summer school at the local junior high to study chemistry (I wanted to be a scientist) and typing. Little did we know how valuable that would be. But another thing happened. All of a sudden, I was surrounded by hundreds of kids, including some I knew from the neighborhood. It was like the world was in color. I told Mom I wanted to go to Glenview Junior High. It was a much-needed fresh start.

With the fresh start, all geek stuff got washed away.

I joined the Boy Scouts and went to camp. I got into the best class, and many of the people in that class remain friends to this day: Dave Lawton, Judy Eich, Shannon Clements, and Linda Christiansen, until her passing.

I went to Glenbrook South High School in the fall of 1969, as *Abbey Road* was being released, and started a band with Mike Weirich, Scott Selbe, Paul Lange, and Doug Matthews. While I was probably the most incompetent person ever to play and sing in a band, we got enough gigs that it was a fun experience, and writing songs was one of the first publicly creative things I ever did.

For reasons that are difficult to understand, English teachers and writing teachers tended to hate me, and other than being in a couple of plays and getting good results in film class, I in no way distinguished myself. My grades were terrible—mostly my initials—until I got scared and turned it around senior year and slithered into UC Berkeley on the strength of my SAT scores. I'd also been accepted at USC and would eventually go to grad school there, but in the spring of 1973, Berkeley just sounded cooler, so I went and majored in ancient history and classical rhetoric. After a depressing first year in an all-male dorm, I joined a frat and eventually became pledge trainer and president. Life doesn't get better than those years.

Setting: The Eighties and the Monoverse

LET'S STOP FOR A moment to talk about the eighties and the "monoverse." I learned that term at Wyrd Con 2016, in the mediascape during a Q&A session. I'm not sure where it came from, but I like it. The monoverse is a way of describing the shared reality of the media universe before VCR and cable, when most of the country had three networks, a local station, a PBS station, and maybe some UHF stations. That's if you were lucky and lived near a major market. Most cities had two papers. Every week, *Time* and *Newsweek* came out with a summary of what was happening in the world, and the television news ran at six and eleven, with local right before or right after.

VCRs didn't infiltrate homes in a significant way until the late seventies or early eighties, and if you missed a show, you missed it until reruns aired in the summer. (I waited decades to see the end of *The Man from U.N.C.L.E.* episode "Alexander the Greater Affair," in which Illya was about to be cut in half with a pendulum and Napoleon Solo was over a pit.)

Then there were *Life* and *Look*, magazines that served as a window to the rest of the world through photojournalism at its best. This was an age where a single image encapsulated an event or an era—the girl hovering over the dead body at Kent State, the girl running down the street with napalm on her, the ubiquitous shot of Earth from space, the moon landing. The unimaginable decadence and luxury of the Cannes Film Festival. Swinging London in a few shots of miniskirts and bell bottoms. The see-through shirt. It would be impossible to encapsulate that era without *Life* and *Look*.

Now, everybody has a video camera and everybody looks at fifty images a day on a slow day, and it is hard for any shot to make an impact. We have more, but less of it sticks. Back then, a single image—almost always without some pompous quote attached to it, telling you what to think about it—could steer an entire civilization. Mario Cuomo, legendary governor of New York, said something fascinating about his generation (the greatest generation) that I suspect is even more true now: "We knew less then, but we understood more."

Politically, all three networks lived in the same universe. There might have been nuances of difference as to what they thought was and was not important, and there was some carefully calculated bias, but by and large we perceived whatever Walter Cronkite or David Brinkley was saying as pure, unadulterated truth. The daily papers all seemed to share similar facts and opinions, and editorials were kept on the editorial page.

The film industry was similarly organized. There were six and a half studios (Disney was its own thing), and there was some low-budget stuff dominated by Roger Corman and a few others, usually "B" pictures and/or garish sci-fi or horror. *Easy Rider* created the "youth movie" in 1969, but the monoverse was largely unfazed. The studios would adapt and survive in the seventies and go through what many would perceive as the golden age of film with a spate of young directors—some of whom are still relevant today.

For film, the monoverse was a small, well-defended universe rife with gatekeepers and moats. Only studios had the equipment to make and distribute movies—except for the small, scruffy, independent counterculture world of drive-ins and dying theaters, which either went "B" movie or "X" movie.

The monoverse didn't die in a day. And some parts of it are still standing. There are still studios and networks, and there's still *The New York Times*, but they are shadows of their former selves and exist more as brands than omnipotent entities. In the seventies and eighties, cracks started to form in the monoverse—Xerox machines would create fanzines, Super-8 would spawn a generation of filmmakers, smaller and cheaper cameras would challenge photojournalism. Syndicated television and toy shows were other cracks. It might have been the first time the networks were really challenged.

Another of those cracks was video games. They evolved heavily during the exact period that is covered in this book. As the book starts, we're in *Space Invaders* and *Asteroids* world. Video games were played in arcades and 7-Elevens and bars, occupying much the same cultural space as pinball machines. Not long after, we had *Galaga* and *Pac-Man*. I never worked on a video game animated show, but there were a lot of them. From the point of view of the monoverse, they were in the same category as comic books and cartoons—which meant they were not taken very seriously.

However, when the Atari 2600 and Mattel's Intellivision were released, they actually competed with networks and cable for the television set itself, although the monoverse mostly dismissed them as toys for kids and drunks.

The Coleco Adam, which would ship with *Buck Rogers: Planet of Zoom*, was forecast to be a threat because it also moved the home computer to the television screen, but for technical and business reasons, it failed and offered the monoverse a reprieve. But they should have seen the handwriting on the wall.

At that moment, nobody but geeks were paying attention to role-playing games, with the exception of CBS, which did a children's version of *Dungeons & Dragons* on Saturday morning. Again, the handwriting was on the wall. An entire generation was being trained by games, and that generation would change entertainment forever.

But for the moment, games were novelties to be licensed and exploited by traditional mediums. They weren't viewed as anything more than that—at least not yet.

Setting the Stage

My "Ordinary World"

"I'M TWENTY-SEVEN YEARS OLD and I haven't done anything."

That would be my first thought as I woke up and smoked my first cigarette, and it would recur during pretty much every dead spot of the day.

And if it happened to slip my mind, there was always someone around to remind me. It would come a number of ways—sometimes cruelly, sometimes as a reality check or mini intervention, and sometimes as a preposterous job suggestion ("Have you thought about working at a bank?")—but it never left my mind. Thinking back, I'm not sure whether it was a motivator or whether it just caused paralysis.

Those years are what I would refer to as my "Hollywood Guerrilla" period. It plays in my mind as a montage of snipe hunts, false starts, Risk games, moves around different parts of Westwood, a series of girlfriends (most ending badly; life ain't easy when you feel like a loser), and an array of amusing characters. I won a screenwriting contest, but nothing really came of it. I wrote more scripts and I got an agent, but he never sold anything. I went on various adventures with John Phillips as he parlayed his "A-Bomb Kid" status into two congressional runs (more on that later). I was an incompetent PA and realized I was a writer, was constantly frustrated with Buck Rogers (again: more later), and so on. I finished a novel called *Fratricide*, sent out a hundred query letters that led to some near misses, but in the end it wasn't published and is still sitting on my shelf. About every five years or so, I think I should polish it up and self-publish for the frat bros, but everybody from Sarah Knapp (my college girlfriend, who eventually became an editor) to my son tells me it's crap and not to do it. So it sits.

That era was a blur of reading scripts for David Hemmings at Hemdale, where I got to read a script for *Eve and that Damned Apple*, which was supposed to be Bo Derek's follow-up to *10*, but I never met her. I did run into Jim Cameron and Gail Anne Hurd, who recognized me from *Battle Beyond the Stars*. It had only been a couple of years, but it seemed like centuries. They were working on a film that would grow up to be *The Terminator*. At one point, I had an urgent overnight read, and Isabel and Donna Daves (who will reappear in this saga) rushed me back to Hemmings, who was on the phone. He motioned me over, and I gave him the treatment. He smiled and started giving my comments to whoever was on the other end of the phone as if they were his.

I was simultaneously flattered, appalled, and amused. I'm not sure whether that word would be flapalled or apmused or maybe flapalmused, but there should be a word, because it is one you feel a lot on good days in the entertainment business.

I did a script reading audition for Jane Fonda of a script called *The Bodyguard* and learned a fascinating thing. The movie was later made with Kevin Costner and Whitney Houston, but this version was tuned for Jane Fonda. The lesson there was that you have to "tune" your scripts for the talent. It's really easy for a writer to be focused on their story and their characters and forget that this is a business, and if somebody of stature doesn't want to star in or direct your film, it is very unlikely that it will get made.

At the exact same moment, we were always pursuing snipe hunts. There was always a remote sucker with money whom you never exactly got to meet who wanted to make "low-budget horror" or some such. Some sucker chases were so bizarre that even I didn't go on them. Bill Winter was working with a couple guys who were trying to finance their film (or at least get seed money) by harvesting golf balls from water holes at golf clubs. I'm not making this up. They used to sneak into swank country clubs at night and fish out lost balls. Then tragedy struck when the LA Country Club buffed its fence and eventually production got shut down; then LA Country Club built a fence.

I have a theory that everybody has to look stupid sometimes. A lot of times, and all things considered, you're better off looking stupid when you are young, because looking stupid in your forties makes you look like you really *are* stupid.

A bunch of us went on silly entrepreneurial missions. John Phillips' project, the "Little Apple," was basically Waze without the GPS. It helped you calculate streets in Manhattan. That was followed up with the "Talking Anusascope" for proctologists or something. I'm not making that up. (It wasn't called an anusascope—but, still.) His girlfriend, Sarah Kershner, made an umbrella with a hand at the bottom of it. I still have a prototype. In a world where magical objects were appearing every week, it wasn't the most unnatural thing to want to make a magic object.

Anyway, my fool's errand was a thing called the ON TAPE (TM) VIDEOCASSETTE LOGBOOK, which was a VHS tape–sized book that people could use to log their videotapes so they didn't have to keep writing over the labels and spines of the tapes. Huge flop. I built prototypes and tried to sell them. They were a turd of a dead-end idea, but with the fifteen hundred dollars my parents lent me for this ridiculous product, I probably learned more than I would have from fifteen thousand dollars' worth of business classes. It was my first experience with prototypes, business plans, manufacturing, pricing, cold-calling, and "transitional technology."

In order to dignify the fact that we weren't accomplishing anything while years were falling off the calendar, we called ourselves Hollywood Guerrillas. The "we" of this was a shifting set of people that included Tony Cinciripini, Larry Leahy, Mike Hill, Bill Winter, Ted Chase, and various other folks. The idea was that when somebody got through a door, they'd "hook the others in." I'd get calls that somebody needed a PA or an assistant art director or something.

The high point of that career was pushing waves onto Lynda Carter's lips while they were lighting a Maybelline commercial. During the real shoot, the professional wave pusher came in and did it, but it was cool to be in a fake pool with Wonder Woman. Most of it involved moving things and trucks and renting lights from Mole Richardson and picking up odd props from odd places.

My brush with upcoming Hollywood greatness came when I got a splinter in my eye while working at Raleigh Studios. For some reason, when one eye is in distress, so is the other. As a result, I didn't see the guy who gave me a ride to the eye doctor—though he did an incredible job of talking me out of near panic. They got the thing out of my eye, and I was back at work in a couple hours, but I never knew who the guy was. I was too concerned about impending blindness to pay much attention to introductions.

Years later, Tony Cinciripini said, "You know who that was, right?"

"No idea."

"It was Kevin Costner."

I could probably do a whole book on the Hollywood Guerrilla Sucker Chase, and for what it's worth, one could make a great argument that this book is a sucker chase. But what's life without sucker chases?

Never *don't* go on snipe hunts. Snipes are real, and every once in a while, you find one. The thing I didn't know as the summer of 1982 was turning into fall was that I was on a launch pad, and the rocket was about to take off.

First Agent, Bushmills, and a Real Live Leprechaun

ONE DAY IN THE 2000s, shortly after reading Malcolm Gladwell's *The Tipping Point*, I was cooling my heels at Disney, waiting for a meeting on a new concept I'd sold them for an animated film. The project never went anywhere, but while I was waiting, I'd begun to make a list—not dissimilar to the link charts used by the CIA—in hopes of figuring out how I'd gotten to this fortunate point. A bunch of trails led back to Joey Thompson, one of the most fascinating people I've ever met.

If you want to try an interesting exercise, draw a link chart of how you got your job or met a significant friend: Who introduced you? Who invited you to the party where you met somebody? How did you meet the person who introduced you to the person who invited you? And so on. Usually, it is a complex chain of relationships and introductions, but as often as not, you notice that most of the paths lead back to a small and specific set of social connectors in your life.

I met Joey Thompson through a guy named Bob Mitchell, and I met Bob through Michael Douroux, and I met Michael Douroux after I got out of USC and was named "Dramatic Finalist" in the USC/MTM screenwriting contest. Bob Mitchell, who might remind you of Hagrid from *Harry Potter*, introduced me to Joey Thompson. He wasn't exactly clear on what Joey did—whether he was an agent or a manager or a producer—but he assured me that he was worth meeting. I figured Bob was slightly muddled or maybe even kidding, but I ended up working with Joey for years and never figured it out either. Part of that was the "blurriness" of Joey (some people are just blurry), and some of it was that Joey was a little bit ahead of his time and thought of himself as a "transmedia" entity a couple decades before anybody had heard the term.

Joey was simultaneously the most present and most mysterious person I'd ever met. He had a company known as Thompson/Starr, and for a long time I was never sure who Starr was, though eventually I gleaned that Starr was his daughter whom I met on several occasions. He had a Century City address, but I never saw the office. He seemed eccentric but was actually quite normal and rational. I could never figure out whether the eccentricity was a cover for his being very normal or if he superimposed normal on the eccentric.

If I were going to classify him as a mythological character, it would be a leprechaun. Joey drove an aging Triumph Spitfire that he kept in good shape. Coincidentally, he also kept himself in good shape. He dressed in a slightly European manner, and his motto was "smell roses," which was his shorthand for "stop and smell the roses along the way." He spoke in shorthand and adjusted his sweater a lot, like he'd gone to some school where you had to wear a uniform and it was inspected all the time. Everything about Joey seemed like he was some English aristocrat who found himself in Hollywood by accident, though the truth, and he was very open about this, was that he was from Chicago, he was a hardcore Bears fan, and he loved Old Town, Chicago beer, and everything Midwestern. He also took care of an ailing brother who was nothing like him at all. I never detected any subterfuge in him. He was extremely amusing, but many of the people we dealt with had no idea what to make of him.

Part of the problem was that Joey spoke so quickly that it was hard to process what he was saying. He seemed to have an accent, but it wasn't an accent; he just spoke in musical cadences. He didn't exactly mumble, but it was often hard to track what he was saying. Bob Mitchell, who I think viewed the world as animated, said his words seemed to fall out of his mouth and curl around on the ground and rise again like smoke.

Our first adventure together was licensing a Buck Rogers game to Sega Entertainment. The game was called *Buck Rogers: Planet of Zoom*. We made the deal with Sega in November of 1982, somewhere around my twenty-seventh birthday. They paid something like two hundred thousand dollars to slap Buck Rogers on a preexisting game called Zoom 909. I'd seen license slaps before and understood them, and I thought it was great to get Buck Rogers back on the field after the cancellation of the Universal show.

In a karmic way, it was great to feel like I was reimbursing my parents for the years of freeform academic and life subsidy. It was a welcome shot of good news, as my parents were dealing with a relapse of my father's cancer. My mother and I went down for the signing and had lunch with Dave Rosen, head of Sega, and it felt, in some way, like my career was taking off.

We were right where we wanted to be. It would be an arcade game and a launch title for the Coleco Adam, which was their follow-up platform to the hit ColecoVision. The Adam, forgotten by all but hardcore geeks, was an incredibly ambitious adventure. The Adam was designed as a "disruptive" game machine and personal computer with a printer. If you remember this in the context of a world where most families did not have a personal or home computer, it was a great idea.

So we were on a rocket ride in more ways than one.

And I was about to get a fundamental lesson in the tech and entertainment industries. As we left for the Arcade Owners Game Convention (I can't remember the real name or location) in Chicago, Illinois, in 1982, we were right there with Zaxxon, Pengo, a new Pac-Man, and numerous other games.

But there was something wrong.

Even I could feel that something was wrong. The bottom had dropped out of the arcade industry. Everything was moving to home machines, which had gotten a lot better. The game appeared at my local arcade, but already the first few arcades were going out of business. It didn't sell that well, but we were still queued up for the Adam.

The Adam bombed due mostly to manufacturing problems. I never got one. But I learned about the business cycle. Boom towns go bust. You have to surf trends, but they always crash. Well, almost always. This would happen over and over. Boom. Bust. Sometimes the busts die. Sometimes they boom all over again.

But all of this happened over time, and there was a moment after the signing and before the bust when everything was virtual platinum. And during that period, Joey Thompson started setting up meetings with people about Buck Rogers.

In the course of this, we met Charlie Lippencott, who was an executive at Columbia at the time. He'd been a publicist on *Westworld* and *Family Plot*, then the first *Star Wars, Alien*, and *Flash Gordon*. In other words, you could not genetically engineer somebody better to work with on *Buck Rogers*, so we began talking about a *Buck Rogers* movie, though we also wanted to pursue a television animation path (and a feature animation path).

Of course, at that moment, I knew nothing about animation and hadn't thought about it since watching *Spider-Man* in the sixth grade. That was about to change, however, as Joey would soon make another introduction that would change my life.

My Call to Adventure

AS I MENTIONED FROM THE jump, one of my not-so-secret goals for this book is to test my theory that epic fiction (or at least regular fiction) mirrors the patterns of real life writ large. I'm going with the Joseph Campbell model because it is the most well-known and the most specific at my disposal right now. So after we get done with "The Ordinary World," we get "The Call to Adventure."

Did I get one? Yep.

In fact, I got two—almost simultaneously.

King Arthur's call to adventure started when somebody said, "Hey, there's this sword in a stone in the market square, let's go try and pull it out." Mine wasn't heralded by trumpets, nor did it promise magical swords— well, that's not entirely true; there were magical swords involved—but it came in the form of my agent, kind of a herald, asking me if I wanted to go to some meetings.

In the real world, calls are fairly mundane, and my advice is to learn to hear the calls when they come. Sometimes they're not nearly as loud as the invites to the latest snipe hunt. The trick is to make sure you answer them.

The next phase is, quite often, "Refusal of the Call," and I'll tell you right now that I didn't refuse the call, so we can flush that one, but suffice to say that in real life, refusal usually takes the form of "I'm too busy" or "I already have plans."

I was about to get two calls to adventure, and my life would not be the same now if I had refused either. In fairness, nobody would have. I think "Refusal of the Call" might be a literary invention.

Point is, when you hear a call to adventure, answer it—unless you really don't want an adventure.

Meeting a Wizard in a Medieval Tower in Anaheim

Summer 1982

ONE DAY JOEY SAID, "You want to go down and meet a fellow named Gary Gygax?"

Flash back to a couple years earlier, at the height of my "trying to figure out what I want to do with my life" era: I walked past a game store on Alvarado Street in Monterey, where they were selling D&D and Avalon Hill and SPI games, thinking, "If I could do anything with my life, I'd design games like this."

It turned out that a friend of Joey's from Chicago who'd worked at Sears for a number of years had just recently gone to TSR (the company that made *Dungeons & Dragons*), and he was going to be at the American Booksellers Association Convention, so Joey and I drove down to Anaheim on Saturday, May 29, 1982, to meet John Beebe. (Jump forward thirty years, and BlizzCon is held in the same convention center—how's that for a flash?)

TSR was becoming the largest imprint house in America, and they'd built a castle in the middle of the showroom floor with a tower at one corner. Joey and I climbed the stairs to the tower, and there was Gary. I'm not making this up. I met Gary Gygax on the top of a medieval tower (well, fake medieval tower made of scaffolding and plywood) at the ABA convention. We hit it off right away.

Gary was in his early forties, and his hair was right between black and gray. He had a goatee and maybe looked like a wizard. He had a big smile. I'll be damned if I can remember what we talked about, but my guess is that it got to something very particular very fast, like how you'd lay siege on the TSR castle complex at Book Fair.

A few weeks later, Gary sent me a letter saying he was moving out to LA and wondered if I wanted to write movies with him. I'm not sure whether I ever got a more exciting letter than that in my life—maybe my college acceptance letter would be in the same league.

And that's how careers work. You do a lot of work, go on a lot of fool's errands and schnook chases. Nothing or almost nothing happens. More hunts for smoke benders and skyhooks. More nothing. There are some monkey junkets, and you get rube wrangled a few times, and then *BINGO*, stuff starts happening—and when it happens, it happens fast.

First, they had to find a suitable mansion for the Dungeons & Dragons Entertainment Corporation (DDEC). They wanted it to be a home, an office, and an entertaining venue all at once. Not a bad concept, but that meant it had to be big, and it had to have a lot of rooms. I rode around with Gary and Joey and John Beebe looking at some potential mansions for DDEC. Some were extraordinary, but they were too foofy—they weren't ragged enough for what we needed. We knew the right place when we saw it. It was a giant LA ranch house, themed like some improbable Craftsman hunting lodge at the very top of the Beverly Hills. There was scrubby property all around it, with the semblance of a lawn and a swimming pool, and there was a general sense that while it wasn't in disrepair, it wasn't fully repaired either. And that's what we liked.

The ostensible purpose of the mansion was to take TSR to Hollywood, but as with many things, there's the ostensible purpose and the real purpose.

The real purpose was more complex. Trouble was brewing at TSR; Gary and his partners, the Blumes, were not getting along. They wanted to get Gary out of town, and for his part, Gary was eager to oblige them.

Some would argue that was the moment the fuse was lit for the TSR calamity, but to me, it was the call to adventure for some of the best days of my life. There were great people, it was a great place, and, as I was to discover, there was no real mission. We'd have to make one up.

Winter 1983

THERE'S A DEFINITIVE MOMENT when my actual cartoon career began, which was right at the same time my game-design career was coming into its own, coincidentally. I was standing in Joe Ruby's office when it happened, and the good news is that I was able to get a firsthand account from somebody in the room who wasn't me. I've been blessed with a more objective version of my first day from Harriet Beck, who ran business affairs at Ruby-Spears. When I started posting about this book, Harriet messaged me on Facebook to talk about various things, and with her permission, here's her version of the "how Flint came to work at Ruby-Spears story."

> Sometime in 1983, Joe Ruby was approached by a guy named Joey Thompson, who offered to introduce Joe to a guy named Flint Dille who, he said, was a member of the Dille Family Estate, which owned the rights to Buck Rogers. Joe was interested in the rights, so we took the meeting.
>
> Joey was a slender, angular, casually dressed man with longish curly graying hair and aviator glasses. He seemed to materialize in my office out of thin air from time to time and then disappear. I could not say how old he was or what he actually did. In any case, he was attempting to broker deals between creatives and producers in the animation business. I never knew anything about Joey's background or his relationship with the people

or properties he brought in, but he hinted that he expected us to pay him an unspecified commission for any deals he might bring us. Other than Buck Rogers, he was shopping around the animation rights to Dungeons & Dragons and Doctor Who. He was also very excited that the year's nouveau beaujolais wine was about to be released, and he later brought me a bottle.

Joey came in with Flint, a big, happy puppy dog with a Buck Rogers spec script. Joe and Flint discussed in very general terms how Flint and Ruby-Spears might work together, but nothing specific emerged from that meeting. After that first meeting, I believe I wrote up a proposal for the Buck Rogers rights. However, a few days later, Joe came down to my office and told me he had decided to put Flint on staff. He said he thought Flint had potential, and he wanted to put him with Buzz Dixon to learn the ropes. I suppose he made that decision based on the spec script Flint had given him. It was my impression that Flint was excited to be there, so I made a deal with Flint to enter the wacky and chaotic world of Ruby-Spears. I often said there was nothing about Ruby-Spears that a supply of Thorazine would not cure.

So, that's Harriet's version of the story. Puppy dog indeed.

To Joe, it was probably just another hire—an out-of-the-box hire, but a hire. He'd try me out and see if I fit. To me, even though it was only two weeks, it was my first shot. You never, ever forget the person who gave you your first shot. To me, it was deliverance. It was my first moment out of the wilderness.

Joe became earnest and businesslike and maybe a little embarrassed; "Listen, we don't pay like live-action. All I can pay is $800 a week."

"Great!" I figured he'd misspoken and it was really $800 a month, but since I had been living like a student, that was double what I'd been getting paid by Roger Corman for a few weeks on *Battle Beyond the Stars*. It was exponentially more than I'd been paid to be a freelance script reader for Hemdale and other companies, and it was infinitely nicer work than I'd been doing in my Hollywood guerrilla days.

My first day at Ruby-Spears, Joe took me and Buzz to the Smokehouse, a classic place across from Warner Brothers that has been around for almost as long as the movie business and at the time had been unchanged since probably 1943.

Buzz was immediately fascinating, and there was no part of me that wondered why Joe put me with him. It was like creative matchmaking. Not that we're opposites. We're not. There's a lot of overlap, but we're different.

Buzz is a big guy. Looks like he would have been the fullback or defensive end on your high school football team. He had a moustache and a haircut that made clear he had spent some time in the Army.. He came from Tennessee or Kentucky, or maybe it was both. I never knew he had a Southern accent until I came in halfway through a voice message on my answering machine and I wondered, "Who's this Southern guy calling me?" He had great stories about growing up in the hardscrabble South. And as I remember it, his father was an efficiency expert who "efficiencied" himself out of work.

In the real world, "creative guy" and "berserker" don't usually show up in the same sentence. In the case of Buzz Dixon, they did easily and often. At Ruby-Spears, I'd hear stories that Buzz had taken off his shoe and pounded on a table in a network meeting. It doesn't matter whether it's true; what matters is that it is believable. He once said of Robert E. Howard that it was amazing how he had transcendently beautiful lines right next to things like "his head smashed like a melon." That was Buzz. Inside of a minute, he'd have three ideas—one of them absolutely crazy, one of them so risque or edgy that it really only served to refocus the conversation, and one of them absolutely brilliant. The hardest thing to do was separate the thoughts from one another, a skill he seemed to lack entirely.

Buzz's career trajectory was the opposite of mine. He'd come back to the US from Korea with wife and child in tow, went over to Filmation, knocked on the door and landed a job on the spot and had moved seemingly effortlessly from Filmation to Ruby-Spears to Sunbow. Buzz might have been in the infantry while I was in grad school, but he's always been as much of as a scholar as I am—maybe more. He's just had a somewhat less formal curriculum.

We were originally assigned to work on a thing called *Cyberforce*. We jammed for a couple hours and came up with something we thought was absolutely brilliant. It was one of those ideas that has morphed and changed over the years, but the basic concepts we hammered out have impacted all sorts of things I've worked on since.

Joe didn't grab the idea at first, so we kept selling it. The harder we sold it, the less he got it. I can't remember the specifics of the cartoon version, but I do remember that all of the computers were hooked together and that the really old computers looked Jurassic and the new computers looked state of the art and that the enemies had ray guns. This meeting led to my second day and the "blue shoes/red shoes" life lesson from Harriet Beck.

I'll default to Harriet's version of the story. I remember it exactly the way she wrote it.

> From time to time, as some of the writers often did, Flint would wander into my office for one reason or another and we would chat about various random subjects. One day, Flint was particularly unhappy because he and Buzz had created a story for the ages that had been rejected by Joe. Flint paced back and forth across the room. It seemed that Flint and Buzz had done their best to sell the story to Joe, to no avail, and Flint was distressed that the world would be deprived of that creative vision. I explained to Flint that Ruby-Spears was a business that sold cartoons to television networks and that this was not Shakespeare. (As I think about that now, I was mistaken. Shakespeare actually made a living by writing plays on deadlines for paying audiences, some of whom were British royalty.) I explained that the networks were Joe's customers and that Joe knew what the networks were looking for. I explained that Joe's rejection of his story was based on Joe's understanding of what he could and could not sell to a network.
>
> Flint was unmoved.
>
> So I asked Flint to imagine that he was in the shoe manufacturing business and that his customers were shoe stores. I asked him to imagine that his customer ordered inventory of blue shoes in a color that he, Flint, did not like. I asked Flint to imagine that he thought the red shoes were more appealing. Then I asked Flint whether he would tell his customer that he hated the blue shoes and liked the red shoes better. I suggested

that Flint would probably not start an argument with his customer about which color shoes to stock and, instead, would rush back to his shop to make the blue shoes.

Flint paused and looked out the window for a few moments. He thanked me and left. I thought I had made a dent, and my advice to Flint so long ago seems to have stuck.

Harriet was entirely right, and it was a great lesson to learn on day two of my first real job. Like all epiphanies, the information was perfectly obvious one minute after the realization, seemingly inevitable even, but this was a big one. I got it. It's the best lesson you could get. It was a rite of passage from film school and trying to do the brilliant auteur thing (that hardly even exists, by the way, and never really did in my estimation) versus servicing a commercial enterprise. You make things for buyers.

It's really easy. Default professional writer strategy: give the customer the best version you can of what they want. Like all strategies, it doesn't work all of the time. If it did, it wouldn't be called a strategy. Sometimes customers don't know what they want, and occasionally they really do want "out-of-the-box" ideas—but not always. For all of the ridiculous and stupid stuff I did there, I didn't make that mistake again, and sure enough, my two-week deal at Ruby-Spears turned into two years.

By the way, the only difference I remember in the story is that I didn't just "wander" into Harriet's office. Rather, I was "called into" Harriet's office. Doesn't make any difference, but I wouldn't be totally honest if I didn't say that.

I was hired to do "development" at Ruby-Spears, and it's important to note that for all of the classes I took at USC, both in the Summer Cinema Program and while getting my MFA, I'd never heard the term before. That doesn't mean nobody ever said it—it means I never heard it. Like most writers, I would spend a significant part of my career over the next few decades in development. Sometimes it was good, sometimes it was "development hell," but it is an ongoing part of every screenwriter's life.

In TV, development is generating and fleshing out a concept in order to sell it and then to prep it for becoming a TV show before production begins.

(Change the "TV" to "movie," and it is pretty much the same thing.) It is the period between when you are hired to do the job and greenlit to go to script. In TV, development usually involves a bible and a pilot script at the very least. In short strokes, a bible in those days involved:

1. Series premise (what the show is about).
2. Series concept (format: hour/half hour, weekly, A story, B story, continuity, etc.) If your show is to end on a cliff-hanger on Tuesday nights and finish on Wednesday nights, you'd mention that in the "format" section.
3. Longer section detailing the main character(s) and the world of the show, though in those days nobody used the word "world." That came later. If you're going to put your effort into one section, this is it. This is a couple paragraphs or pages that sell the show.
4. Character bios. A few sentences about the characters and how they relate to each other.
5. Pilot or sample episode outline.
6. Story springboards. A few sentences on episodes. Sometimes people write up the season arc.
7. Now that you've read all that, just think of it as guidelines for what a bible is. There are no hard and fast rules, but the strategy is—and again, if strategies always worked, they'd just be called "the way"— to do all of those things. As the show goes deeper into development, it all grows. The outline turns into a script, the bios turn into fleshed-out characters, etcetera.

Developing in Development

THROUGH 1983, RUBY-SPEARS WAS developing a wild array of shows. I can't remember all of them, and figure that for every one that got picked up by a network, at least three went nowhere. *Cyber Force* (at least the Buzz/

Flint version of it) was left in a development landfill, while all around the Ruby-Spears writing team was working on things like *Turbo Teen, Q*bert, Donkey Kong, Donkey Kong Jr., Kangaroo, Pitfall Harry, Frogger, Space Ace,* and *Dragon's Lair.* If you're noticing a pattern, you're right. Most of them were popular arcade games of the day. All of them would make it onto the 1983 Saturday morning schedule, with several being bundled into a thing called "Saturday Supercade."

Before I leave that list, take a look at the ephemeral nature of culture in those days. Now, once something is noticed, it is never forgotten. It lives on at conventions, on T-shirts, on the Internet, etc. Not then. Stuff came and went.

Try this experiment. If you were around in the eighties, how many of the aforementioned shows have you thought about in a decade? *Frogger* comes to mind every time I cross a complicated street, but that's about it.

I drifted on and off developing different shows. It's all a blur now. I do remember me and Paul Dini sitting down one day working on some forgotten action show project and creating a character called "Ninjar." I wince now, and Paul, who has gone on to do a lot of epic stuff, probably winces, too, but it was the eighties, and putting an "r" at the end of "ninja" seemed like a perfectly credible way to create a fully licensable, trademarkable, merchandisable property.

Ruby-Spears occupied pretty much the same real estate in popular culture that it had in Cahuenga Pass. Located in an urbanomaly (urban anomaly) near where Barham sweeps down from Warners, bridges over the 110, and hits Cahuenga at a dead end. Turn left, you're at the Hollywood Bowl and eventually the Magic Castle and the Chinese Theater (before it was baked into a mall). Turn right and you're free fallin' down to Ventura Boulevard and the Valley. The Ruby-Spears office was a three-floor mock Tudor office building with a front door that nobody ever used (we went in the back). Nearby was a hamburger joint that looked like a riverboat that had come loose from its moorings on Universal's backlot and drifted down Barham to run aground between the fast-flowing Hollywood Freeway and its sleepier tributary, Cahuenga, which turns into Highland when it hits Hollywood and Ventura when it hits the Valley. The riverboat was as cartoony as the shows we wrote (and would inspire a *Mister T* episode), served horrific food but housed the Zaxxon game I was obsessed with until I decided it was unbeatable. Down the street, there was an underground and cult film VCR rental store, a mini market that sold Unknown Jerome chocolate chip cookies (in order to compete with Famous Amos), a sort of "no-tell motel" called the El Rodeo hotel, and a variety of other adjunct TV and film industry buildings leading to the iconic Hanna-Barbera building.

In other words, we were just downstream from Quick Draw McGraw, Huckleberry Hound, Wally Gator on one side and Bugs, Daffy, Foghorn, and Porky on the other. If there was ever good karma for an animation studio, that was it.

Add to this that the real people inside of Ruby-Spears were at least as interesting and comical as the ones they animated. Little did I know that I was seeing the heyday of the Saturday Morning animation studio. So vivid is Ruby-Spears in my mind that I can almost walk through it like a memory palace. And it's a journey worth taking for a moment, because so many of these people would figure prominently not only in this entire era of my journey, but in the animation world of the day.

You'd step off Cahuenga and walk past the Tudor façade, and there'd be an elevator in an empty hallway. The elevator would open upstairs, and there would be Kathleen Capps. If she sent you right, you ran into the executive area and you'd see Joe Ruby's admin, Stacy McLaughlin, who was funny and always seemed to know everything that was going on. Behind her was Joe Ruby's office. The door was closed. Ken Spears' office was all the way across the administrative pit, and I'm not sure if I was ever in it. I never really knew much about Ken, other than the fact that he had silver hair and drove a cool Corvette. Everybody said he was very creative, but in this incarnation, he rarely interfaced with us.

If you went left from Kathleen's desk, you'd hit Mark Jones' office. Joanne Sanchez sat there. She worked with Mark and appeared to do a lot of other things around R-S. I can't remember if she was a comical actress, but she could have been. She was very funny.

Mark Jones, unlike any other writer, had a big, swanky office and was working with Glenn Larson and Steven Cannell. If Steve was the creative's creative, Mark was the closest thing we had to a mogul-in-training. He even acted like one. It is no accident that he had the best office and seemed to be operating on a different plane than the rest of us.

If you spun around from Kathleen's desk, you could walk back past the elevator and down a long hallway to the writer's area. The first thing you'd see was the typists' room. It might have had a different name, but that's what I remember. The thing that didn't really dawn on me at the time was that I was seeing something that would soon be eliminated by the word processing technology that the early-adopter writers were just picking up.

Several people would come and go, but I particularly remember Cheryl Scarborough and Katy Kuch were trying to break out of the typing pool and into writing. Joe gave them the chance, and they went on to write a lot of scripts together. One day, I walked in and there was Donna Daves, the very same Donna Daves who gave me scripts to read at Hemdale two years earlier. My guess is that I might have met Meg McLaughlin in there. She was Stacy's sister and she also went on to write scripts. The first time I saw Liv Tyler, she reminded me of Meg.

Gordon Kent and Jack Enyart lived in the next office. Gordon Kent was Ruby-Spears' Woody Allen, able to do everything in animation (writing, drawing, in-betweening, editing, directing, etc.) and seemingly a vet of every animation studio in Hollywood. He had Albert Einstein hair and was an incredibly warm and sweet guy who would, multiple times, give me "just in time" education that saved my career. Jack Enyart, Gordon's partner, first struck me as somebody out of a forties musical with a top hat and cane.

In the next office were Cliff Ruby and Elana Lesser—Joe's son and daughter-in-law—a husband and wife who anchored the team. They were like the Special Forces of the office. For years, they would follow me onto projects after I'd been fired or failed out so often that the joke was, "What are you working on now? We're trying to figure out what we're doing next." They wrote *Balto* years later, among other things.

Marty Pasko resided in the office next to that. Marty was rumored to be related to William Shatner and seemed to have inherited his dramatic flair. Marty was brilliant and seemed to overthink everything. A twenty-one-minute script would come in somewhere between forty and forty-five pages—roughly two pages per minute of show. Marty was known to turn in seventy-page scripts.

Gary Greenfield was across the hall. I never really worked on a project with Gary. He was a clever comedy specialist and an amusing character to run into in the hallway, though.

Michael Maurer had the corner office and seemed to command the most status in the outside world, other than Mark Jones. Michael was the brother of Jeff Scott, the most successful writer in animation of the day. He was also the grandson of Moe Howard of *The Three Stooges* and son of Norman Maurer, a prolific writer, producer, and comic book illustrator, so basically he was comedy and Hollywood royalty. (One of the legendary moments at Ruby-Spears was when Joe Ruby said, "Michael has a very fine mind," and somebody, Marty or Buzz, said, "Michael has a Larry Fine mind.")

If you followed the cloud of smoke, you'd wind up in Steve Gerber's office. Steve had already created *Howard the Duck* and cocreated *Thundarr the Barbarian* (which, like all things creative, is somewhat disputed. I wasn't there. That's somebody else's battle to fight). If there was a most revered writer at Ruby-Spears, it was Steve. He'd had a long career before he ever got to Ruby-Spears and would go on to have a long career after.

There were a bunch of offices for production people whom I never really got to know. At the end of the far hallway was my first office. My officemate was Janis Diamond. She was also established and very patiently taught me a lot.

Buzz, at that point, was in exile in an inside corner office, as I recall. Funny. His is the one office I don't remember, and he was the writer I probably worked with the most.

Shortly after I came on, two new writers came to Ruby-Spears: Rick Merwin, who reminded me of a cross between Tom Selleck and David Hasselhoff—I'd go on to do the *Agents of Fortune* books with him later; and the prodigy, Paul Dini. Paul was the only writer on staff who was younger than I was, but he was already established in the animation world. Paul buzzed with the joy of childhood and cartoons back then and still does now. More on him later. We'd go on more adventures in that period and still do to this day.

There was some secret area down on the ground floor run by John Dorman. I never had reason to go there, but from the stories I've heard, it would have been a very interesting place to be.

I'd like to write about a typical day at Ruby-Spears, but the truth is, there wasn't a typical day. Some days were centered around writers' meetings in Joe's office, which had a couch, a couple chairs, a big desk covered with developments, and Joe's ashtray and a glass-topped coffee table that Rick Merwin crashed through one day. Joe tended to think of the world as action adventure and funny animals, and I was in the action adventure meetings. Funny animals were still far in my future at that point.

At some point in 1983, I purchased a second Decmate II. One was for home, the other for whatever office I needed it at, as the Decmmate II was fairly portable. I treated it like a laptop. However, like most writers, I did ninety percent of my actual work at home/alone. Corporate offices are not conducive to writing scripts, hence why no studio I know of has a "writers' building" anymore. Offices are for meetings. Having to come into an office to write is usually only a penalty for people who blow deadlines.

Nevertheless, I brought in some of my own furniture and started working with my feet up on the desk and the keyboard in my lap. I adapted that from a writing book that suggested you had to be in a comfortable position. I figured leaning back was about as comfortable as it gets. With my rattan chairs, the place was a little like a tiki hut.

This was low on the scale of aberrant behavior for Joe Ruby, so he put up with it. I didn't miss deadlines. Instinctually, I knew that while 90% of this business is subjective, deadlines are objective. A client can like or not like what you do—that is subjective—but there's no *objective* sin if you deliver on time.

My offices always seem to be tucked away. Usually I was alone because I smoked and people didn't want to be around it. In fact, smoking, not seniority, was the best way to get a solo office. Steve Gerber and Rick Merwin had solo offices too. For a while, I shared an office with Janis Diamond, but she probably got sick of the smoking.

My office wasn't the sanctus sanctorum of Ruby-Spears, however—Joe Ruby's was. I learned more in his office during story meetings than I had in multiple semesters of film school. It was the place of golden ashtrays and notes that said things like "Fix/make better," "Too much yap yap," and frankly a lot of the rules I still teach. Joe had a pure vision. Like all of the best, from the Beatles to George Lucas, he snagged a lot of stuff, but by the time it was done, it was something original. Yeah, we can say that his *Scooby-Doo* was a morph between the Hardy Boys, Nancy Drew, Dobie Gillis, and Marmaduke processed through James Whale films, but the brew he came out with has outlasted and outplayed them all.

"I Want You to Work on Some Action Show Ideas with Jack"

ONE DAY, JOE RUBY called me into his office and said, "I want you to team up with Jack and come up with some concepts." He didn't actually introduce us. Maybe he thought we already knew each other. He motioned to Jack, who looked like he was in his mid-sixties (and that seemed old) and was of the World War II generation, but as Buzz Dixon described him, he had this unique twinkle in his eyes. He literally shook with energy. That's not some literary fabrication. He seemed like he was shaking, like a dog really excited about going for a ride in a station wagon. He was ready to go. As it would turn out, it doesn't matter how old you are if you've got the twinkle.

The introduction was brief, and off we went. Joe didn't seem to have much of a specific idea what the concepts were, but by that point, I knew enough about Joe to know that he wanted straight-ahead action, "boys'" stuff.

I'd had no formal training on how to come up with TV series concepts, and all these years later, after having been exposed to pretty much every theory there is on how to generate creativity, I've realized that the best way is to just start talking about stuff. And as best I can remember, we just started talking about stuff.

Pretty quickly, we figured out that we were both into ancient history and mythology, so we used ancient gods as a kickoff. Well, more specifically, the Titans. We hit on Prometheus—always a good place to start. At the time, I'd either forgotten or was entirely unaware that Mary Shelley had titled her most famous work *Frankenstein; or, The Modern Prometheus.* Joe drew amazing stuff as we talked. He was full of ideas, and everything he drew meant something—the belt, the sword, the eagle. Prometheus, as a punishment from Zeus, had an eagle eat out his liver every day. We decided to give him an eagle buddy. Not really a nya-nya, but a hunting companion. Somebody to talk to. (Also, my guess is that the eagle was kind of sorry for all the liver-eating.)

Pretty soon, a whole mythology grew up around Prometheus. It bore no relation to mythologist Robert Graves, but that didn't matter. Prometheus was just a kickoff point. No part of me believed that any of this stuff would show up on a medium dominated by blue elves in funny hats, but we kept barreling along. And, man, it was exciting to just talk about stuff and then see it drawn to life.

This went on for a few days. Finally, we were talking about something and he casually said, without airs, "Yeah, back when I created Captain America…" I was no comics expert, but even I knew who Jack Kirby was. A montage of comic pages flashed across my mind that looked a lot like the animated Marvel Productions logo at the beginning of a Marvel film. Thank God I hadn't known Jack was *Jack Kirby,* or I would have been too intimidated to function when we were starting out.

If he noticed or cared about my sudden epiphany, he didn't show it.

It's not hard to find the obvious lessons in this story. It's that even geniuses (and Jack Kirby safely falls into that category) have to start somewhere, and that somewhere isn't necessarily some obscure place. Classic mythology always works. It is no accident that Wonder Woman is named "Diana" after the Greek huntress, or that Flash has wings on his feet like Mercury. Aquaman is Poseidon (or Namor, which is "Roman" backward, in which case he's Neptune), and then there are Thor and Loki—granted, they're Norse gods. Hawkman, if you squint, looks like an Egyptian god. Sometimes it's not as obvious. You can get into an argument over whether

Batman is Pluto or Daedalus (with Robin as Icarus), but it's impossible not to see how comics reach back to primal myth, and let's not even get started on messiah stories.

You keep developing and talking, and slowly but surely, your "Prometheus" evolves into something different and new as you add new characters and situations and strip away all of the stuff you don't need.

For instance, Optimus Prime started out as John Wayne. "John Wayne" was really just code for a strong, reliable hero at the center of the story. Nobody took it literally or had Optimus saying "pilgrim" a lot, but you have to start somewhere, and a well-known hero is as good a place as any to start.

But it's not the only place to start. If you know who your hero is, it tells you everything about who surrounds him and who opposes him. If your hero is a "consulting detective" who figures out things through incredible brilliance, it's pretty evident that he's going to have a sidekick who lacks his brilliance and is constantly amazed by it, and that he's going to run into a series of opponents—either people on his own side who lack his brilliance and get in the way or come to wrong conclusions that have to be corrected (LeStrade), or opponents who are as brilliant as he is (Moriarty) and who have infinitely more resources at their disposal.

Then you have a series of decisions to make. Is your hero arrogant and well aware of his capabilities? Or is your hero an idiot savant who continues to amaze themselves as well as everybody around them? If this is the case, you need surrounding characters who are amazed at his brilliance and request it.

Is your hero physically formidable, or is there another character who handles the fisticuffs? Does your character ever consider using their powers to less than noble ends (see early Spider-Man)? Does your hero mask their capabilities—literally with a mask, or perhaps by pretending to be an idiot (Columbo)? And if your hero hides their abilities, sooner or later you're going to create other characters who mirror these things—in this case, idiots who think they're brilliant.

Then you ask questions like, "What sort of world needs this hero?" Welcome to world building. If your hero has great lockpicking skills, you have to create a world with a whole lot of locks in it. If your hero is a disguise expert, they have to have a good reason to keep disguising themselves. One reason might be that they are famous. Or maybe they live in a surveillance state where everybody is recognized. Maybe they are really great at disguise and need to fool people who know the people that they disguise themselves as. This leads to *Mission: Impossible*–class skills and high-tech voice modifiers and perfect masks.

And what are the limits of their disguise power? Can they be the other gender? Can they be a foot taller than they really are? Or, harder still, a foot shorter? Now we're into hologram and shape-shifter territory, so it's a world with either extremely advanced technology or high magic. And where does the magic come from? Do they hypnotize their opponents into seeing the wrong thing, or do they literally change their DNA on the spot?

And whoever this character is, who's their nemesis? Is it another shape-shifter, or is it somebody who can see through their powers? Or do you have both, and start your rogues' gallery, because as Paul Dini once told me, "Any hero is only as good as his rogues' gallery."

Batman probably has the best rogues' gallery, and all of his opponents are some reflection of him.

Batman dresses like something dark and sinister, while the Joker dresses like a clown. Batman solves mysteries, the Riddler creates them. Catwoman is a frenemy. She's a cat. He's a bat. Normally, he'd be prey, but he flies. They only touch at a midpoint. Oliver Cobblepot, aka the Penguin, is of the same social class as Bruce Wayne, but he uses his wealth and status to opposite ends. (It's not like this in some iterations, but that was the original concept.) Batman uses fear to do good. Scarecrow uses fear to do evil. Around the time we realized Batman used a powered suit, Bane showed up in a more powerful one. And so on.

Let's go back to Jack. While it is more likely that somebody who has had success in the past will have success in the future, it is not guaranteed. There are a lot of one-hit wonders on the billboard charts. In the creative business, nobody wins by reputation. All reputation can do is raise your price and get you a good introduction, but it never makes success any easier.

I like to think that's why Jack Kirby didn't feel the need to inform me about who he was. He was an old guy (at least from my perspective) and he'd done epic things by any standard, but he was right there, in the moment, still creating—and either these new creations would be worthwhile, or they wouldn't.

Here's another interesting thing about Jack. I spent probably dozens of hours with him, but I never got the sense he knew me in any individual way. I had the impression that Buzz and Steve and I all sort of merged into one person in his mind: the Ruby-Spears guys. It was like he'd met so many people over the years that his mental Rolodex was full and he now clustered people into groups. Maybe he'd have remembered me as the Prometheus guy, and if he did, that's good enough. (I'm also prepared to accept the explanation that I'm just forgettable, but in this case, it seems that the other explanation fits better.)

Of course, the Prometheus show never sold, but what I learned there powered a whole lot of things later on. I'd love to know what happened with the stuff we worked on. My guess is that it's sitting in a warehouse somewhere, controlled by some lawyer who has no idea what he has.

Jack did tell me one joke that blew past me at the time but has rattled around in my head ever since:

"When was the golden age of comics?" he asked, challenging me.

Truth is, I didn't even have a good stock answer. I knew whatever answer I had wasn't right, but this wasn't about being right, it was about not looking stupid. I probably answered "World War II" and waited for him to correct me.

After a beat, he said, "Twelve."

First Script Ever

The Puppy and the Badlands

THE FIRST ANIMATION SCRIPT I ever wrote was for a show called *The Puppy's Further Adventures*. I haven't thought about the show, much less watched it, in over three decades, so forgive me if this sounds hazy. It was about a gang of dogs who went on adventures. I think the titular puppy was looking for his master—or maybe it was just any suitable master. To be honest, I don't even know whether there was a wrap-up episode where he actually found his master, but somehow I doubt it.

That was an era when shows had fictional end states—in other words, one of those shows where the main character has a problem, the solving of which would end the show. *The Fugitive* ran for several years, Ben Gazarra had a terminal disease that never seemed to kill him in *Run for Your Life*, and the poor guys in *The Time Tunnel* never seemed to be able to get back home—or if they did, they got flushed back into the time toilet one more time.

Mark Jones was the story editor of *The Puppy*, and he was doing animation and working with Stephen Cannell and Glenn Larson at the same time. He was a talented guy, but it wasn't the kind of talent taught in film school. In film school, we worshipped guys like John Milius, for whom writing scripts was supposed to be a Bushido mission. I'd get done listening to him and head back to writing like I was heading into combat. Mark Jones was about getting the job done as quickly and correctly as possible. He wasn't trying to write the "Great American Cartoon," he was just trying to get it done. I remember him telling me that I should get an act done in one sitting. He was right. I got "The Puppy and the Badlands" done in two days and told him I'd taken some extra time going over it. (The truth is that the extra time was spent getting Vicky Shellin to proof it, because spellcheck hadn't been invented and I was too embarrassed to take it to the script typists at Ruby-Spears. My excuse is that I'm dyslexic and have mixed dominance and can't spell or punctuate. It may or may not be a legitimate excuse, but I'd made serious efforts to correct it and mostly failed.)

The lesson I learned from Mark Jones is that working quickly does not necessarily mean that the final product is worse, nor does fretting over every detail necessarily lead to a better result. My favorite rhetoric professor, Larry Green, theorized that when you're working really fast, your writing tracks your thinking very well and there's no fear of overthinking, whereas when you labor and fight over every line, sometimes the life gets beaten out of a project and it's easy to lose the vision of what you were originally intending to do.

And writing the script was the least of our problems. "Network approvals" could be brutal. Luckily, Mark had a genius for sussing out what networks would balk at and what they'd buy. He didn't have to be told the blue shoes/red shoes story. He was born knowing it. In fact, I think it might have been him that told me, "Sometimes you want to leave some crap in there, so they'll focus on that and leave the rest alone."

What Mark didn't care about was expropriating stories. "The Puppy in the Badlands" was a flat-out snag of the set pieces from *North by Northwest*. As I recall, the pooches were buzzed, for no real reason, by a biplane and actually ran across Mr. Rushmore. I can't remember who the "baddies" were (they used terms like "baddies" back in the day) or what they were trying to accomplish. It didn't matter. They wanted gold and either the puppies got in their way or they thought the puppies knew how to find the gold. We didn't spend a lot of time on villain identity or motivation. This was all about three acts, cliff-hangers, set pieces, and hero motivation. And they wanted a beating "heart," one of those terms that always seemed to be used like a weapon. My basic thought was that heart was for wieners, but at this late date, I've given up the point; heart makes things go better.

In fact, as much as it pains me to say it, I'd argue that if you have heart and action, most viewers don't care if your story makes sense. Heart and action (especially anger, which is a subset of heart) deaden cognitive powers. Intellect comes later on, and when heart and mind come together, it's magic.

I don't remember Mark's reaction to the draft, but it got made pretty much as I wrote it. However, the thing that rattled around in my head was him telling me how hard he'd worked to convince Joe not to put me under contract. He actually told me this. The amazing thing about Mark Jones is that I think he was absolutely sincere, but also charming enough that I just shrugged and laughed along with it.

So "The Puppy and the Badlands" was approved and went into production. It wasn't going to push my limits as a literary luminary, but it did teach craft. And that's important. People often forget about craft. The art is the profound stuff. The craft is how you execute. And if what I learned was how to write a script in two days, that was a good thing to learn.

At the end of the day, I think the show did well. It had three seasons, which is no small achievement. In those days, if you had good ratings, that meant millions of people watched your show. Yet somehow, *The Puppy's*

Further Adventures has vanished without a trace. It doesn't even have a proper Wikipedia entry, and as of this writing has virtually no fan presence. Why do some things stand the test of time and others disappear?

For me, the show served as a proof of concept. Whatever Mark told Joe about the script and whatever else happened, Harriet called me into her office not long after "The Puppy and the Badlands," and I figured I'd be thanked for my work and told that development season was over and they'd call me next year. Which was okay with me. If the ride was about to be over, it had been a great one.

Instead, she offered me a contract for two years. Wow. Joey wanted to negotiate the offer, and my only directive was, "Don't blow it." This was about a lot more than money for me, and the money was, in my opinion, already great.

I'd passed the audition. If I were to pick a moment when I'd broken in, this was it. I was in for two years, and that's about as good as it got in the entertainment industry back then and probably better than it gets now.

There is a lot I don't know and will never know about how all this happened, but it doesn't matter. I was in, and the only thing I wanted to do was stay there. I'm not sure I was very consciously ambitious, and I had no plan whatsoever as to how to advance, but instinctively, I was doing something I have done ever since, and that is building up a skill, doing something parallel or on the side that would often lead to the next advance.

I was learning how to design games.

Most Expensive Classroom Ever

Game Design 101 from Gary Gygax

WHILE GARY AND JOHN Beebe were looking for the Dungeons & Dragons Entertainment Company (DDEC) mansion, Gary stayed in a bungalow at the Beverly Hills Hotel. If you've never been there, you've seen it in a hundred films and TV shows. "The Pink Palace" has been the epitome of Beverly Hills and LA luxury since the 1920s. Everybody who was anybody cavorted in the cabanas, was photographed in the pool, and made deals in the Polo Lounge.

Somewhere in the winter of 1983, at exactly the same time as I was writing "The Puppy and the Badlands" and working with Jack Kirby, I had my first game design lesson.

Gary's bungalow was well shaded by giant tropical plants, and I remember it as being art directed by Rousseau or Gauguin. Gary had presumably identified me as a promising noob and was now lecturing me in game design 101 while he smoked Camel straights and I smoked Camel filters.

He said, "The first thing you have to figure out is the ecology of the dungeon."

"What eats what…" I said.

"Right. Who built the dungeon and why? Who moved in? What is it protecting? Start answering those questions and you have a dungeon."

To this day, a hundred projects later, I think about this every time I approach a project. A dungeon is a microcosm of what any world is really about. A dungeon is about keeping things out, and in some cases, keeping things in. Most dungeons perfectly represent what is both valued and feared in a world. In a horror film, it can be a basement or attic. It doesn't have to be huge. It just has to be the home of the fear and the treasure.

To me, there are basically two kinds of writers. There are some who see a story clearly, and the whole exercise is to figure out how to tell that story the best way. Every set, prop, character, event, etc. is there to tell that story. The other kind is a person who simply loves a "world" and can see twenty stories in a given world, and their biggest problem is figuring out which one to tell.

A dramatic script is about the biggest moment in somebody's life. "Dramatic storytellers" build worlds in order to tell human stories. They're really only trying to answer the question of "In what world could this story happen?"

"World builders" are people who tell stories as a means of exploring a world. The product of world builders tends to be "franchises." James

Bond is a world as much as it is a character or story. It is a world of secret headquarters, tropical islands, lavish casinos, beautiful women, henchmen, and menacing villains bent on world domination. Which is to say, franchise characters aren't about arcs. We don't want Captain America, Indiana Jones, Batman, Harry Bosch, or Jack Reacher to change. Everything in the real world changes; that's why we go back to places where things don't change.

Personally, I like figuring out worlds. If you know what's valuable in a world, you know where a thousand plots come from. You know the look of a world, you know about who's in it. You know the ecology, you know where your character is in it. But a world doesn't start from nowhere.

Ironically, worlds can come out of dramatic situations. If you have a character or a situation, you can begin to create a world. Bruce Wayne's millionaire parents are killed in an alley near an opera house during the Depression by a robber, Joe Chill, who apparently wants their money. Already we know quite a bit about the world. It's the Depression. People get killed on the street for jewelry. We're in a world of rich and poor. We're in a lawless city where people get shot in alleys. It's a desperate world. Even if we find out that the real motive was something quite different than robbery, we know we're in a world where random robbery is rampant. We know that the value system of this world is money.

Even without the backstory footage about the ring, the minute Gandalf shows up in the Shire to inquire about a ring, we know that we're in a world of magic and that certain rings are powerful (we can guess that from the title)—so powerful that even when an old Hobbit has one, he becomes a person of interest to the most powerful people in that world.

Even if your story is set in the real world, there is an ecology. There is a value system. If everybody in the story is a multimillionaire, then power in the social structure is what's most valuable. James Bond, in any incarnation, operates in a world where technological superiority sets the victory conditions, where rogue billionaire sociopaths with beautiful girlfriends can threaten entire nation states. But strip down to the surface, and what is usually at stake is control of destructive or disruptive technology. (And as a side note, without getting too far into it, worlds can be largely defined by what is *not* in the world. I don't think Walmart exists in James Bond's world).

Scratch the surface of *G.I. Joe*, and it was a counter-terrorist force that took on a multifaceted terrorist group known as Cobra. Cobra was evil. But it was lawful evil; they had uniforms, a clear leader, rules, equipment, infrastructure. (I think of neutral evil as being more related to business, money, evil corporations, and mercenaries, while chaotic evil is things like the Dreadnoks, who were just chaotic and evil and weren't even trusted by Cobra but were sometimes used by them. If the story played out, Cobra Commander would have as many problems with his own side as he has with Joe and the lawful good guys.)

Transformers was a product of the eighties, a period of fear of the global control of oil. The seventies had gas shortages, the threat of oil wars, OPEC, and an overriding existential fear that we were going to run out of oil. So when you're structuring a story around a toy line of robots who disguise themselves as cars and planes, you have to figure out why they would do that. Why do they have to hide? What are they doing here? What do they want?

Well, the answer is simple. They want Energon. Their world is running out of it and Earth is basically an oil field. If they run out, they cease functioning. They disguise themselves both from each other (Autobots from Decepticons) and from humans, who have their own set of weapons and might, in aggregate, be dangerous to them for two reasons. First off, humans have primitive weapons, but they have a lot of them, and they might actually be able to defeat the Transformers. Second, humans might destroy the Energon reserves in order to get rid of them—though I can't remember that we ever played directly with this implied threat, it was always lurking about. So the entire premise was based on a metaphor for our real-world worries during the eighties and a dramatic need to make sense of the toy line.

It's important to have this in the back of your mind when looking at different franchises. What is valuable in the world? What is the ecology of the dungeon? It may be conscious, or it may be unconscious, but our fictional worlds somehow speak to our real worlds. What is the audience jeopardy here? What is this really about?

There would be many more lessons from Gary. And just like we probably adjourned from that day to the Polo Lounge, I'll now adjourn back to Ruby-Spears, because that's how life worked in those days.

The Golden Ashtray
Animation 1983—Ruby-Spears

Spring 1983

BEFORE I STARTED WORKING AT Ruby-Spears, Joe Ruby (co-creator of *Scooby-Doo*) had coined the term for a mythical object in the network animation business in those days called the "golden ashtray." Harriet said it happened in New York after meeting with Erno Rubik to talk about Rubik's Cube. The golden ashtray was whatever huge license was out there that everybody wanted. Pac-Man had been a golden ashtray a couple of years earlier. *ET* and *Star Wars* were golden ashtrays, but they were unattainable. That year, Marvel went in with *Dungeons & Dragons* and we went in with *Q*Bert* (a video game).

Mr. T. was a person, but he was also a golden ashtray. He is a giant African-American guy with a mohawk and gold chains who said things like "I pity the fool who..." followed by an action that Mr. T does not want the person to take. He'd been introduced to the world in *Rocky III* as the self-made hard counterpart contrast with Rocky, who was going soft because of his fame and money. Apollo Creed had to train Rocky to beat this monster. Mr. T then took his image to *The A-Team*, an action-comedy show.

Our mission was to turn him into a cartoon show. I had little or nothing to do with the early development of the show, but I was very much involved with the execution. I think it was Steve and Marty who developed it, but I could be wrong. Maybe it was Cliff and Elana. Maybe it was everybody.

The premise of *Mister T* was that Mr. T was a gymnastics coach who traveled around with a bunch of teen gymnasts, a bulldog with a mohawk, and an old lady, and they solved mysteries using their wits and gymnastic skills. It was like *Scooby-Doo* with Mr. T. in a gymnastics world. It sounds more incongruous than it really is.

Joe Ruby assigned me to the show, and I was invited to my first big meeting in the entertainment business. To this day, I'm not sure I've been at a bigger meeting. There were at least fifty people around a giant conference table at the Universal Sheraton. As I recall, there were six writers: me, Steve, Buzz, Cliff, Elana, and Marty. Joe was there. Harriet might have been there, but as a businessperson, she would have been in the "adult area" of the meeting. Phyllis Tucker-Vinson and Winifred Hyde-White ran NBC Saturday Morning. They each had an assistant. Then there were panels of three people representing every ethnic group in the show, whose job it was to read the scripts and look at the art and make sure we weren't doing anything racist and were providing "positive role models."

Our show included a Hispanic character, a Native American character, a couple black characters, and an Asian character. Each week our "A" story was solving a mystery and our "B" story was one of the characters learning a moral lesson. Point is, we had fifteen people reading the script to make sure nobody did anything offensive and we were sending the "right messages."

There was also the "violence" group. That accounted for nine or ten more people in the meeting. Violence divided into two groups. One group concerned itself with imitatable action—that is, preventing a kid from putting a towel around his neck while pretending to be Superman and jumping off his garage roof. The other was generally morally opposed to violence and didn't want to have anybody, including our villains, do anything to intentionally harm another person. In other words, a character could not throw a chair at another character, but if a character were fleeing, they could knock it in such a way that the other character might be impeded by it and have to use their gymnastic skills to get around it.

It's obvious that there were good intentions behind this, but once this type of doctrine is actually enforced by humans, it can get increasingly silly and frustrating. Gordon Kent used to tell a story about a script he was working on that involved a pirate ship. Broadcast Standards and Practices (BSP) at the network told him that could not have both a cannon and a cannonball. It was too violent. It's hard to see how any of this really changed the world for the better. Steve Gerber put it another way: "It's like they think kids are completely stupid and are all Charles Mansons in training." Joe Ruby was more practical: "It's hard to do action and adventure when you can't have action and adventure."

The Network Violence Count System worked something like this: You got forty points of violence. Guns, knives, etc. were out of the question. Slamming a door was three or four violence points, getting hit by a wave was one point. Getting hit by a big wave was two to five, raising your voice was a couple points, and so on. Most importantly, as Cliff Ruby explained to me, "You can't save it all up for a disemboweling."

Navigating BSP was like a game, but it wasn't a fun one. The fear object here was a show called *Rickety Rocket*, which had come out a couple years earlier. *Rickety Rocket* was basically a parody of *Star Trek* where everybody was stupid. At the last minute, they decided to make it an African American show, using African American voice talent. The mix was toxic, and the result was extremely racist by all accounts. Interestingly, there was no record of anybody complaining, but Phyllis, who had been an executive on *Rickety Rocket*, didn't want to take any chance of that ever happening again.

So, in all fairness, there are no bad guys in the BSP story. There are people with different concerns and agendas that struggled every day to find a middle ground. The problem is that, looking back thirty years later, almost none of the Saturday morning shows of this period (note the word "almost") left any cultural ripple. Sure, people remember them, but you never see them at cons. Nobody talks about *Mister T* or *The Puppy's Further Adventures*. They came and went and hardly left a skeleton because, at a certain level, they weren't really about anything. And the more they tried to be about something, the more they were really about nothing.

The eighties, for all of their wonder, were the real dawn of political correctness at exactly the same moment the Baby Boomers were having children. It was called the "baby boom echo," and there was particular attention to this huge demographic bulge of the children of hippies and yuppies passing through the cultural system. Mommy and Daddy wanted a safe world for their kids, and there was no shortage of pressure groups.

Peggy Charren had a group called Action for Children's Television that focused on this issue.[2]

And no discussion of eighties censorship is complete without mention of Dr. Thomas Radecki.

The Twisted Trail of Thomas Radecki

No SMALL PART OF our current culture was defined by the children's entertainment wars of the eighties. The attacks came from multiple sources, including televangelists who claimed that Dungeons & Dragons pieces *screamed* when they were thrown into the trash, which in turn prompted *60 Minutes* to do a segment on Gary.

Thomas Radecki ran an outfit called the National Coalition on Television Violence. As far as I could tell, it wasn't national, it wasn't a coalition (it was just him), and it wasn't really about television violence. He seemed most obsessed with the Dungeons & Dragons game.

My biggest personal encounter with him was one day when Gary and I drove over to KABC radio station, went on the *Michael Jackson Show* radio show, and were "ambushed" by Mr. Radecki.

Radecki's stance, in his own words, was: "The evidence in these cases is really quite impressive. There is no doubt in my mind that the game *Dungeons & Dragons* is causing young men to kill themselves and others. The game is one of nonstop combat and violence. Although I am sure that the people at TSR mean no harm, that is exactly what their games are causing. Based on player interviews and game materials, it is clear to me that this game is desensitizing players to violence and causing an increased tendency to violent behavior."

---

2   At one point, Joe Ruby asked Peggy Charren if she'd stop if she got what she wanted. She said yes. And, indeed, she actually did shut down Action for Children's Television when she got what she wanted.

He made similar attacks on *Transformers* and *G.I. Joe*. Smug, pompous guy. And the media, long before anybody called them "fake," lapped it up.

Oddly enough, I was probably the best equipped member of the staff for dealing with political correctness at the time because I'd been in the Berkeley Rhetoric Department when they were making all of this stuff up. At the time, it seemed like radicals were amusing themselves by floating ever more outlandish ideas that they didn't actually believe. Now, something like "cultural appropriation" is a common charge; back then, it didn't feel like I was hearing serious arguments. It felt like we were playing with words and constructing silly arguments from them.

Times change.

The results of the *Mister T* dilemma were predictable in hindsight. A minor character, a Jewish male named "Woody," became the only guy who could make mistakes, while the other characters learned very soft lessons. And although action without violence was actually a good piece of training for young writers, two years later, when Steve Gerber said, "I'm working on a new show [*G.I. Joe*] where guys can hit each other with real fists," it was extremely liberating.

Oh, and we were not allowed to use Mr. T's tagline "I pity the fool who..." We never received an explanation for why, but that was the rule. There are a number of possible reasons why "I pity the fool" was not acceptable. Maybe some writer or studio owned the tagline. The crusade against bullying started with not calling people names, and "fool" was considered a name. There might have been more than one reason.

All of that having been said, *Mister T* was a great experience for me and changed my career. I learned how to write animation from Steve and Marty in all-night, smoke-filled sessions on "The Mystery of the Forbidden Monastery." I learned that the page ratio was two pages to one minute in animation, as opposed to the live-action one-to-one ratio. I learned that everything had to be described. Every actor and action had to be called out (you didn't have actors sitting around on the set waiting for instruction). If a character was going to be in a scene, they had to be written into the scene. Actions had to be described in what felt to me like excruciating detail—a far cry from the extremely fast and light dialogue with a lot of white space that I was taught by Jim Boyle in film school at USC. Of course, there I was being taught to write "spec" scripts. At Ruby-Spears, I was making actual product. That is a very different art.

Mister T also marked an interesting point in my writer's journey. I hadn't pulled the sword out of the stone yet, but I was hanging around with the knights, and they didn't really know what to make of me. That was okay, because I didn't entirely know what to make of myself. I was a strange animal. Unlike everybody else, I had no credits, had never written a comic book or done much of anything. However, I had been to film school, and I'd been born a form of geek royalty as the descendent of the creator of Buck Rogers. This sounds like nothing today—and let's be honest, it really isn't anything. Being related to somebody who did something bears absolutely no relationship to actually having done something yourself, which I guess is just like real royalty, actually. It also carries with it the implication of vast sums of money, which adds an English all its own to relationships. It was a talking point when people would introduce me, and it always made me cringe slightly, because…who cares.

As it happens, everybody at least pretended to care—some actually did.

The other thing was that I'd just finished up at USC. This was, at that moment, about the equivalent of having come out of West Point or the Air Force Academy, and I was the equivalent of some newly minted second lieutenant showing up with a bunch of sergeants who have been in numerous battles. USC was legendary for the directors and writers it had produced, and thus, I was an elite noob. The fact that I looked more like I belonged in the NFL than in a writing room added yet an odder drift to it.

And there was the issue of interest. Everybody else was either from deep animation, comics, live action, or even books. I, on the other hand, was into games. That was weird, too. Yes, video games were huge and D&D was a phenomenon, but games were a very strange place to come from in the spring of 1983.

So, it was neither my fault nor the fault of anybody else at Ruby-Spears if they didn't know what to make of me. And in the numerous all- and late-nighters that would make up the experience of trying to crack *Mister T*, I was a dubious junior partner. If I was going to get any respect, I was going to have to earn it. Most of the time, I was like a spectator at a tennis match, watching the far more experienced Steve Gerber and Marty Pasko attacking the series. If there could have been a more perfect training ground, I have no idea what it would have been.

My best moment on that project was during the aforementioned "Mystery of the Forbidden Monastery," as I happened to know that a table at a monastery was called a refectory table. Marty and Steve looked it up. Sure enough, I was right. They were amazed by this piece of trivia, and there was an air of *"Maybe he really does know something."* The truth was that my family happened to have a refectory table; I'm using it as my desk as I write these words.

After that came the "Fortune Cookie Caper." The network still wasn't entirely happy with the way the show was coming out, but it was still approving things and the show was moving forward. I didn't understand how big a win that was at the time. I was a little better and more confident.

As a follow-up to the "Fortune Cookie Caper," I had this idea—and it still seems weird to me as I type it—that there would be a sunken riverboat and the smokestack looked like a gravestone, but our intrepid kid investigators would discover treasure in the steamboat below and solve a hundred-year-old mystery. As I said, the idea sounds preposterous right now, but the network bought it, and Joe Ruby let me write the first draft myself.

The training wheels were partway off.

"The Hundred-Year-Old Mystery" came out fast. Oddly enough, my mother, who in no way fancied herself a writer or comedian, supplied a joke for it, and that was that Mr. T saw himself in a funhouse mirror and jumped. Cliff and Elana were assigned to edit it. I'm not sure why it wasn't Marty and Steve. Maybe they were running ahead with other episodes, maybe they were sick of the noob (I wouldn't blame them), but either way, I had new story editors to report to. At any rate, I'd never had my script edited before and thought that it was a negotiation. I quibbled. Elena offered to take my name off the script. I stopped arguing. If I hadn't known my place in the pecking order, I did now. They sent the script off to NBC.

I walked in the following Monday afternoon a little late. Mark Jones had told me that if I was writing, I didn't have to come in. That wasn't entirely accurate, but Joe put up with it. People were acting strange when I got there. It was like there was something nobody was telling me. It felt weird, but not entirely bad. Not entirely good, either. Then Marty said something about the "fair-haired" boy, and I'm not sure I'd ever heard that phrase before. Eventually, somebody told me that the network had loved my episode, and I thought that was great. Later on, Joanne Sanchez explained the implications of it to me. The network wanted me to be lead writer on the show. This was incredibly lucky for a rookie. It was the first unequivocal praise I'd ever received for anything I wrote professionally.

In the end, if I had to pick a moment when I realized that I actually had a career coming, it was "The Hundred-Year-Old Mystery." You have to take your victories when you can. *Mister T* was a hit, number one on Saturday morning. I'd be knocked back down a few pegs not long after that, but at least I knew winning was possible. I don't care how long your career goes on; there are not that many "clean kills."

And it wasn't just me. Ruby-Spears was on a hell of a roll. From 1983 to 1986, a number of their shows were hits in their time slots, and they were riding the wave of arcade games and golden ashtrays. On ABC, there was *The Pac-Man/Rubik, The Amazing Cube Hour, The Puppy's Further Adventures, The Puppy's Great Adventures, Dragon's Lair, Turbo Teen, Mister T,* and *Alvin and the Chipmunks.* On CBS, there was *Donkey Kong, Donkey Kong Jr., Kangaroo, Pitfall Harry, Q*bert, Frogger,* and *Space Ace.* There would also be something called Bad Cat, which I have no memory of, and a couple of specials, including *The Cabbage Patch Kids' First Christmas.*

For Ruby-Spears—or anybody, for that matter—it was a hell of a run. Joe and Ken had built an amazing machine. And I'd go so far as to say that if somebody went to Joe Ruby today and took a lineup of shows that he developed but never sold in that period and produced them properly, they would have hits.

Joe Ruby had a focused, clear, classic vision of entertainment that would work almost anywhere, almost any time. Working with him and working with Steven Spielberg a few years later were not entirely different experiences, and I mean that as a compliment to both men.

After "The Hundred-Year-Old Mystery," which brought unexpected money and membership in the Writers Guild of America due to the live-action Mr. T. wraparounds, I realized I could move out of the old Spanish house in Westwood.

As I hadn't figured out where to live yet, my sister set me up in a place in the Marina. I went over to visit it, and the guy who took me around said, "Don't leave your gold chains anywhere somebody can see them through the window." I didn't know whether being in a world in which people wore gold chains or a world in which those chains were subject to probable theft bothered me more, but I ate my deposit and went on a hunt. This was Thursday, and I had to move out of the apartment on Saturday.

I got lucky. I drove by the house I'd lived in two years earlier, probably ditched my car in the middle of the street, went up to fill out a contract, and wrote a check faster than parking enforcement could find me—which, in Westwood, that's quick.

In movie terms, this was a matching scene. I was moving into the exact same building I'd lived in two years before, but my circumstances were totally different. This time I was paying for it myself, and even though I had a worse view, I was thrilled to be there. I'd never live with other people again until I got married, though there seemed to always be somebody living on my couch.

At this point, I felt like a completely different person. Probably because I was.

The Girl in the Polo Lounge

VARIOUS NEW HOLLYWOOD HOT spots come and go, but the Polo Lounge remains to this day. Dinner might cost you a down payment on a house, but it will be worth it. To Gary Gygax, the Polo Lounge was like a dungeon, or at least a game board, and I think there is a great retro strategy game to be made about becoming the king of the Polo Lounge. Gary explained it to me. Not all seats were equal, and the most unequal was the power booth, which was centrally located and easily visible from the door. The person in that spot was the most powerful person in the room at that moment, and given that the Polo Lounge was where half of the deals in Hollywood were made in its day, to be in the power booth conveyed real power. The booth next to it was the second most powerful, and every other booth had its own power level. If you were sitting in a table off to the side, you weren't powerful.

The power booth was Boardwalk, and the other front booths were like Park Place and the greens. The tables were the yellows, and the seats outside and in the next room were the reds. Baltic and Mediterranean were somewhere deep in the garden. And, like their Monopoly counterparts, they had their virtues.

In this scene, I'm sitting at the bar lining the west wall, out of sight upon entering the Polo. It is the perfect place to see and *not* be seen. In other words, the perfect place to set an ambush.

If this story were a game scenario, it would start like this: "You are in your mid-twenties. You're not naïve anymore, but you're not experienced, and there's a lot of stuff you've heard of but never actually seen. This quest starts in an inn called the Polo Lounge, where you are drinking a Diet Coke, waiting for Mordenkainen (aka Gary Gygax) and the DDEC entourage to arrive. Mordenkainen is an extremely powerful wizard in the world of Greyhawk, but as your party is about to discover, you're not in Greyhawk anymore."

I was early, milling about aimlessly. It felt like being at a stadium before the game. I would have felt like a schnook sitting alone at the power booth, which Gary gamed for the night, so I went to the small bar. There was barely enough light to read the paperback I usually carry in my pocket, and a girl about my age came and sat two seats away. She was well turned out, but there was nothing gaudy about her. And she was beautiful. I figured she was an actress waiting to meet a director or something.

I can't imagine that I started the conversation, so she must have. It was probably about the paperback. And at some point, I must have asked if she lived in LA or was visiting—after all, we were in a hotel. Something innocuous, doing everything I could to give her the impression I was not hitting on her, because I wasn't. I had a girlfriend and don't think I've ever picked anybody up in my life, and this wasn't going to be the night.

And, of course, I had dinner plans.

She said she had a date. Didn't surprise me. But the way she said "date" was weird. I can't remember how the conversation went in this direction, but a few minutes later, she was explaining to me that she was an escort working her way through grad school at UCLA. At that point, I probably thought "escort" meant she literally went to events with men who couldn't find dates, though I may not have been naïve enough to actually believe it. *Pretty Woman* hadn't come out yet, so I didn't know that prostitutes could look like Julia Roberts and act like well-heeled ladies. I thought they stood on Sunset with visible needle tracks. It was eye-opening. I did my best to act like this was the most normal story in the world.

I went into interview mode, and she explained that a couple girls in her sorority introduced her to the job as an undergraduate. Her sorority? I'd been ATO at Berkeley. I immediately started going through my mental Rolodex to figure out if I knew any girls who were having paid "dates."

She said her boyfriend at UCLA didn't know what she was doing the two nights a week she didn't see him. Her employer would call her up and it would be arranged like an appointment. This was just a way to get through school. She didn't want it to follow her. She didn't go under her own name, and it was forbidden for her to give out her phone number to one of her dates, and on and on it went.

A few minutes later, the phone rang near us, and the waiter gave it to her. Her date was calling. I told her the story was at least worth paying for her drink. She asked me what I did, and I told her I wrote cartoons. She laughed, then caught herself and left. I've sometimes wondered what happened to her.

I'll never know. But I tell that story because for me it was one of the first real-world instances of a concept that I'd learned in film school—namely, "the presence of other realities existing simultaneously." Here I was in a Hollywood "dungeon" (and a beautiful dungeon it was) alongside another adventurer with a completely different set of goals. She could have been a spellcaster in training or any other thing. There was no way I could know what her real motivations were; I don't have mind reading in my skill tree.

As anybody who's ever played D&D (or World of Warcraft, for that matter) or read much fantasy knows, almost every adventure starts out in a bar—usually called an "inn." And in some ways, my adventure with the Dungeons & Dragons Entertainment Company began in the Polo Lounge.

Like all of the best fantasy inns, the Polo Lounge (seemingly) offered multiple quests promising all kinds of fabulous rewards, from fame to money to power and more. Adventuring groups were assembled here, and powerful wizards spoke to people on retro phones that didn't have dials on them and which never actually rang.

The quest givers and adventurers—in this case producers and moguls—would be told that there was a call for them and the phone would be handed over. A really powerful producer could refuse the call, though I never saw that happen. I mean, it's always good to look like you're talking to an extremely powerful sorcerer.

Along these same lines, I realized sitting at the bar was like sitting on "chance" or "community chest" on a real-life Monopoly board. You get a drink and maybe something happens. Moments later, other women showed up. They were far more glammed than my grad student friend. I have no idea whether they were millionaires or escorts. I was close enough to Hollywood to know that little is what it appears.

It was around then that I realized the real world was a game. Maybe it was a badly designed game with unclear and unfair rules, but a game nevertheless. If I had to pick a moment when the seeds of what would later be called "gamification" started growing in my mind, that was it. And, inadvertently, this would serve as research for an upcoming project.

It's wonderful when life gives you free research.

The Post-College Era Ends

IF RUBY-SPEARS MARKED THE beginning of one era, moving out of 1901 Camden marked the end of another: the "post-student" era. The actual move-out was, in and of itself, a *Mission: Impossible* style adventure.

I moved back into the same apartment building in Westwood (the same neighborhood I've lived in the entire time I've lived in Los Angeles), up on Kelton and Wilkins between Santa Monica and Wilshire. I'd briefly lived in the building before, so it was with a reset that a sub-era had begun.

It was an all-white, well-designed studio apartment, and if this book were an art film, the sparseness of the white in that apartment would be the symbol of a tabula rasa, a blank slate.

Westwood was cool back then. Paul Schrader (*Taxi Driver*) would shoot *American Gigolo* there in 1980 and make Westwood look like Rome. Mel Gibson, Kurt Russell, and Michelle Pfeiffer would star in a cryptic movie called *Tequila Sunrise* set largely in the neighborhood, and a Curtis Hansen/ David Koepp movie called *Bad Influence* had Rob Lowe living in a building catty-corner from my apartment. As a result, living in Westwood in the 1980s felt a little bit like living in a movie.

Whatever else that move was, it was the end of the post-student era and the beginning of the professional era for me. I'm not sure I ever met any of my neighbors except in passing, though I remember Vanity, one of Prince's singers, lived in the building—I used to see her on the elevator. It was fascinating to me that somebody that cool and hip would live in the same building I did.

Then there was the cool blonde woman with the cherried-out '63 Corvette convertible who parked next to me. The only time I ever saw her was when I'd be leaving really early or coming in really late and she was coming in. She looked like a vision from the new MTV network and didn't entirely seem to live in the same dimension of reality that I did, let alone the same apartment building. She was more hallucination than anything. I've often wondered who she was and what she did. There was no way to know, and asking wasn't an option. Without the Internet, people could be very mysterious in the 1980s.

It's hard to see things when you're actually living them, but in Campbell terms, after answering the call and crossing the threshold, often as not, the ordinary world changes. In a few short months, mine had changed dramatically, but I was too busy living to really notice it.

The D&D mansion wasn't what you might expect. It wasn't some gothic castle or a *Beverly Hillbillies* mansion or a "stately Wayne Manor" type of place. It felt more like a giant Craftsman hunting lodge somewhere in the Sierras than a medieval mansion. In fact, it was so high in the hills that from one part of the property you could look down at the San Fernando Valley, and on the other you could follow Sunset from downtown to the ocean.

The house was built by King Vidor, an actor and famous director from the early days of cinema. The house, I believe, plays a cameo role in a book called *A Cast of Killers*, a great early Hollywood noir about the real murder of William Desmond Taylor. If you read the book, it might be the house where he did his research on the murder. And if it's not the right house, well, it should have been.

For our part, we knew it was the right place the minute we saw it. The front gates were wooden and wouldn't sustain a heavy assault, but they'd serve as a deterrent, and I knew I was part of the family when I got the access code to the gates. Next to the gates was the caretaker's house. It was staffed by Matthew and Christina. Matthew was a down-to-earth, all-American guy; Christina was his very inordinately pretty Swedish wife. While she didn't exactly wear a uniform, she was always dressed like something out of *Heidi or The Sound of Music*. I vaguely remember John Beebe, who was the head of DDEC, thinking they should have uniforms so the place looked more like a business, but that might be a manufactured memory.

The gate led to a long oval-shaped driveway with grass in the center. The grassy area seemed like it was about half a football field, but things are rarely the size you remember them. The top of the oval was the front door of the mansion. It was a mansion, but it was one story, except for Gary's master suite above and some storage rooms that were converted to offices below.

There was a reception area, which led to a lanai with a fantastic view of Los Angeles and the Jacuzzi area. I can't remember whether the Jaccuzzi was already there or Gary had it installed. I'm guessing the latter, but I can't be sure.

If you turned right, there was a warren of rooms where John Beebe and his wife Ingrid lived, as well as Gary's driver/bodyguard. When Ernie and Luke (Gary's two sons) came into town, they stayed in rooms down the hall.

If you turned left in the front hall, you entered the living room, which was also a screening room because there was a projection booth in there with a secret door in the wood paneling, through which was a large dining room where I remember playing D&D more than I remember eating, an enormous kitchen, and some more rooms for staff and visitors. The crown jewel of the mansion was the bar room. It had a sunken bar that looked like something you'd expect at the Playboy Mansion down the hill. That led to a sprawling cliffside yard and the pool at the corner of the property.

My office was a converted stable situated hard left from the entrance gate at the front of the property, a minute's walk from the main building. In its day, the stable had room for three horses, a bathroom, and big doors at the front. We threw down carpet and did a few other minor things, and I had the coolest office anybody will ever have. My office took up one of the original stalls, and the largest ex-stall became a guest bedroom that I don't remember anybody actually using.

There was a large open area, which had a couch and chairs and an assistant's desk, and Matthew built us a giant hundred-square-foot sand table. There were some cubby shelves that contained Gary's three thousand Elastolin medieval miniatures, which we used for playing Chainmail.

Gary lived in the suite upstairs in the main house, directly above the entrance. There was a master bedroom and an office with an epic view. There might have been dressing rooms off to the side. He had a huge baronial desk with all sorts of interesting artifacts on it.

Gary and I realized early on that we were like the old joke about an atheist funeral: all dressed up with nowhere to go. We knew we wanted to create something together, we just didn't know what. We needed a project. Something tangible.

As it happened, TSR had optioned *Conan the Barbarian* from a colorful fellow named Arthur Lieberman and produced a Conan role-playing game. Gary and I were interested in writing a Kull movie, but for now, there was a slot for Conan *Endless Quest* books, and Gary and I took it on with the goal of designing a more robust gamebook system that involved combat and dice, something that moved beyond the *Endless Quest* pick-a-path formula.

So we had a clear, defined, real project that we could start on. But we also needed something BIG. Hyper-ambitious. World-changing.

Also, very early on, we came up with the movie/game idea called *The Sceptre of Seven Souls*. We knew that would take a while to develop.

Gary and I got the opening scene early on in the DDEC mansion days. We were sitting together at my Mac, which was a terrible thing to write screenplays on but looked really cool. We would come up with an idea. Laugh. Write it down. Top it. Come up with another idea. Write it down. I'd delete it. He'd complain. I'd hit "undo," and it would come back. That seemed like magic to him. Seemed like magic to me, too, but I tried to act blasé about it.

We decided to lead from strength. Hollywood would trust Gary Gygax with a sword-and-sorcery scene, so the opening scene was a dungeon crawl.

The MacGuffin of the series was a sceptre forged by seven ancient sorcerers that divided into seven parts. Each part was a portal to a different world. I have no idea whether we thought we could fit all of this into one movie or we were selling them on seven movies or we had a "back pocket" idea of a TV series. We just thought it was a cool idea.

Our hero was tentatively named Dart. He was a rogue/bard kind of a character. I had this goofy idea that he infiltrated enemy kingdoms guised as a magician with a traveling group of cutpurses with magical musical powers: one could hypnotize with their instrument, another could charm animals (like a snake charmer, but also birds, lions, dogs, whatever animal was necessary). Of course, all the wrong people were immune to his charms, and other wizards could turn his charisma into negativism.

This band of loveable, musical, medieval thieves would always get wind of some treasure or some tyrant who needed assassinating or something and go on a mission. Of course, they'd always get in way over their heads and a desperate adventure would follow.

We even figured there was a musical tie-in. After all, what are synthesizers, fuzz pedals, and the like other than magically enchanted musical instruments? So it was a heavy metal take on *A Hard Day's Night* set in a D&D world. Except the world changed. In fact, the genre changed. The only constant were the characters and the quest.

The following is my reconstruction of our teaser scene. It's funny how I can forget all sorts of details about the life I actually lived but remember, beat for beat, a script from thirty years ago. I think that's because the fictional takes effort to create while the real just happens. Here's a reconstruction written in the feathery, fragmented way we'd beat out stories:

OPEN ON—DART, OUR HERO

Is being chased out of—

A LOST TOMB

by DISGUSTING DARK ELF ENEMIES and looks like he's going to be trapped at the edge of a cliff but suddenly jumps—

It looks like he is going to fall to his death. The pursuing Dark Elves...

Fire arrows at—

DART

—anyway.

He spins in the air and fires his one-hand crossbow, killing one of the Dark Elves.

Then, Dart activates his cape, which spreads out to control his descent until an arrow pierces it—

He is losing altitude. Going to die for sure until—

HIS FLYING DRAGON

Swoops down and snags him out of the air.

Just as we think they're safe.

A blast of fire nearly engulfs them.

Behind them is a bigger, nastier fire-breathing dragon ridden by some truly terrifying-looking guy.

No match for this foul beast, Dart's Dragon seeks refuge in—

A MAGICAL CAVE

And races through its seemingly endless tunnel.

THE EVIL DRAGON

Follows.

DART

Pulls out a piece of the sceptre he's just received and activates it.

(We didn't know how he would do this. Magic words. Rubbing it. Twisting it. We'd figure it out.)

THEN SOMETHING MAGICAL HAPPENS.

The world begins to change. The flapping of wings turns into the roar of a steam locomotive. Same happens to his pursuer's dragon

WHEN DART

Emerges from the tunnel, he's on the top of a steam locomotive. His hand-held crossbow is a six shooter.

The evil wizard is a DESPERADO.

They're firing at each other.

Sword and Sorcery suddenly turned into Enchanted Western.

(/end scene)

And it works the other way around...

The end of the act is that he's on a train, activates the Sceptre and comes flying out on his dragon, back to his world, where he has to find the next part of the Sceptre.

I think I wrote both of those scenes, and they were matching scenes. We were showing that magic helped our hero move between genres and that genres were really just different props and costumes. In the middle, he'd find his musicians in dance halls, traveling carnivals, opera houses, wherever. He'd reassemble the team, and they'd go hunting for another part of the Sceptre. Of course, the big bad guy was always a step behind him or even a step ahead of him, and he'd lose pieces of the Sceptre as quickly as he got them. And he'd face the same ambient villain and his endless minions in numerous different worlds, whether as an enemy spymaster in a *Top Secret* world or Fu Manchu in the Gangbusters world or as a demented computer gone mad in *Gamma World* or the XXVC Space World.

As whacked as this was, there was a practical business hook to it. The marketing piece of *The Sceptre of Seven Souls* was designed to be a genre-morphing story that connected all of TSR's franchises at the time: *Dungeons & Dragons, Boot Hill, Top Secret, Gamma World,* and *Star Frontiers.* Players would twist the sceptre, translate the stats and characters to another world, and continue the adventure. For instance, I remember in *Gamma World* that a warrior's shield morphed into a stop sign scavenged in a post-apocalyptic world. *The Sceptre of Seven Souls* was a wild idea in some ways and a natural eighties progression in another way.

And, yes, this is frustrating, but I can't put my hands on a copy of *The Sceptre of Seven Souls*. I'm not sure how many scenes we had, but we had enough that we were able to pitch it to Gary's first choice for Dungeon Master, Orson Welles, at the Magic Castle.

Here's the weird thing, and it gets back to what I was saying about the unreliability of memory. I'd utterly forgotten about Gary and I meeting with Orson Welles until I was reading Gary's blog after he died. Even now, the meeting at the Magic Castle is a hazy memory, partly because of what happened later that night.

But, still, how do you forget something like Orson Welles? Memory plays strange tricks. And, of course, that memory would be utterly overwritten two years later, when Orson Welles came in to play Unicron in *Transformers: The Movie*.

So, under normal circumstances, you'd think that *The Sceptre of Seven Souls* was just another fool's errand. I mean, really, how would you have produced it in 1984? It was never finished. I might have a copy somewhere in storage, but it has never left my mind, and various bits and pieces of that idea forged at the dawn of my career have been stuck in there like a puzzle that I'm trying to solve. It's not so much the actual execution that mattered. It was pretty ridiculous stuff. But it was the engine that started turning, the reactor core of Sceptre that started burning that has, one way or another, fueled half of what I've done since then, from *Diablo* to *Ingress*.

The idea of shape-shifting worlds is lurking somewhere in the background of *Transformers*, which is just a metal shape-shifting idea. It would continue to be this unresolved thing in my mind but somehow inform everything I do. And though I'm not a superstitious person, I do have this strange fear that if I finished *Sceptre*, I'd never write or design anything again. The concept of the "essential unfinished" is as close as real life comes to a magical concept that I sort of believe, and I both love and fear it.

John Beebe is a guy I appreciate more in retrospect than I probably did at the time, and that's no slight to John. He was the most conventional corporate person in this mad world. He was on the last stop of a long corporate journey, much of which was spent at Sears. I'm not too sure whether it gets all the way to cynical, but he would offer up wisdom that most of the time I didn't want to hear. Of course, he had an annoying habit of being right. I remember him chastising me once for speculating on the budget for *The Sceptre of Seven Souls*.

"What do you know about making budgets?" he asked.

Okay, he had a point; I'd never done a film budget in my life for more than student films. Nevertheless, I stuck to my guns. "Not much, but I do know what's already built on Universal's backlot. We shoot the western sections on the old west town, the ancient in Spartacus Square, the gangster stuff on New York Street. We go to lots of different worlds, but on that lot they're only about a hundred yards from each other."

"That's clever. I'll give you that," he said.

It was a test of sorts. And while I hadn't aced it, I hadn't flunked it, either.

"And if I can figure out how to throw in the psycho house for a horror bit, we'll use that," I said.

He laughed, but the weird thing was that I did find a use for the psycho house.

Sucker Chase with the Lounge Lizard

Spring 1983

"So you've been out of circulation and you're looking for some action. You've come to the right place…because if you can't get it here, you can't get it anywhere."
—The Lounge Lizard
Intro to Lounge Lizard *Video Game*

IN A SCENE AS wild as any cutaway from my life in this book, we do a sudden change of world and I'm standing in Doubles, a singles bar in Norwalk,

Connecticut, with my old college buddy (and future best man) John Aristotle Phillips. We're looking at two of the highest-grossing models in New York that year, Wendy and Patty Determan, who are tall, blonde, and stunning in a Kim Basinger, Daryl Hannah, Sharon Stone kind of a way.

John was going out with Patty, and she'd agreed to act in an interactive video game called *Lounge Lizard*. The premise of *Lounge Lizard* was what my students would now call "elegant sketchy," though maybe without the elegant part. John's cousin, Ted Spirakis, played the titular character. It was a pick-a-path video game designed to work on RCA's new Interactive LaserDisc program. Basically, you have a choice of pickup lines that your character says to the girl. Say the right thing, and you get her phone number or she'll go out with you. Say the wrong thing, and you get flushed.

The problem, of course, was that besides our actresses being hugely successful models, they were identical twins. I hadn't bargained for that when I wrote the script, but it was a classy problem to have.

John and his brother Dean owned Aristotle Industries and still do. They're the preeminent makers of political software in America and have all sorts of ventures, including Predictit, but on that particular afternoon thirty-three years ago, they were scrambling around trying to figure out what the next move was. John had just run for Congress and lost for the second time. His "A-Bomb Kid" luster had worn off (he was famous in 1977 for designing a functioning atom bomb while flunking out of Princeton). He needed a new incarnation. They were working out of a crumbling house nearby donated by their campaign angel, which also served as the headquarters of Aristotle Industries 1.0.

I'm not sure how he'd done it, but he got a deal going with RCA, and I had the material from a schnook chase I'd gone on several months earlier with some rube who thought he had an "in" at RCA. *Lounge Lizard* was part of a planned series, including *Gold Grubber*, in which the player was a hot woman trying to "separate the schmucks from the bucks"—in other words, figure out who was the rich guy by asking the right questions.

The big win that day in Doubles was that we figured out how to shoot interactive. More specifically, Dean Phillips figured it out. What would have been a brain-buster for me was child's play for a Summa Cum Laude engineer from MIT. I've relied on engineers ever since. It's an entire skill set I don't and never will possess, though I've gotten good at understanding the issues and the practical aspects of what they say.

We shot it that day and had both discrete elements and a *Lounge Lizard* optimal path run-through on VHS—though, in those days, we didn't know language like "optimal path run-through." Of course, *Lounge Lizard* turned out to be a partial schnook chase—I think we got paid a little bit for it—as the product never appeared.

The road to Doubles started back in sixth grade. My teacher assigned us to write the first page of a story. The idea was that another student would write the second page and another would write a third page, and eventually we'd have a multi-authored story (the technical title for this type of exercise is "exquisite corpse," but that's not the term sixth-grade teachers use). After a few false starts from other students, I wrote a thing called "Ben and the Mini-Men." I have it somewhere, but put simply, it was the story of a kid named Ben (I can't remember, but I think I knew that was the teacher's first name) who had what amounts to a Mattel Creepy Crawlers set, which was basically an Easy Bake Oven, but instead of making food you filled critter molds with goop and baked them until they solidified.

At some point, they sold molds for army men along with little wires that you'd bake in to make the arms and legs bendable. Of course, they self-destructed with the first bend, but that's not the point. I had the idea that a kid got one of these and figured out how to bring these army men to life. In fact, he made a whole population of them. Then they escaped, and he had to go find and rescue them. Mr. Thomas loved "Ben and the Mini-Men." It was the first and only time a teacher saw any merit in my writing until college, as best I can remember, and that's probably no small part of why I'm a writer today.

Some other student followed me and took the story in some funky direction, and I think the whole project wheezed out. I kept thinking about my version, but more importantly, I got this idea that the story could branch. I could write my "Ben and the Mini-Men" story and everybody else could write theirs, and everybody was happy. And this was all happening the same year of the Ultimate Night of Television (*Green Hornet, Time Tunnel, Wild Wild West,* and *The Man from U.N.C.L.E.*). In some ways, I was just like a creepy crawler. The Plasti-Goo had been poured into the mold, and now it would only have to bake for about twenty years.

The next baking phase was in high school, when I decided to write what I called a "diamond story." It was a sci-fi story very derivative of "Kaleidoscope" by Ray Bradbury, but people had their brains put in boxes in orbit in case the human race was wiped out. The story probably sagged, but I did more or less create a pick-a-path. The difference was that my pick-a-paths all led to the same ending, there were just branches in between. At that point, I couldn't wrap my head around terminal paths. The diagrams I drew in my little composition book with the different branches were almost exactly what I ended up drawing up for video games later on, until we just made templates. This would pay off in *Soviet Strike, Terror T.R.A.X., Riddick: Butcher Bay, Uncharted*, a little bit in *Diablo III*, and in book form in the Sagard series with Gary. In fact, in the majority of games I've written.

It had never occurred to me in high school to do a branching movie. Of course, in fairness to myself, that would have been a real number with synchronized Super-8 projectors. The whole medium of branching game videos in that period would die with the death of the RCA LaserDisc system. I think they did a whodunit type game and some other experiments, but *Lounge Lizard* wasn't one of them.

And *Lounge Lizard* skittered off to oblivion for a few other reasons that had nothing to do with "not ready for primetime technology" or sleazy concepts. As fate would have it, a guy with whom I'd been on a previous snipe hunt involving *Lounge Lizard* suddenly popped up at RCA, claiming it was his idea. Ignore the fact that there was no record to support his claim and that all of the documents for *Lounge Lizard* were written by me and there were no other names on them, and ignore the fact that the snipe hunt had died because the guy was a limp shrimp (by my recollection) who couldn't really deliver what he said he'd deliver. I can't remember his name and probably wouldn't put it in here if I could.

My big lesson, and I'm still learning this, is that you have to be very clear in your relationships with people. Good ideas and the talent to express them are rare, but parasites are common. If something is your property, you have to say it, and you have to say it in writing. In informal situations where you don't want to call lawyers in, you have to say something like, "This is mine. Happy to have you explore it, but if nothing happens, it's mine until we formally change the relationship." This works in an email. It's a tough conversation to have, but not nearly as tough as it will be later on if you don't have a paper (or digital) trail.

In this case, I think that RCA figured out what was happening, but it cost time, and given that we're in the fruit business (green today, ripe tomorrow, rotten the next day), it ran out the clock on *Lounge Lizard*, and the project died. Not that I mourned it much even then, as I knew I didn't want my legacy in the world to be something called *Lounge Lizard*. And just so I'm clear, this had nothing to do with *Leisure Suit Larry in the Land of the Lounge Lizards*, which was released four years later. That was a totally different project by totally different people, and *Lounge Lizard* is now a VHS tape in some box in some storage area somewhere.

So was *Lounge Lizard* a waste of time?

No.

I harvested a lot from that schnook chase. I'd actually done an interactive video (if you didn't mind fast-forwarding a VHS), I'd met great people who I still know (Patty Determan would edit the third Agent 13 book, *Acolytes of Darkness*), and I sort of had something on my résumé. And when it comes to emergent technologies (we didn't have that phrase back then either), having *sort of something* on your résumé is a whole lot better than having *clearly nothing* on your résumé.

Little did I know that *Lounge Lizard* was just a dress rehearsal for my future adventures on the edge of tech, and frankly the adventures that have defined my later career. So, I'll say it straight out: just like in "Jack and the Beanstalk," a magic bean sometimes takes you into whole new worlds that exist in the clouds of not-yet reality.

Jack got a golden harp and a goose that laid golden eggs. I got my first practical experience in interactive media. The metaphor to a harp that I've been playing ever since isn't lost here, and it has laid many golden eggs for nearly four decades. Long live fool's errands, magic beans, fairy tale princesses, magical places, ogres, and treasures.

Lounge Lizard had all of them.

Meanwhile, Back at DDEC

BRANCHING STORIES, DECODED FAIRY tales, and "schmucks and bucks" were about to play a major role in my life, but first, a little context.

This is neither the time nor the place to write an elaborate history of TSR and Gary Gygax—Michael Witwer and others have done a great job of that—but it needs to be briefly summarized in order for the next part of the story to make any sense. Most of what follows is fairly uncontested history of TSR, but I'm quite sure that every single part of it could be a heated discussion. I have no interest in entering that discussion right now, only in telling this part of the history from my point of view, which may or may not be as valid as anybody else's. That's for somebody else to decide.

To me, TSR was a puzzle. At one level, it was a super-successful company with a huge intellectual property and the market cornered on a whole demographic of players. TSR was a giant sequoia in a forest of shrubs. It was a new and exciting entry into the world of games and media. Even then, I knew the ideas in D&D would change the world. Anybody with any instincts knew that it was not some passing fad but a portent to a much bigger change. While vilified in media by various televangelists and well-intentioned but ill-informed do-gooders, TSR was respected.

But it felt like there was something wrong.

There were whispers about financial issues, and it was clear Gary was on the outs with his partners, Brian and Kevin Blume. In short, the storm clouds were on the horizon, but the physical reality at that moment was that I was sitting in a mansion and I had a cool project to do. Another benefit to me was that as a result of Gary's falling out with his partners, he was exercising his right to do a project outside of TSR. Next thing I knew, the Conan book was moving to Simon & Schuster. That meant it couldn't be a

Conan book, which was fine with me, as I was all in for developing my own world and mythology.

We plotted away on *The Sceptre of Seven Souls*, but that was stuck in this "TSR or not TSR" world. So TSR seemed clogged to me, and if it was clogged to me, what could the future of DDEC possibly be? I'd wave these thoughts away like buzzing flies or mosquitos because I didn't want to think about these things, but they were there, and they kept buzzing.

The Simon & Schuster deal was very fair, and Gary split it with me, which was extremely generous, though we both knew that I'd be doing the heavy lifting. As it would turn out, Gary would be very present for the inception, plotting, gaming system, etc., though it was another Ernest Gary Gygax, Gary's son, who would drive the project home with me. That would be EGG III, aka Ernie Gygax. Speaking of whom, before we get rolling, a couple introductions are in order.

I have no memory of when I actually met Gary's sons, Luke and Ernie, but I think Ernie showed up first. My recollection is that, in the beginning, he'd surf back and forth between the family home and TSR headquarters in Lake Geneva and Beverly Hills. I have no clear memory of Luke showing up. I'd met him a year earlier at their house in Wisconsin, along with the three Gygax daughters—Heidi, Elise, and Cindy—who for some reason never made it out to the mansion.

What I do remember is that we started hanging out almost instantly. Luke was the first person in my lifetime that I ever felt any particular responsibility for. God help him, but he came out great despite an amazing amount of bad influence. Luke is now a Lieutenant Colonel in the US Army and a real buff soldier. At the time, he was a soft thirteen-year-old kid. I was trying to write Sagard from his point of view, and Sagard was thirteen. Editor Wendy Barrish correctly pointed out that nobody wanted to be thirteen, and so we made him sixteen, but Luke's presence was amazingly helpful.

To an extent.

Just as I was somewhat professionalized in evaluating potential comic strips for my father's newspaper syndicate by the time I was eight, Gary Gygax's son was not exactly a noob to sword and sorcery stories. Still, he was thirteen. He was also old beyond his years and both intellectually and emotionally intelligent enough to have a strong intuitive understanding of where he was. At least, it seemed that way. When I was taking a break, we'd play *Bogus League Football* on their Intellivision, and I'm not sure I ever won a game. We joked about the *Beverly Hillbillies* aspects of their life. We'd call the pool the "cement pond" and wondered why there were so many Elly Mays around and no grannies. He was extremely cognizant of his family's financial upgrade. I only abstractly knew it, but I had no idea how dire their finances had been.

Suffice to say that Luke had to have been amazed by the fruits of a different financial status. Still, we laughed about Gary's fifteen-hundred-dollar blue jeans (they did look good) and some of the shocking wastes of money. I was utterly unaware of the strict Jehovah's Witnesses upbringing the kids had, because Gary was living about as far from a Spartan religious life as he could get. (He'd return to it later, but in that period in the mansion, Jehovah was looking in a whole different direction.)

I've known Luke from his early teens to his late forties, and while there have been incredible ups and downs for D&D and the Gygaxes, he is virtually unchanged since then. And that is notable. Talk about a child at risk in an incredibly dangerous golden ghetto. He was going to school at the time, but I had no idea where. Never crossed my mind. He didn't seem like an actual thirteen-year-old kid, and he was so much more sophisticated than I had been that I treated him as a miniature adult or member of the creative team.

At that juncture, I was a well-paid animation writer. Money just wasn't something I thought about. I was living very cheaply. I didn't want for anything and I didn't really want anything, and if I did, I bought it. I always knew I had more than enough to cover any check I was likely to write, so I didn't bother to balance my checkbook. My mother came down every year and did my taxes.

At the time, and still, I was extremely paranoid about drugs. My only addiction was cigarettes, and they were still cheap and easily available, and you could smoke anywhere. No part of me grokked why people would go broke to get cocaine or why women would do the "poke for the coke." I'm not a teetotaler, but alcohol is mostly a "take it or leave it" proposition to me. Yeah, there were the Trader Vic's nights, but left to my own resources, I'd forget it existed. This, of course, caused me to miss the fact that there were alcoholics and budding alcoholics all around me. In short, I more or less went through life thinking everybody was like me and missed a whole lot as a result. In my own defense, I was young. Looking back, lots of things should have been obvious.

While it's fun to make fun of the circus, let's look at the world from Gary's point of view for a moment. When D&D hit the world like a hurricane, Gary hadn't been to the circus before. He'd done cool and significant stuff, some sideshows and maybe a few roadside attractions, but not the big circus. Then, all of a sudden, he was the ringmaster. Not only was old Jed a millionaire, he was also Midas and Mephistopheles all rolled into one.

There's no question in my mind that Gary's alignment was good, but being good doesn't make you a saint. And for much of his life, as a Jehovah's Witness, he'd tried to emulate a saint. He studied the Bible (it's hard to look at D&D and not see that, though I didn't get it at the time), and it is impossible to imagine how somebody who'd been laboring in obscurity, clonking away on a basement typewriter by night and being the Lake Geneva shoe repairman and on food stamps by day, could handle the amazing number of threats and opportunities coming his way. Of course he couldn't avoid being affected by it. Could anybody?

The money flooded in faster than Gary could figure out where to put it. TSR grew faster than anybody could keep track of it. A large pile of unguarded money attracts sleaze monkeys like blood attracts sharks. In rolled the advisors and the lawyers and various other predators and parasites, and before long, he wasn't in control of the company he'd created.

Once something's this big, everybody wants a piece of it. Some cajole, others reason, others flat-out steal. You have to make deals to get things done. In the beginning, there was no money for lawyers, and a deal hashed out over a card table in 1972 sounds very different in a courtroom in 1982.

Gary had gone from Lake Geneva to the ocean, and as any dive instructor will tell you, once you step into the ocean, you enter the food chain. He'd gone from an aquarium to the Great Barrier Reef, and the threats came from everywhere. Nobody does anything alone. How should he reward or not reward all of the other people who were components of the D&D breakthrough? There would be legal action for decades after. Dave Arneson, Will Niebling, and others would want their piece of the pie. Did they deserve it? Who knows. I wasn't there. However, I have been in enough situations where people squabbled over credit for an idea to know that if five people are in a room when a good idea happens, all five of them think it was theirs. And it's not that they're bad people; that's just the way the human brain works. No idea is real until you can imagine it, and from your perspective, the idea is born the minute you have it. All that came before is irrelevant.

But imagine what this all looks like to Gary, when old friends are suddenly showing up with lawsuits and he goes from obscurity to being brown-mouthed by the media. Most of the people who played roles in D&D eventually found a happy place somewhere in TSR, got their moment in the spotlight to take the bow, and moved happily on. But not everybody did.

And, if you're Gary, what are you thinking at 3 a.m. when you're all alone? Was it really you? Did you just get lucky? Or are you really that good? Wasn't it you who kept soldiering on when everybody else drifted away? Wasn't it you who had their family assembling the box and mailing the orders and, in the case of your daughter Elise, posing in your ads?

Yes. Others participated, but would all of this have happened if you hadn't been in the center of it? Unlikely.

And then there's the fame. People you don't know are asking you for autographs. You are suddenly a celebrity and you are handled by PR people who want to help you with your "image." Funny, your image was just fine while you were creating Gen-Con, but now you need to fix it.

People are calling you a genius. That's not the problem, because you are one. The problem is that people are attributing all sorts of things to you that just don't feel real. Are you really a business genius, or are you just somebody who invented a product with so much merit that people are willing to pay for it? The answer might seem clear a few decades later, but when you see your company on the cover of *INC* magazine, you have to wonder if you might not also be the greatest businessman in history. Maybe you were right all along and everybody else was wrong.

What would that feel like? Imagine reading articles about yourself praising or damning you, and almost all of them get the facts wrong. Some of the errors are honest, some of them are simplifications of incredibly complex stories, some of them are downright libel. And then you become a news story because some kid in Michigan vanishes and the press goes into a frenzy, blaming D&D.[3] Nobody bothers to apologize when they find out the story is bogus.

And your wife is still asking when you're going to take out the garbage.

At what point do you lose track of who you are?

Next thing you know, televangelists are accusing you of Satanic practices (and in this case, you're a Jehovah's Witness and have raised your family strictly that way).

And you get called names. You're "King of the Nerds." And that was before nerds got their revenge. At that point, it was downright insulting, and it was meant that way.

You've got weendanglers from *60 Minutes* lighting and shooting you like you're the star of a horror film. Don't believe me? Just watch the segment online. You don't need a degree in cinema to see the cheesy tricks.

And you're getting calls from Hollywood.

Never underestimate the pull of fame and celebrity—especially when you're being called the "King of the Nerds." Maybe you don't want to be a nerd. A trip down the red carpet with famous people will wash that stench clean.

And you know the pitfalls. You know Hollywood is one big nasty dungeon. You know you can't trust the treasure map some guy sold you. You know it's filled with other wizards and sorcerers and enchantresses, rogues and thieves. You know they serve stuff a lot stronger than Elvish Ale there and you know, intellectually, that if they have one core competency, it is "separating the shmucks from their bucks." But, still, you want to go. You

---

3   James Dallas Egbert III disappeared from his dormitory room at Michigan State University on August 15, 1979. The fact that he was a D&D player who might have "vanished into the underground tunnels at the University" was seized upon by the press and investigators alike and lifted D&D from obscurity to national fame and big sales. It turned out that he had a number of psychological problems and D&D had nothing to do with his disappearance.

know it is very unlikely that you'll win the game. And you also know that you'll never forgive yourself if you don't try.

Hollywood pays off in the form of the CBS Saturday Morning *Dungeons & Dragons* show. Gary met Stan Lee in that period. So did I. At that point, Stan Lee was a walking cautionary tale of what could happen to Gary. He was basically golden handcuffed (or maybe silver or copper handcuffed, I don't know what his deal was) at Marvel Productions and used as a "closer." That's how I met him. They wanted to do Buck Rogers and brought him in at the end of the pitch. Charming guy. He was an icon of my childhood even though I wasn't a comic reader after eighth grade, but still, it was a big deal for me. And it made me sad. He seemed so domesticated.

Of course, forbearance is an underrated virtue, and Stan Lee got the last laugh against the world. I'd work with him years later on a Spider-Man TV show in the early nineties. But right then, it just seemed sad. At least Jack Kirby was doing what he loved to do and was respected. I vaguely remember Gary sharing my feelings about Stan Lee. What I don't know is if he saw a potential future in being like Stan Lee, or what he would have thought about it.

Gary still maintained all of his creative powers, but he wasn't working them out as much. If he were a body builder, I'd say he was in maintenance mode. He wasn't crashed on the creative couch getting flabby, but he wasn't buffing, either. He was frying different fish. Exotic ones. I don't remember talking much to Gary about comic books, but certainly he was literate in them. The one thing I remember is him saying that Advanced Dungeons & Dragons (AD&D) was created so players couldn't suddenly have the Silver Surfer show up in an adventure.

Along those lines, *Dungeons & Dragons* had a unique problem: it was a world without specific characters. Tracy Hickman and Margaret Weiss were changing that with the *Dragonlance* series (which would, to this day, be a great TV series; I'm surprised that it hasn't happened in the wake of *Game of Thrones*).

In any case, that's my best picture of what was going on in Gary's mind as he hit Tinseltown. But there were other pressing matters to attend to.

Our first challenge was a set of "fight-a-path" books while we incubated *The Sceptre of Seven Souls* and various other projects.

I remember the day Gary Gygax and I named Sagard. It wasn't some sensitive writer moment, where we asked something like, "What do I feel about this character?" There was no writing class exercise along the lines of, "If this character could speak his own name, what words would emerge from his lips?" That's the brand of writer hoo-hah that I simultaneously find both embarrassing and marginally intriguing.

The way we came up with the name Sagard was that we had a contract sitting in front of us from Simon & Schuster and a great young editor named Wendy Barrish. The setting was Gary's upstairs suite at the DDEC mansion. The light was falling at that "it can be any time of the afternoon" angle. You live in LA, you become your own sundial, because the sun is always there.

Gary and Gail were leaving for Andre Moullon's place in Morocco, so we had to sign the contract before he left. And in order to sign the contract, we had to have a name for the project.

Our character was a young barbarian. Nobody in the story knew his name, thus nobody had a reason to use it, thus Gary and I had no reason to know it. I thought he was kind of a Nordic hero. I always thought the name Asgard, home of the gods, with a whisper of Thor and Odin was cool. So we flopped the first two letters and saw Sagard.

Looked good to us.

Done.

Never looked back.

Was it a good choice? Sagard is hardly a household name, but I've never looked back and winced. Nobody ever vomited on it. But then, maybe it never really excited anybody. Naming books, movies, shows, and games is a tricky business. Sometimes we'd come up with the name in the beginning with the premise, and sometimes we got near the end and got a better idea. Or the names came out of a piece of dialogue and we thought that would be a great name for the episode. Sometimes we'd make a list. But rarely was an episode referred to during production by its name. Episodes were slowly born with a number attached to them and a working title on the charts.

Naming characters is incredibly hard. You can argue a plot from the point of view of logic, but how do you logically argue a name? Ian Fleming called his most famous character "James Bond" because he thought it sounded boring. I think the opposite. I think of Bond Street, bonds as instruments of big money. I think of a sacred bond. And then James seems like an aristocratic action name, but what do I know?

Or better put, what did Ian Fleming know? That name would emblazon an action film series that still sells tickets well into twenty-first century. I've always wondered why he'd want a character name that was boring, but then, having worked on multiple characters with names like Samantha Strong and Max Fury, maybe boring is good.

To be totally honest, I would never have named a character Han Solo, or Napoleon Solo for that matter. I would only have named a Native American character Luke Skywalker. And Sherlock Holmes? What kind of name is that? I can understand Bruce Wayne, sort of. Clark Kent at least hits me as Midwestern and solid.

And then real life gives you names that only seem to come out of fiction. Just look at American football. Joe Montana? Bart Starr? Johnny Unitas? Peyton Manning? Can any of those names possibly be real? Casino owners named Trump and Wynn? And this is coming from a guy named Flint Dille. Names are tricky.

The hardest thing to remember is that life is irrational, and art is especially irrational. That's where you get to the "rule of cool." If you think it's cool, it rules. Ignore the rest of the world.

Liberated from *Conan* (and this is no slur to Robert E. Howard, but I wanted to do my own thing), Sagard morphed a lot. Obviously, it had to stay in something like a D&D universe or what's the point of buying a book from Gary Gygax, but we had a lot of latitude. The first thing I thought of was that this barbarian world was built on the ruins of a tech world like ours. It's hidden under the surface. The irony is that at that exact moment I was working with both Joe Ruby and Steve Gerber, who had explored very similar territory with *Thundarr the Barbarian*. I knew the title Thundarr but had never seen an episode.

The lead-in for the first Sagard book, *The Ice Dragon*, was a great sign of the times. In the eighties, you began a character with his origin story and leveled him up. The *Conan* movie was in the air, as of course was *Star Wars*, and this was an opportunity to monetize the ancient history my parents paid for.

As far as game design, it was basic. We had one good wrinkle, which was that the reader, if they didn't have dice, could flip the pages for a die-roll outcome. We decided to go with D4, partly because I thought D4s looked cool (they are pyramids) and partly because the player could also use two coins to get results. I'm not sure I'd go for that now, but in fall of 1983, it seemed like a really great idea.

We wanted a Robert E. Howard feel to the book, so before we could start, Gary challenged me to a test—something of a literary version of the test Sagard would take in the book. Since the book was told in second person and present tense, I was to translate some Howard passages of my choosing to the same POV, reimagine the particulars, and then write samples of my own. When he couldn't tell me from Howard, we could start. In hindsight, I strongly recommend exercises like this and should do this more often.

So off I went. The interesting thing was that I'd never written a book or really designed a game before, but I don't remember being afraid of it. After all, I had the greatest game designer in the world, maybe ever, by my side and a number one show on Saturday morning. What could go wrong?

It's great being young. It was great for Sagard, and it was great for me. Sagard's first adventure began as follows:

YOU ARE SAGARD

You are sixteen years old.

All your life, you have wanted to enter the Warriors' Lodge. Though you are strong and have already reached a height of over six feet, the warriors of the tribe think you are still a boy. You will not be a man until you pass the Ordeal of Courage.

To do so, you must perform a brave deed and bring back a trophy as proof. Your trophies, whether they are the fang of a death viper or the scalp of a mountain bandit, will be presented before the Warriors with your tale. If they approve, the elk's-horn goblet will be presented to you. If they reject you, you will be greeted with ridicule and will leave the hut in shame, never again to return to your tribe. Can you pass the Ordeal of Courage...?

It was freezing cold when I wrote *The Ice Dragon*—or at least as freezing cold as Los Angeles gets. LA isn't set up for the thirties. I grew up in a suburb of Chicago, so I know what real cold is, but Chicago is ready for cold. Houses have heat and are insulated and you have the clothes for it. The converted stable without proper windows and doors at the Dungeons & Dragons mansion was the coolest office ever, in multiple ways.

Gary and I wrote out the first chapters of Sagard together sitting at my DecMate II. It was fun as hell. We'd just write away and laugh all the way through it. The funny thing about a lot of geniuses is that you'd be amazed by how much time they spend laughing over the stuff they do, especially when the final product isn't something you would describe as comedy.

Gary and Frank Miller are both like this. You think of *Sin City* as dark, but when Frank was actually working on it, he'd call me up laughing about all of the various undignified ways thugs could die, and pretty much everything else. It was always "top that idea" or "let's go one further." This was true of Sagard, though by nature of being a "fight-a-path" book, they were short chapters and the fun was in finding surprising ways to pay off the consequences of winning or losing or fleeing a fight.

The first few encounters probably show how I was freezing when I was writing this book more than anything else:

"A mistral wind blows across the icy moors, blowing back your thick, dark hair."

"The night winds howl, and stray bits of Icy Cold sleet sting your eyes."

Okay, so there were no icy moors and no sleet in LA. I'd left all that back in Chicago. But even with my lame heater in the converted stable, it felt like an icy journey. So if Sagard was Luke when I wrote him, was the Ratikkan girl Peggy Wilkins, who referred to me as "her barbarian" but who looked more like a seductive princess than a thick-limbed, barbarian Frazetta?

Who knows, but what's fascinating—and this was not evident at the time—is how much what I was writing reflected my real life. Of course, the Gamesmaster would bring this all home in an almost prescient way, but that was later.

I sent the first Sagard book, *The Ice Dragon*, out to Wendy Barrish at Simon & Schuster, and she liked it. Ordered three more. Months fell off the calendar. Gary was out of town a lot in that period. I got sucked into *Robo Force* and plotted the next three novels and didn't worry about the fact that I had to write three more books. Non-linear was, and still is, much easier for me than linear. It's not an accident that I've spent so much time in the game world. The problem is that game writing didn't really exist then the way it does now. Pick-a-paths and modules were the outer edge.

If DDEC had a golden age, this was it. It was a magical place stocked like a fantasy story with beautiful women, colorful characters (some of the beautiful women were also colorful characters), odd knights errant on unknown missions, sand-table conquerors, flim-flammers, magicians, studio executives, agents, evil sorcerers (literally), dubious business characters, and run by a real-life wizard.

At that age, for someone in my shoes, could life have been any better?

Enter the Robots

Ruby-Spears—Winter 1984

SOMEWHERE IN THE LATE winter/early spring of 1984, I started hearing vague things about *Star Wars* animated shows called *Droids* and *Ewoks*—first from Joey Thompson, then Charlie Lippencott. Charlie asked for writing samples and said he was going to submit them to Lucasfilm. It was incredibly exciting, but not something I took very seriously. There was zero chance that I was going to get to be a story editor on a *Star Wars* TV show.

It would be hard to be more dominant than Lucasfilm was in 1984. The *Star Wars* trilogy had been released and had broken record after record. The toy line was booming, still, and the movie I knew as "Indy

2" was set to come out that summer. *Raiders of the Lost Ark* was, and still is, one of my all-time favorite films. I had no idea what the next movie was going to be about, except that I'd seen a trailer in which George Lucas and Steven Spielberg were all over the world shooting what would become *Indiana Jones and the Temple of Doom*. All you saw of Indy in that trailer was Harrison Ford saying, "Trust me."

And I did.

This was going to be great.

Around that time, I was working on my first foray into robots with a thing called *Robo Force*, which was based on a toy line launching from Ideal Toys. Frankly, most of what I know about the deal and the sponsor is what I found on Wikipedia. I remember meeting with Joe Ruby and a couple executives and seeing some prototypes. The gag with the toys is that they were various R2D2-looking robots with suction cups on the bottom and various claws and things.

I didn't visualize suction cups when I wrote it. Instinctually, I knew our show wasn't supposed to be about the reality of the toy, but the fantasy that the toy evoked. Much later, I'd learn that sometimes you can't get past the reality of the product, but I didn't know that as I started on *Robo Force*.

I also didn't know that *Robo Force* would be a dress rehearsal for something much bigger. If I were trying to encapsulate the stories being born in 1984, *Robo Force* is it. The very nature of the plot (putting human brains into robots) is a huge step darker than where cartoons had been in the past, mixed with the fact that real people were interfacing with technology in ways they never had.

I had nothing to do with casting *Robo Force*, but take a look at it and see if you see the same thing I did.

Michael Bell—Cruel

Rodger Bumpass—Mark Fury

Arthur Burghardt—Nazgar, Sentinel

Peter Cullen—Coptor, Vulgar

Ron Feinberg—Hun-Dred

David Mendenhall—Jason Fury

Robert Ridgely—Councilman Frost

Neil Ross—Blazer

John Stephenson—Dr. Fury

B. J. Ward—Deena Strong

Alan Young—S.O.T.A.

I went down the list and, without trying, found Optimus Prime, Duke, Scarlett, Destro, and about fifty other Sunbow characters. I'd also run into several of these actors working on video games in the 1990s and 2000s. I only found two of them who were never on any of our shows, and one of them was on *GoBots*, our competitor. Whatever else you want to say about *Robo Force*, you could make the argument that it formed the backbone of the Sunbow cast and is a collection of voices that defined multiple eras and mediums (just look at their video game credits).

And notice the names. Except for S.O.T.A. (which was an acronym for "State of the Art," a big phrase in the early eighties), the names were "action" names. They were names designed to give the figures a sense of power and hopefully translate into "empowerment" for the boys, because the theme of boys' toys in that era was empowerment, even though terms like that wouldn't become fashionable until much later.

There was another backbeat to all of this that I felt but didn't really grasp, and that was that we were living in the last moment of old-fashioned childhoods when cartoons were for kids. Yeah, the boys at Termite Terrace (Warner Brothers Cartoons) slipped things in for adults, but that was because they made cartoons that were made to be shown before movies that adults would watch.

At that time, everybody in America knew the Bible quote: "When I was a child, I spoke as a child, I understood as a child, I thought as a child; but when I became a man, I put away childish things. For now we see in a mirror, darkly, but then face to face." I left the "mirror darkly" bit in there because it sounds cool, and also, people were no longer looking into onyx mirrors, but shiny big-screen TVs, and the only way to tell fantasy stories was either through extremely expensive feature films and TV shows or animation. And so animation began to serve as a kind of methadone for sci-fi addicts.

All of that having been said, in the early eighties any adult male would rather have been caught with porn than toys. I got a pass because I was in the business, but only sort of. There were dates who definitely thought it was weird (most notably the woman I ended up marrying). Blue for Boys and Pink for Girls and lines between childhood and adulthood and masculine and feminine have rainbowed since then, but in 1983, the lines were sharp and nobody crossed them.

Robo Force aired somewhere in 1984 and it vanished without a trace.

Recently, Toyfinity did some great models of them without the suction cups. They looked a lot better.

Journey to the Fabled Land

Spring 1984

IT'S THE FINAL SCENE of *The Maltese Falcon*. If you haven't seen it, see it. Setup: Sam Spade, our hardboiled PI protagonist, finally gets his hands on the Maltese Falcon. He realizes that it's worthless. The guy with him asks:

Polhaus: *[lifting the fake falcon]* It's heavy. What is it?

Spade: The, uh, stuff that dreams are made of.

We can debate whether he was talking about the Falcon or the relationship he'd entered into with the ultimately treacherous femme fatale, but it doesn't matter. It's a great scene. By the way, this final scene came from two great writers. The first was Dashiell Hammett, who wrote the novel; the second was John Huston, who wrote the script.

So what happens when your ultimate dream comes true?

Well, my dream and the dream of just about every other writer in Hollywood that year—was about to come true. As I was finishing *Robo Force* and contemplating new episodes for *Mister T*, the *Star Wars* Saturday morning show came bubbling up to the surface. It was for real, and they were interested in me. Charlie Lippencott and Susan Nicoletti, who made the connection as we were working on an ill-fated *Buck Rogers* movie project, cautioned me not to talk about it. Everything at Lucasfilm was super secret. I had no trouble keeping my mouth shut. I'd like to believe it was because I can keep a secret, but it was probably because I didn't want to have to "un-tell" people about it when it didn't happen.

I met with Miki Herman, who would be the producer of the *Star Wars* shows, and it went well. Miki looked and dressed like a character from *Star Wars*, or at least a Jedi, and with her white flowing clothes and short-cropped hair, you could put her in a modern episode and she'd fit right in. My biggest impression of the meeting was that the Jedi were real, and I'd met one.

I can't remember the exact moment I got the job, but it seems to me that I had some warning. Maybe it was from Joey or Charlie Lippencott. I just can't remember. What I do remember was hearing that the fact that I went to the USC film school was the determining factor in Lucas's mind—welcome to the power of academic networks.

In somewhere around two years, I'd gone from loser noob to story editor on a *Star Wars* property. Two years might seem like a long time, but it sure seemed like it was happening fast.

Story Editor on A *STAR WARS* TV SHOW!!!

And in true mythical fashion, there was a prophecy. Steve Gerber had said, "You haven't figured it out, but you live a charmed life. You're going to end up writing the next *Raiders of the Lost Ark*."

Even as I sit here, I'm trying to put together the incredibly complex set of emotions that were surging through me at that moment. I'm quite sure that in spring of 1984, somebody was having a better geek experience, but I can't imagine who it would have been—other than my partner in crime, Paul Dini, who had been hired to story edit the "Ewoks" half of the *Star Wars* show.

As elated and inflated as I might have felt, there was still the everyday business to get done. Joey negotiated the deal, and it was a good one, but the money wasn't silly. I also had an uncomfortable task ahead of me, and that was telling Joe Ruby. I don't think I had a formal contract to be let out of, but I wanted it to go well. Joe gave me my big break, and I didn't look at *Star Wars* as something that was going to take very long. I had this idea that I'd be up there for a couple months and then be back.

It wasn't a formal meeting. I ran into Joe in the parking lot and just blurted it out. Joe being the great guy that he is, he understood that no twenty-seven-year-old guy could pass up working on *Star Wars*, and he knew I was a loyal guy and that far worse things could happen than having an ally at Lucasfilm. I said I'd come back when it was done and Joe went for it. It was just that clean and simple, and it was a big favor that I wouldn't be able to pay back for a few years.

Miki Herman had been at Lucasfilm for a long time. She'd worked her way up the ranks, and *Droids* and *Ewoks* seemed like a reward for her meritorious service. She'd never produced an animated show before, but that didn't seem to matter. We were Lucasfilm. The normal rules didn't apply to us. We were going to change the face of Saturday morning, and the attitude, which didn't just come from Miki but from all of us, was a combination of starry-eyed idealism and a certain amount of arrogance. But you almost can't fault the arrogance, if that's what it was. Lucasfilm could do no wrong. With three *Star Wars* films already a success and the second Indy film coming out, they were flying.

Paul Dini was the perfect person to go on this adventure with. Paul was in his mid-twenties and already a vet of Filmation, Hanna-Barbera, and Ruby-Spears. Animation and comics were in his blood. He writes from inside the characters out. I don't know where I write from, but it's not there. Paul has a wonderful ability to describe what characters are feeling in a completely fantastical world. I mean, you'd think that characters in fantastical worlds would think fantastical things that we can't imagine, but Paul always seems to be able to get inside of everything from goofy cartoon characters to Batman. Later, he would create Harley Quinn.

Very early on, Miki got me and Paul Dini into a prerelease screening of *Indiana Jones and the Temple of Doom* on the 20th Century Fox lot—my first prepremiere. Strutting onto the lot with my pass and ticket, there is no way to overstate my sense of having made it.

The movie started out great. The scene in the Chinese restaurant with the sleazy gangsters, the archeological artifact—it was everything I liked about hero pulp.

It was all great until Short Round showed up.

I'm not sure why this broke it for me, but it did. I felt like I'd already seen that character in *Goonies*, and there was something fundamentally wrong about Indiana Jones hauling a kid along on an adventure. And I missed Marion Ravenwood. Not that there was anything wrong with Willie Scott, but come on. Of course, I realized that Indy was more like James Bond than a family man, but I was invested in her and that relationship in a way I was never invested in Pussy Galore or Domino or even Solitaire. You'd marry Marion. Nobody in their right mind was going to marry Honey Ryder or Holly Goodhead.

I'm not sure I entirely processed the thought that I was disappointed by *Indiana Jones and the Temple of Doom*. If I had that thought, I didn't let it very far in. I tried to keep it at bay. Not only was it a depressing thought, but it was a useless thought.

We got working on the bibles for *Droids* and *Ewoks*. I approached it exactly the way we did at Ruby-Spears, except this was the first time I was translating a very well-established franchise from one medium to another. There was no way I could have known at the time that this was how I would spend no small part of my career. The *Star Wars* Saturday morning show had two parts more or less divided along the younger/older and the boy/girl (remember, it was the eighties) parts of *Star Wars*. *Droids* was the metal and machines and ray guns, and *Ewoks* was the soft, cuddly part (or the "squishy" part). Of course, *Ewoks* had battles and *Droids* had soft moments, but the lines, in eighties terms, were clear.

Paul and I worked on both franchises, but for all practical purposes, I was on *Droids* with Art Cover assisting me. Charlie knew him, and he was a good choice. Art somewhat reminded me of Joe Walsh. He seemed like a rock 'n' roll guy. He was smart as hell, and his girlfriend at the time owned a sci-fi bookstore. He knew a lot about the medium, and having him around was like having the Sundance Kid around, what with his long blond hair and ice-blue eyes.

Paul was paired up with Bobby Carrau, who was George Lucas's friend and who reminded me of Luke Skywalker. He'd written *Caravan of Courage: An Ewok Adventure*, a television film that aired in 1984, and so he knew the characters and world extremely well. His friendship with George gave us a sense of proximity to him that we didn't have with Miki, who seemed to have a more formal relationship with him.

At one point, Miki decided I needed a more up-to-date haircut and took us to some elite place in Beverly Hills. I remember the cut looking pretty extreme, but as I didn't comb my hair in those days and rarely looked into mirrors, I'd forgotten all about it until I got up to San Francisco and Sarah Knapp, the college girlfriend with whom I wrote my first novel, saw me and immediately said, "Great punk haircut." At some point it grew out, and I returned to my more familiar "it's curly so he doesn't comb it" haircut.

Some eras of your life are defined by your haircut.

Eventually, we went up to Northern California. The Ranch was just opening, so we were based in the Kerner Building in San Rafael. It was a standard eighties office building. They didn't have anywhere to put us, so we moved into the president's office, which was vacant because the president had just been fired.

Paul and Art and I seemed to rattle around in the gigantic office. It weird, but there was something cool about it, and I liked being back in Northern California near Berkeley. It made me feel a little bit like being back in college. There was something kind of metaphorical about being in San Rafael, in that in one direction was Marin County (and that seemed like the future), and looking the other way out of the window I could see Berkeley (and that was the past). Those were heady days, though, and I was constantly thinking in terms of metaphors and symbols. It's a great way to be if you're a writer, but it's not terribly useful for real life.

As a film industry noob, I remember being amazed at an office pool going on over the first weekend box office for *Indiana Jones and the Temple of Doom*. The thing that struck me was not that there was a bet over whether it would break the all-time weekend box office record for a film, but that the bet was over *by how much* it would beat the all-time box office for that weekend (May 8, 1984). I distinctly remember thinking, "It is never going to be this easy again." I'm not sure why the thought struck me, but as their next film was the Steve Gerber–created *Howard the Duck*, I was certainly proven correct.

As a side note, I've never seen *Howard the Duck*. You'd think I would have, given that I had worked with Steve Gerber since 1983 and would work with him until 1987 and occasionally after that. However, I happened to be out of town the weekend it opened, and the news was so grim that I just didn't want to be on record as having an opinion about the film. I just kept saying, "Haven't seen it yet," until the subject dropped. This was cowardly, yes, but sometimes you just don't want to be in the middle of a controversy.

I'd raise this to an art when the Michael Keaton *Batman* came out. No part of me wanted to be in the middle of that conversation, though in that case I actually *had* seen it early on and kind of pretended I hadn't. I was very interested in knowing others' opinions but extremely uninterested in expressing my own. There was a "caring" differential. Frank Miller and Paul Dini and others in our crowd really cared, and everybody else had a big reaction, and part of the fun for me was betting on what people would think.

The funny thing is, I don't remember anybody ever asking my opinion.

The Sanctus Sanctorum. Holy of Holies.

Summer 1984

THE *DROIDS/EWOKS STAR WARS* Saturday morning show team—me, Miki Herman, Paul Dini, Bobby Carrou, and Art Cover—left from San Francisco on a postcard-clear summer morning and drove north across the Golden Gate Bridge, under the rainbow tunnel into Marin County, and kept driving for a long time into the countryside up Lucas Valley Road, past a Mewok Gas Station and a rock that looked like Darth Vader's head, up another road to Skywalker Ranch.

In the summer of 1984, there was no cooler place in the world to be than Skywalker Ranch. It wasn't fully operational yet, but close enough. The main structure was a giant white Americana Victorian building that reminded me of Main Street at Disneyland, and for some reason I remember seeing glass chips in the ground like little jewels. I figured they were remnants from the stained-glass windows. I have no idea why that detail is locked in my head.

I don't remember what security we went through or how long we waited before being led through a labyrinthine set of corridors and stairs to George Lucas's office. It felt like a game quest where only the locals knew the path. It's all a blurry set of shots now. The office itself was perfect. Big desk. Bookshelves. Props. Posters. Memorabilia. I did note a set of D&D monster manuals and players guides just like I had at the D&D mansion.

And then, finally, the real George Lucas was sitting in front of us. He looked exactly like George Lucas was supposed to, with his black hair with stripes of gray that lived right on the edge of cool hot-rodder and auteur filmmaker. This was the guy who had changed the world seven years earlier, and now I was actually getting to talk to him.

The meeting was mostly him giving us his vision of the show. I don't remember being nervous so much as being in awe, mostly that I was actually in that place in that time and doing what I was doing. And I realized it at that moment—that's the good thing. Life doesn't give you a lot of moments like that, so you have to snag them when they happen. Anything was possible. If this were a movie, I would have been hearing Steve Gerber's echoey voice saying, "Haven't you figured out that you have a charmed life…" and kind of believing it. At that moment, it felt like I was exactly the right person in the right place at the right time.

It was one of those situations where you're trying so hard to hear everything that you hear nothing at all. We grabbed onto stuff. John Ford. The Cavalry Trilogy. Laurel and Hardy, even *Beverly Hills Cop* (maybe that came later). I didn't know how all of those things synthesized, but I'd figure it out or die trying. In a nutshell, the premise of the show was the adventures of Artoo and Threepio before they met Luke Skywalker. The idea was that they had a number of different owners/masters, and we'd follow their adventures. We didn't get to use any of the other *Star Wars* characters so as not to bump into the upcoming prequels.

There was a transcriptionist. Somewhere in a box in my semi-mythical storage area near the lost *Transformers: Secret of Cybertron* script and all of the other stuff I hope exists, there might be a transcript of the meeting, though I couldn't print it or quote it here even if I wanted to; it's not my property.

I walked away from the meeting with a bunch of notes and two books. They were the secret formula for writing. They were the holy grail of entertainment. The two books were:

1. *The Uses of Enchantment* by Bruno Bettelheim. Bettelheim was not an alien to me. I'd read *The Informed Heart* in college.

2. *The Hero with a Thousand Faces* by Joseph Campbell. As an Ancient History major, Joseph Campbell was not an alien to me either, but I'd never read the book.

After the meeting, I drove down to Carmel, where my mother was living, and read the books twice, highlighting everything. I utterly believed that I now had possession of the holy grail of successful popular entertainment. At least, part of me thought that. Another part didn't really believe there was a holy grail. I'm still not sure.

I'd study Campbell's book like it was the Dead Sea Scrolls that weekend. Joseph Campbell would become doctrine in Hollywood for a generation, and the echoes still linger on. The thing I didn't know was that I was on my own Hero's Journey, or that thirty-five years later I'd be writing this book, loosely structured in the same exact way.

The time up north writing the first bible was a blur. I wrote it on my MacIntosh, on MacWrite or whatever their bare-bones program was called. Microsoft Word wasn't available. The great thing about the first Mac was that it was semiportable. It had a sleek bag that carried the keyboard and mouse. Ignore that it was almost unusable; that didn't matter. I was at Lucasfilm and working on the coolest computer in the world. Miki sprung for a dot matrix printer. Along with the Campbell and Bettelheim books, George told us to look at the John Wayne Cavalry movies—*Fort Apache, She Wore a Yellow Ribbon,* and *Rio Grande*—for inspiration.

There never seemed to be the intensity around *Ewoks* that there was around *Droids*—either that, or Paul is just cooler, calmer, and more collected than I was. We were in a hurry, so the bible had to get done fast. We wrote it, thought it was great, printed it out. It was a very exotic-looking document for the day, printed on Mac fonts and not daisy wheel. I felt like I was living on the cutting edge. Then we went back to LA and waited for the verdict. But we were confident.

The bible felt like a bullseye.

Joseph Campbell doesn't talk about the Nervous Blissful Moment, and in fact, nobody else does either. It's that moment when you're done with a project and feel great about it. But you don't know how well it will be received. Rumor had it that George Lucas went to Hawaii when his movies were about to come out. It's that moment when you've done everything you can do. You feel good about it—but you don't know.

You're relieved and depleted. The mad-dash paper chase is over. The pressure is off. I was sure George was going to love it. We'd done everything he'd asked.

I came back to my apartment that had been vacant for a couple days and got about the business of catching up with people and other projects. It was great to be back in LA. It was great to be back at the D&D mansion, where things ran at a different pace. I had a great office with no phone and I started working on Sagard again.

I was too velocitized not to do anything.

The Loser Ex-Boyfriend
Or
Achievement Unlocked

"What is this place?" she asked.
"It's the Dungeons & Dragons mansion. I'm doing a couple projects here."
"I thought you were working at Lucasfilm."
"I am. I'm doing both things."
"So you're working on Star Wars and Dungeons & Dragons?"
"Yeah."

SOMEWHERE IN THE SUMMER of 1984, an ex-girlfriend of mine drove up the long and winding road to the D&D mansion to drop something off or pick something up. The reason for the visit is lost in time. I hadn't seen her for a while, but we were in loose touch. It was what we call magic hour in the film business—the moment when the light is just a little softer than when the sun is at full pitch. She looked beautiful. She was the optimized version of what you expected to get as a girlfriend when you moved to California: blonde, brilliant teeth, bikini worthy. But there was no "bimbo" component. I remember seeing *Mosquito Coast* in that period and thinking that she was kind of like a younger version of Helen Mirren.

We'd both been aspiring writers. It had been that relationship you have when you don't know if all of your efforts are going to pay off. You don't know whether you're going to make it or slink off to become whatever the eighties equivalent of a barista was. She got her break first as a stringer for a big-time magazine.

She'd been with me for a couple years of snipe hunts and schnook chases and eventually concluded, and not without ample evidence, that her boyfriend was a loser and it was time to move on. Starting out is a dicey time. And when the dice are rolling, you have to place bets, and frankly, I looked like a losing bet in this period. So she met somebody else and moved on.

You can't blame her.

She was the physical manifestation of the "Ordinary World" before this story started. The world where I lived with a bunch of deadbeats in a rundown house, had agents tell me not to quit my day job, was going nowhere, and where time was running out. And I probably would have run out, too, but I had nowhere to run to. That was all less than two years earlier. It was a marker. In a movie, it's called a "matching shot." The shot of her standing there, it advances the story, but it also reminds the viewer of what has changed in the story.

Now she's standing at the D&D mansion noticing/not noticing that Donna, Penny, and Peggy are wandering around looking like Bond girls. I'm hoping it kind of bugs her. We had no unfinished business and no future. It wasn't about getting her back. It was about vindication. Maybe her loser ex-boyfriend wasn't such a loser anymore. At least, that's what I wanted her to be thinking, and it's hard to imagine that she was thinking something much different.

It was a moment when I thought I'd made it. It was a moment when it looked like I'd made it. And in that moment, I had made it. The whole time Kipling was rolling around in my head—something about treating victory and defeat as the impostors that they are. Kipling is right, but, face to face with the "loser" period, I felt like I was checking a big box in life.

Of course, this was only a small boon in the adventure, but you need those. You need those moments when you realize where you are and where you've been. You never know where you're going. Right then, at that moment, I also realized how far I'd come. And it was a good feeling. You have to take those moments when they come. They're rare. They're incredibly private, playing out in your own personal universe and the real world at the same time.

It was also a moment of closing off the past. It was one of those moments that felt like it had already receded into history even as it was happening. I feel like that even now, at my kids' graduations. It feels like the actual moment only exists for the photograph it will produce. It's a moment of pure ego exhilaration. And it's not all illusion, and it's not necessarily a bad thing to have moments like that. They make a lot of other not-so-stellar moments worth living.

There are also about fifty lessons in moments like that.

The one I'll extract right now is that almost everybody I know who went on to have an interesting life had long periods of looking stupid. We live in a culture where you never want to look stupid. You script out this life of effortless victories and one long ramp-up. No dips. No problems. You get the right grades, get into the right college, choose the right career, move quickly and effortlessly up the ladders, and your mother is constantly proud.

You then have the right spouse, buy the right house, have the right number of kids, and eventually retire to the right private island. The ultimate end state is hard to haul up in your mind in an exact way, and nobody wants to see the elderly version of themselves smiling weakly and shaking as somebody helps them back to their seat at a dinner in their honor.

But real life doesn't work that way.

Anybody who is anybody spends a considerable amount of time looking stupid or looking lost or looking like they haven't hit the mark they should have hit. We construct elaborate illusions to mask these moments, because being in life arrears is a bad feeling, and thinking that other people think you're in life arrears makes it even worse. We are pinned to a timeline like life is a script template where you've got to get to the half-hour act break, but we never know how it is going to play out. The great thing about writing about a period thirty years ago is that you know how that whole period played out.

As the sun was setting, she got back into the yellow VW bug that a couple years earlier we'd taken into Earl Scheib for the $29.95 paint job (that wasn't really the price, but I remember thinking it was the price of an expensive car wash), and the moment was over.

Achievement unlocked.

I can count moments like that on one hand.

In the meantime, while we were awaiting the verdict on the show bible, the *Star Wars* team moved into a building called the Egg Company just across the street from Universal Studios. It was not all that far from Ruby-Spears, interestingly, but it felt like a million miles away. It was a cushy luxury office building that Lucasfilm owned, but other people rented. I used to run into Ed Asner in the bathroom. At that point, I was so cool that it didn't seem out of the ordinary to be running into famous stars at the urinal. The Egg Company was highly decorated and had a kitchen area that was not unlike the Google office I'd be in years later, except smaller. I remember Paul and I opening up all of the *Star Wars* action figures one day. A whole set.

Then the bad news came. Miki called to say that George's reaction wasn't good. I was stunned. How could anybody not like it? It was John Ford, Joseph Campbell, and Bruno Bettelheim all rolled into *Star Wars*.

Heaven turned into hell in an instant. It wasn't like I was fired, but there wasn't a clear direction to go in. I didn't know whether to put in more cavalry, or Hansel and Gretel, or Odysseus. But we needed to fix it, and we needed to fix it fast.

After the blow, I was in full flail mode. I'd like to believe that all these years and projects later I'd know how to handle it, but I doubt I would. We cobbled together another story, did every fix, and sent it in. At that point, I didn't know whether I liked it or not—only that I'd done everything I could.

Rinse and repeat the waiting. Only this time there was that creepy edge to it. It felt bad and lonely. I just got things done. Worked on Sagard. Maybe did the last of the *Visionaries*. Washed the car. Just kept in motion.

The second response wasn't much better. Miki wasn't a very experienced producer, so she might have missed the secret sauce, or maybe I just wasn't the guy, or maybe the show just wasn't something that was supposed to happen.

Now I was in full panic mode. I couldn't do anything right. To his credit, John Beebe had great advice, but I didn't have the guts to act on it. It seemed impossible. His suggestion was to set up another meeting with Lucas. He was right, but I didn't think it was possible. I was desperate and flailing.

At one point, I went over to Steve Gerber's house, and he and Buzz helped me through the story. It was all new. Something completely different. I thought that maybe if I just chucked what we had, we'd hit on something new.

When it was all done, we had a story that Steve, Buzz, and I thought was really good, and I sent to Miki via FedEx. Or maybe we faxed it. I can't remember. What I do remember was her response.

It was first thing in the morning. Miki had flown down. We were in the Egg Company. It was just Paul, Miki, Bobby, and I. Miki walked in with the outline in her hand.

"What is this?" It was hard and edged and aggressive.

"It's a new story."

"What is this?" This was one of those moments in life that really is art directed. It was sharp spotlight.

I had no idea how to respond. "I thought maybe—"

"What is this?!"

She might not have really said it a third time. And Miki was a very nice person, but it was a moment that just froze there. It was really over then, but it would play out that I'd write another draft, as I recall, and after that draft, I was standing in my apartment and the phone rang. I knew who it was and what it was about. I didn't answer and let my answering machine take the hit. I'm tempted to go off on a riff about answering machines and how, almost as much as computers, they changed the world in the eighties, but I won't. I'll just get straight to—

"Flint, this is Miki Herman from Lucasfilm. Well, George wasn't happy…" And then something like, "I think we have to go another direction. I'm sorry."

I wasn't surprised. Yes, I'd hoped there as some off chance that this one would get a better response or something good would happen. But I knew it wouldn't. Doom was in the air.

I waited a few minutes and then called her back. It's easier to have those calls when the news is already out. She told me I could keep the printer, but I don't think I ever wrote anything on that Mac again. It was my unlucky computer.

As it happens, *Droids* did go forward and get made. Counter to our high hopes, it didn't revolutionize Saturday morning, and it only lasted one season. *Ewoks* lasted two. Interestingly and ironically, Cliff Ruby and Elana Lesser left Ruby-Spears to replace me on *Droids*.

Years later, Paul Dini mentioned in conversation that George Lucas had asked, "Whatever happened to the original story editor? He had some good ideas." Paul was probably just trying to make me feel good. But even if he's going to make up the story, I'm more than happy to believe it.

I saw Miki one more time a few years later. She'd finished out the show, left Lucasfilm, and had become a psychologist. She seemed very happy with the transition. I don't think I ever saw Bobby Carrau again, though I'd hear about him now and again. In my mind, he's still in his twenties up at the ranch, though I suspect his life has moved on. At any rate, he's no longer in his twenties. It's been a long time. Lucasfilm has been sold, and I have no idea whether George Lucas is still in that office at the ranch or whether the fired president's office is still vacant at the Kerner Building.

The gate to that secret world closed right then and right there for me.

So, yeah. This was the hero's journey for a hero who doesn't make it. I died somewhere on the Road of Trials. There was no Master of Both Worlds. No Elixer or Boon. No Magic Flight. None of that stuff.

The thing that did change, however, was after that moment, I really was a freelancer. There was still the Sagard book, and I could return to Ruby-Spears. It wasn't over, but I was surprised to find that I didn't respond to things quite how I expected I would. I figured I'd feel really depressed, like my career was over. In fact, I was quite relieved. It was like I'd been handed a get-out-of-jail-free card. I was sorry I'd blown my big break with George Lucas, and I knew I was going to have some humiliating moments, but there was good news. For one, I didn't have to think about John Ford and neckerchiefs anymore.

I remember Tom Brady's response when Peyton Manning retired. He said something to the effect of, "He doesn't have to think about all that stuff anymore." He meant Manning didn't have to puzzle out the edge blitz or how to split some seam. He was done. He'd never do that thing that he'd done ever since childhood again. Not for real. I didn't have that luxury, but I didn't have to work on that exact puzzle anymore, and I wouldn't be waiting for bad responses.

Some humiliating moments came, though. There were a couple sack dances. One guy who I didn't think hated me (and I didn't really know) at Ruby-Spears said, "Looks like the big deal at Lucasfilm didn't pan out." It was impossible to miss the edge in his voice.

How can you respond to that stuff? Maybe I deserved it. Maybe I didn't. I said something like, "You got that right." Not much for him to shoot back at me. People can be mean, but when you see that kind of meanness, you're really just getting feedback from some horrible drama that's playing in their head. It has nothing to do with you. I obviously didn't know him very well. I don't remember his face or name.

I did wind up heading back to TSR and started finishing the Sagard books. I had outlined the second book, *The Green Hydra*, before going up to Lucasfilm. Just to get started, I went back through *The Ice Dragon*. Amazingly enough, it followed the Joseph Campbell paradigm perfectly, and I didn't even know what the paradigm was when I wrote it.

There's a lesson in there somewhere.

The Bold Claim, the Rallying Cry, the Paradigm Buster:

Why are you doing this project?

PROJECTS HAVE ALL SORTS of origins. Some are somebody's dream or pet project, and others are a business deal disguised as a movie or TV show.

But when you're setting off to do a project, there should be some kind of a "bold claim" attached to it—a rallying cry, a goal bigger than the money. How is this project going to change the world? If you're a creative, try it for whatever project you're working on. What is this project trying to do for the first time, or better than any other project has done?

Sometimes the idea is big, like the heady days of *Droids*, when we were going to change the face of Saturday morning, and sometimes the idea is smaller, like with *Inhumanoids*, through which we hoped to make the scariest animated monster show ever. Sometimes these outsized goals and proclamations stick, other times they are forgotten after the first setback, and occasionally they change when something exciting happens. But rarely does a good project start without bold ambition. I've seen it happen that a project starts out relatively unambitious and then suddenly pops—somebody has an insight or a vision, who knows—but very infrequently will a flat project take on a messianic zeal. Usually, unambitious projects end up getting mediocre results before being deleted from the next iteration of your résumé. Messianic zeal gets you through the long voyages and slow trudges. Something about the project has to be radically different or radically better, or what's the point of doing it?

Here's the other edge of the same dagger: the more ambitious and the more inflated the goal is, the more likely it is to go horribly bad. It's like playing with explosives. That's not a lobby for unambitious projects, but rather a caution that you don't win on passion alone. Often, passion projects are very personal and esoteric and end up art damaged. So make sure the rallying cry is something that involves the audience.

I'd be tempted to offer some advice here about the best way to approach a project, but I don't have any. Every project is different. Some projects start in the weeds. Mark Turmell, one of the best game visionaries in the world, had this idea that he wanted to do a "two-stick game." He told me about the fun of playing with two joysticks. I thought, "That's interesting, but what's the game?" The result was *NBA Jam*, a huge surprise, groundbreaking hit. Did Gary Gygax know, when he published a small supplement for a medieval miniatures game called Chainmail, that he was on the brink of changing the gaming world and the rest of the world?

He couldn't have. However, he did know he was doing something nobody had ever done before.

Did George Lucas know, as he was shooting *Star Wars*, that he was going to change the face of movies forever? By all accounts: no.

Probably not. But he did know he was doing something different, because he got rejected by pretty much every studio in Hollywood. Still, he stuck with it. There are always going to be times of bleak self-doubt and there are going to be times when everybody around you will tell you you're on a schnook chase. You've got to think of that mantra, that bold claim, that *whatever* that will keep you going.

GEN CON 1984

My next get-out-of-jail-free card came from Gary Gygax, who shortly after my dismissal from *Droids* invited me to stay at Stone Manor for Gen Con, so I headed out to Lake Geneva, Wisconsin. It was a slightly historic Gen Con, because this was its last year at the University of Wisconsin, Parkside, before moving to MECA in Milwaukee. But my memories of Gen Con itself are extremely spotty, other than Luke Gygax and I inventing the "funkador meter," which we used to evaluate the strangeness of the costumes walking by.

The thing that's funny about remembering the funkador meter is how much the world has changed. In those days, it was weird for anybody in America to wear a non-work-related costume any time other than Halloween, and fandom itself was a relatively new phenomenon. The whole idea of dressing up like a wizard or a barbarian to go to an event was not standard stuff. Yeah, there were *Star Trek* conventions and some costumes at Comic-Con, but in the summer of 1984, it was still funkador. Little did I know that I was getting a dress rehearsal for the future. In fact, everything at Gen Con was a dress rehearsal for the future.

And there was nothing weirder than Stone Manor.

To understand Stone Manor, you have to understand Lake Geneva, Wisconsin, and to understand that, you need to know a little bit about Chicago. Back in the days before airplanes, when wealthy people in Chicago wanted to get away, they headed north to the lakes of Wisconsin—Lake Geneva being the best of the nearby options. (That's my opinion, of course, but obviously a lot of rich guys agreed.) Lake Geneva is great for motorboating, sailing, fishing in the summer, and ice fishing and I'd assume skating in the winter—though I never once did that. It also happens to be beautiful. So famous Chicago millionaires—ranging from Wrigley of Wrigley's Gum and Wrigley Field to Al Capone—had places up there. What would later be known as the Battle of Barrington, which ended with the death of Pretty Boy Floyd, began at Lake Geneva.

Sometime in the seventies, Hugh Hefner, a Chicagoan, built a Playboy resort up there. Other than backlit centerfold shots and bunny-costumed waitresses, it wasn't that risqué a place, but it still seemed incredibly cool when we had our high school graduation party at the Playboy resort. Lake Geneva also had the only ski slope in the area, Alpine Valley, which was a fake mountain with fake snow. Stevie Ray Vaughan was killed in a helicopter crash on that ski slope.

By the time I was back there in the eighties, the Playboy Club was gone and there was something called the Club Americana. The mansions had mostly been repurposed as apartments and condos, and TSR was the single biggest employer in town. Most importantly for the purposes of this book is that Lake Geneva, for some reason that's not easy to explain beyond long cold winters and charismatic proselytizers, had an inordinate number of gamers and seemed to be the hobby game capital of the world.

Gary was going through a divorce when he moved into Stone Manor, which was a mansion by any definition. It seemed to be built out of stone, and driving up felt like the beginning of a *Scooby-Doo* episode. Everything about the building was "off" in the way a haunted house should be. Its stately lines were shattered by a gigantic four-story elevator in a three-story building that ripped out of the roof, which supported a good-sized swimming pool. Somebody had stuck a high dive board over the pool at the very top. For some reason, that freaked me out. I froze on that board. It wasn't the height of the board that bothered me; I'd done a higher dive at our local park a thousand times as a kid. It was the idea that the whole building was underneath it. I remember standing on the board and imaging the Michael Bay version of diving off, crashing through the bottom of the pool with the water draining down to the ground floor, which housed—I'm not making this up—a Christmas tree museum. I could see myself swimming amongst the trees. There were no drugs involved in this story, just plain organic fear, and I finally backed off the board. Nobody ever let me forget it. Gary's daughter, Heidi, later sent me a card with a jungle creature cowering on a diving board. I deserved it.

In fact—and I'd never made the connection before writing this—Stone Manor reminded me of the Overlook Hotel from *The Shining*. I know the real Overlook, or at least the hotel Stephen King based it on: the Stanley, which is in Estes Park, Colorado. We used to stay up on the hill in a place called the Craigs, but my grandparents used to stay in the Stanley, down in the flats. If I were ever going to write my version of *The Shining*, I'd set it at Stone Manor.

You walked in the front door, and there was nothing. No doorman, no lobby furniture, nothing—except, of course, the aforementioned Christmas tree museum, which never seemed to be open, and the remains of a high-end restaurant that had closed down a few years before. Gary was on the third floor. You could get there by taking the elevator or walking up the stairs. Knowing that there was nobody to hear me scream if the elevator got stuck, I always took the stairs.

Gary rented half of the third floor. You turned left off the stairs, and the first thing you saw were the porcelain foo dogs, Chinese creatures that looked more like dragons or something out of the *Monster Manual*. I'd never heard of them before or again, until they were the objects of interest in a Philip Marlowe radio show. Gary had furnished the place nicely. Maybe it was the foo dogs, but it seemed like some ex-pat's place in an exotic land. I got my own room and set up my unlucky Mac.

There were stories about ghosts in Stone Manor, and frankly, I believe that if ghosts exist (I'm on the fence), Stone Manor has them. There was the usual Indian burial ground story, of course, as after *Poltergeist* it suddenly seemed like everything had been built on an Indian burial ground. But Stone Manor would have been a great dungeon in a horror RPG.

One night we sat around talking about where the ghosts of Stone Manor might have come from. I'm reconstructing this conversation, but it's probably close. I likely led with, "So, you think there are ghosts here?"

Gary probably responded with something like, "Any old mansion has ghosts. Mansions come with money, and where there's money…"

"…there's murder. So how'd they die? Candlestick, rope, gun…" After all, Stone Manor really was the Clue Mansion.

"Maybe they not-so-accidentally drowned in the pool. Midnight on the rooftop. The killer knew they took midnight swims…"

"Sounds like a good rich guy murder. People who don't have money don't drown in their own rooftop pool."

In game terms, you have to design the murder around the reality of the dungeon.

Gary responded, "People who don't have money don't 'accidentally' tumble down their three-story grand staircase and break their neck at the foot of the grandfather clock…"

"…Only to be 'found' by the beneficiary of their will."

"If you don't have money, you don't get trapped in the elevator and suffocate because the help is asleep." He paused to light up a Camel Straight. That was Gary's blend. Apparently, he got excommunicated from the Jehovah's Witnesses for smoking. It is interesting to note here that at the time, and the entire time I was with DDEC, I had no idea Gary was a Jehovah's Witness or had any particular religious beliefs. I knew he knew the Bible very well, but he also knew Frazer's *The Golden Bough* very well.

"And pure logic tells you that when you have multiple generations living in a house, people get old and die there. Fortunes rise and fall."

"Maintenance doesn't get done. Chandeliers fall out of the ceilings, balconies collapse. There are a lot of ways to die in a mansion. It only stands to reason that it's going to be haunted."

"Think about how creepy it would be to have portraits with faces that look like yours looking disapprovingly down on you all day…"

"Especially if you killed them."

Real or not, this conversation reflects the way Gary and I used to jam ideas. Conversation with him was like a creative game. And usually it was for no particular purpose. You'll note that at a certain point I stopped attributing the quotes. When you're in that kind of creative sync, it's like guitar weaving. It doesn't matter who's talking, you're thinking the same thing. Just building.

Gary didn't think of D&D as just being medieval sword and sorcery. He thought that *Big Trouble in Little China* was a great D&D movie. Squint at it, and he's right. That statement opened my mind. I'd always taken D&D too literally.

We should have had a gangster ghost dungeon crawl with Stone Manor. It's seemed obvious to me that Baby Face Nelson stashed the Dillinger loot in Stone Manor before leading the G-Men on a wild goose chase to the Battle of Barrington. And it was equally obvious that the guys who helped him move it there were silenced so they wouldn't spill the beans, and that their corpses are interred somewhere in some forgotten room in the basement. And the fact that it was built on an Indian burial ground feeds some of the nastiness that can happen there—reanimating things that should have stayed dead. The bones of some Loch Ness–type creature that died horribly on the shores of Lake Geneva might well transmogrify into something horrible if the conditions are right. Or maybe the real Lake Geneva Monster rises out of the abyssal depths to pick somebody off the roof now and again.

And let's not forget about what happens in the Christmas tree museum if you enter during the right phase of the moon. I'm quite sure it works like the King's Cross pillar in *Harry Potter* or C. S. Lewis's wardrobe or Doctor Who's TARDIS. Whatever world is in there isn't bound by the confines of Stone Manor. And don't get me started on things creeping around the secret passages or plastered into the walls.

In any case, I was there for weeks and have no recollection of what I did all day. I'm quite sure I was working on Sagard. That's the fate of a freelancer. You're always working on something. Some projects are more real than others. But the ones that start out not real and end up real are always the great ones—I'm quite sure of that.

There were some other notable landmarks in Lake Geneva. The TSR office was at 201 Sheridan Springs Road. It was an average office park building, but without the park. The only notable thing about it was an odd silver tunnel, which seemed to lead from nowhere to nowhere. As I recall, there was a reception area in the front of it that was rarely manned. I can't remember the geography, but I'm sure somebody out there has used it for a *Dungeon* blueprint or a *Top Secret* HQ.

There were cubicles upstairs for the writers and designers, along with some utilitarian offices and conference rooms. Gary had a swank office, and there was a cafeteria area with vending machines and dining booths, though it seemed like most lunches happened next door at a sandwich and pizza place, the name of which is lost to me at this point.

TSR even had a color scheme that I liked quite a bit. Mary Kirchoff referred to it as "pomegranate and puce," but it looked medieval and seemed to fit. Those are close to my personal colors, so I approved.

TSR had a bookstore in downtown Lake Geneva that doubled as a warehouse and mail-order fulfillment house. Amazon didn't exist in those days. Neither did the Internet, for that matter. You had to clip an order form, mail a coupon and a check, and at some unknown point in the future, the product arrived. I remember it as a wonderful place—a kind of mecca where players could come and buy any TSR product they wanted. When it closed, sometime in the mid-eighties, I had this feeling that TSR had lost something vital.

I've got a theory about meccas. A mecca is a place where you can go and "touch" the franchise and the company. It's a place in the real world. Disneyland is the ultimate mecca. Companies should have meccas, and characters should have meccas. 221B Baker Street never existed in the real world when Conan Doyle was alive. He made it up. But you go now and there's a Sherlock Holmes museum sort of where 221B Baker Street would have been. James Bond has an interesting set of meccas, and that's any swank resort, preferably in a tropical place—especially if it has gambling. That's an abstract mecca. My favorite place in the world when I was a kid was the 007 bar at the London Hilton. Not only did the London Hilton (at the time the tallest and most modern building in London) feel like a Bond place, and not only was it down the street from the Playboy Casino, but it also had Trader Vic's, which is a mecca for the whole genre of Tiki (see: TikiWikiFiki).

Decades later, my son felt that he'd found the epicenter of the universe when he visited the Blizzard Library. That's not a publicly accessible mecca, but it is a mecca of sorts. You could argue that the Star Tours ride was *Star Wars'* mecca. The Grand Ole Opry is country music's mecca. And the studio tour is Universal's mecca. You get the idea, but it is relevant in the modern age. Virtual is really great, but we are primates. Physical really matters.

Lake Geneva had some other memorable places. There was Jane's Bar. Gary had some peculiar love of that place. Thousands of miles away in Los Angeles, he'd spin yarns about the colorful characters in Jane's. Jane's Bar looked exactly like what you'd expect a Midwestern biker bar in the eighties to look like. It was slightly sinister, but when I'd go in there with Gary, I had a kind of invisible protection. If memory serves, there were a couple guys, Skip and Randy, that I associate with the place. Skip was known as "Skip Town," but I don't think that was his real name. Jane's was the kind of place where people had nicknames. Skip Town reminded me of Bob Seger, and if there were a soundtrack for Lake Geneva, it probably would have had a lot of Bob Seger songs on it.

Lake Geneva itself was like a beachfront town transported to the Midwest. There was a Playland Arcade, ice cream and cotton candy stores, and some diners. Lake Geneva had a main street with all of the stuff you'd expect a main street to have. If I remember right, the first Gen Cons were held in the American Legion hall.

In the summer, Lake Geneva had an exciting Venetian Festival with boats lights and fireworks, and in the winter, it was a cold, snug town. It was exactly the kind of place you'd go to write a book or design a complex game. There's a reason why the TSR artists of the time—Larry Elmore, Jeff Butler, Jeff Easley—drew such great winter scenes. They saw a lot of winter.

As I said, I'm on the fence about ghosts, but one incident in Stone Manor made me wonder. It was late afternoon, but it seemed later. A good old-fashioned Midwestern summer electrical storm was brewing, but it was still hot. I headed past the closed Christmas tree museum and up the stone stairs. Lightning struck and thunder crashed and the rain started in earnest. You couldn't get a more classic horror setting. It was one of those great moments when life is better than fiction.

As I went upstairs, past a dead gourmet French restaurant, I had this feeling I was being watched and followed by something not exactly human. I kept thinking I was seeing somebody out of the corner of my eye. My hair stood on end. There were no lights on, and it was dark when there wasn't lightning. By the time I finally got up to Gary's apartment, I was convinced I was not alone.[4]

Did I see a ghost? No. Did I think I heard somebody muttering? Yes. But it's an old place, and old places make strange sounds. What was true is that it was one of the few moments in real life when I was supernaturally scared. And this is advice for writers. Savor those moments when you actually experience things like supernatural fear and use them in your work. They are, hopefully, rare and precious.

The cool thing about hanging with the Dungeon Master was that I got to see a lot of cool dungeons. Cool dungeons, or workspaces, are essential to a golden age. And remember, the only difference between a secret lair and a dungeon is whether you control it.

"Real Fists"

AT SOME POINT, I FLEW back to LA. It may have been after two weeks and it may have been a month. One thing about having a "big epic fail" is that time didn't matter anymore, not in the hourly sense. What mattered was doing the next right thing. When your life turns into a pick-a-path adventure, all that matters is making the right choice.

---

4   When I asked Luke Gygax to review the manuscript before I said anything untrue, his note was, "That happened to me at Stone Manor more than once!" So I guess I'm not the only one who saw the ghosts.

And sometimes paths pick you. Not long after I got back, Steve Gerber called and asked me if I could "ghost" edit some *G.I. Joe* episodes.

Of course I would. And that was when I stepped into the Osterizer of Geek culture.

In the same day, I could be working on the Sagard game books, editing Marv Wolfman's *G.I. Joe* script, and playing some new vampire western game or seeing *Ghostbusters*, which was released during that period. I was now in the kitchen of elements that would become pop culture for that period. We were working from multiple recipe books. Everybody was a chef in the kitchen. Me, Steve, Gary, Buzz—all of us were making meals on some reality creative cooking show. We were all throwing our own meat, vegetables, and spices into this stew at the same time. The taste was constantly changing. It hadn't had time to marinate, but it was alive and always interesting.

G.I. Joe was something that had been in my life since I was a kid. They would advertise the *G.I. Joe* frogman on TV and on the back of comic books. I thought of the Spectre guys, and I wanted an orange suit so I could have a James Bond that looked like Sean Connery in *Thunderball*. I never had many G.I. Joes because my mother essentially embarrassed me out of G.I. Joe by referring to it as "playing with dolls." Terry Stewart, my patrol leader and friend to this day, tipped me off that I'd become the laughingstock of the school if people found out I had a Captain Action G.I. Joe figure. In my defense, I didn't buy it; it was given to my father when Ideal Toys licensed Buck Rogers for Captain Action. The point is that Terry and my mother both saw it as boys playing with dolls. And I'll give them the point.

Here, by the way, is something ironic that I didn't know until I was doing research for this book: It turns out the original design for G.I. Joe was done in 1963 by Stan Weston, who was not a toy designer but a licensing agent. And to bring it closer to home, he was the licensing agent who represented Buck Rogers and had a long relationship with my father. He was the guy who had introduced me to Stanley Ralph Ross, David Gerrold, and Mark Evanier (I think), and the whole world of licensing. His son, Brad Weston, would become a major player in Hollywood. I had no idea that Stan had created G.I. Joe. This gets to a fundamental point about networks. It's a good idea to know all about the people who are in yours. All of these paths created by Stan circled around in my life and still do to this day, except for the people who died, and they're still around in their own ghostly way.

Apparently, Hasbro was aware of the "sissy effect" of playing with dolls, and so the new G.I. Joe figures were about 3.75 inches tall (depending on the height of the character), so they were much more identified with toy soldiers, which were very acceptable for boys at the time. Then Joe Bacal and Tom Griffin (a.k.a. Griffin-Bacal, a.k.a. Sunbow) got the idea that Cobra would be a counter-terrorist squad. There was no changing outfits anymore. Instead, they came fully painted in unique uniforms with violent-looking guns, bazookas, and other things concerned mothers weren't thrilled about. The point is, there was no "sissy" attached to G.I. Joe anymore.

My first exposure to 1980s G.I. Joe was Ron Friedman's miniseries pilot. It was a perfect launch. It bridged the WWII era and the Reagan era perfectly, skipping the Vietnam sixties antiwar protest vibe. There were F-14s (called Skystrikers), the USS FLAGG (a giant aircraft carrier), colorful characters from Larry Hama, and various other designers with names and identities that hit the seam between reality and fantasy. The "counter-terrorist" spin made it as politically palatable as possible, and since we were on syndicated television, there was no giant conference table with sixty people overseeing every script.

And there was Steve Gerber. Let's underscore a point: Steve was brilliant. Beyond brilliant. He had created *Thundarr, Howard the Duck*, and was working on a project called Void Indigo. In retrospect, I realize how much he was influenced by Robert E. Howard. Steve had tried to save my butt on *Droids*, and he and Marty had gritted it out with me in tow on *Mister T*. In a year or so, he would reveal his secret tech geek side, but that was in the future. Still, for all of his virtues, there was at times a flip side to that coin: Steve wasn't the king of organization or deadlines. He was also that rare and almost toxic mix of wild imagination and perfectionism; two traits that, at first blush, wouldn't seem to be in opposition, but sometimes they are.

I would have done any project he wanted to do. With *G.I. Joe*, his pitch, though he didn't really need one, was, "And they can hit with real fists!"

Fresh off of *Droids*, where one of the violence notes was, "Limit the density of violent abuse to Imperial Stormtroopers," this was a whole new world.

We were mostly working out of Steve's apartment in Burbank. Hildy Mesnik, whom we knew from Ruby-Spears, was already working with him. She was perfect if we ignore the fact that she's a Redskins fan. I have no idea how she made it to LA. If Steve existed in a hyperkinetic fluster most of the time, she was like Velda to Mike Hammer. Hildy was a New York girl—come to think of it, a New Jersey girl—who never got flustered. She would be part of every incarnation of my life from Ruby-Spears to TSR over the next decade until she moved back to the East Coast, got married, and thought she was done with geek world. She wasn't, but that's another story. Hildy would later run the Sunbow office, be my and Frank Miller's assistant simultaneously, and be a lead editor at TSR and edit the *Barbie* comic. Extraordinarily talented. Later, Hildy would tell me when my scripts for Steven Spielberg and the studios sucked, and after momentarily getting angry, I'd realize she was right and go back and redo it. That takes incredible skill.

And just as an aside: ignoring her corporate and organizational skills, you'd have to be something far outside the human/empath/social skills norm to deal with Steve, Frank, or myself that gracefully—much less all three of us *and* the collection of lunatics who came in and out of Sunbow and TSR—while remaining sane. She was either very discerning or had amazing survival skills. I don't remember a single innuendo or scandal around Hildy, and sometimes it's important to notice what doesn't happen.

It would be easy to say that around this time I thought I was gornished and my career was over, but it didn't really feel like that. In fact, when all was said and done, the epic fail was more embarrassing than anything else. There were a number of lessons to learn from slipping on a banana peel.

1. Nobody really cares. Yeah, maybe there was some Schadenfreude from people who didn't like me for one reason or another—but people who don't like you, well, they don't like you, so it's not like you really lost anything or like they won anything.
2. We're all commodities. When I got flushed by Lucasfilm, I was like any other commodity. "Copper is down; buy copper."

3.	Always have more than one iron in the fire. In practice, I still had the Sagard books to finish, and it's a lot easier to sink back into things when there's continuity. Always have your own project going.

4.	Always fortify your bridges before leaving. As awkward as the conversation was with Joe about going to Lucasfilm, I had an open door when I got back.

5.	But you never really can go back. Ruby-Spears was a great place to work. In fact, that whole era was a huge part of my life, and I loved it. But the world is a dynamic place. Pick your aphorism or cliché. I'll go with Heraclitus, who put it as "you can't step in the same river twice." Already, Ruby-Spears had changed. Steve was gone to Sunbow. Paul stayed at Lucasfilm. I think Buzz was gone. Gordon was either gone or about to go to Southern Star—I don't remember. Three months isn't a long time, but it can change a world.

I never really made a decision not to go back. I told Stacey I wanted to lick my wounds for a while. The thing that amazed me was that she bought it. It happened to be true. And that's what I'd intended to do.

There's an odd phenomenon in life. Sometimes the periods that are supposed to be the most miserable are the best, especially when you look back on them. I'd been fired. Humiliated. I was gornished. But that was a month earlier. And, still, there's an odd quality to failure, especially at a job or a project. Once you've failed and it's over, something happens that you didn't anticipate: the environment in which you failed goes away. You tend not to see the people anymore, you don't have to go to the office anymore, you don't have to think about that stuff anymore. And given that it was a fail, it's probably not a bad thing. In fact, it was probably miserable, but the misery goes away. That doesn't mean you don't feel bad about it, but if we think in terms of lifescaping, the landscape of your life has been cleaned out. I remember when I got a new car. I was kind of sad to say goodbye to my Jeep Grand Cherokee. It was the car I drove my kids around in when they were small; my wife and I bought it during a great period of our lives, but it had accumulated dents and defects and stains and problems, and I remember when it rolled away, all of those things were out of my life forever. It was a relief.

One Small Legacy of Lucasfilm

THOUGH LUCASFILM, *DROIDS*, AND *Ewoks* was a disaster for me, I did leave some small legacy behind by contributing to the creation of two of the most minor and obscure action figures in the *Star Wars* universe. "Gornished" was a word that Dave Marconi and I used a lot. He got it from a friend of his, Rich Martini, who had misunderstood a couple of producers he was eavesdropping on at the Universal commissary. They were talking about actors to cast, and when a name would come up, one would say, he's "gornischt." Not speaking Yiddish (though I would write a Yiddish-centered movie later), we thought it was secret producer code for a "gornished list," and so we took up the word.

Paul Dini and I needed some washed-up royals, so we created King Gornishe and Princess Gornishe, and while I felt gornished after the whole *Star Wars* experience, still, King Gorneesh and Princess Gorneesh became part of the *Ewoks* toy line. It's great to have inspired perhaps the most obscure characters in the *Star Wars* pantheon.

The bottom line is that, in the post–Lucasfilm summer and early fall of 1984, I edited several *G.I. Joe* scripts, wrote the *G.I. Joe* episode called "The Gamesmaster" (for which this book is named), and wrote three Sagard books. I was in the zone. I remember it in repetitive shots. I'm waking up and snaking my car high into Beverly Hills to the DDEC stable office: writing, playing Chainmail and Risk, smoking cigarettes, looking at a flow chart, scribbling notes as to what I should write next, rolling four-sided dice to test the combat. Talking to Ernie about what would work and what wouldn't. Playing bogus league football with Luke. Standing next to the hot tub late at night while women from *Playboy* bubble away in the Jacuzzi, looking down at the lights of LA.

The next day, I'd do the same thing.

In the afternoons or at night, often until late, I'd head over to Steve's Oakmont apartment on Barham, near the falls of the river that flowed down from Warner Brothers to Ruby-Spears. It was probably the best mix of "extremely eccentric guy in bland boring apartment" I've ever seen. I remember lying on my side on the floor, my head propped up on one hand and handwriting notes on a script with the other.

I remember Steve pitching me the episodes he was really excited about. There was "Red Rocket's Glare," written by Mary Skrenes. Steve, normally a sophisticated guy, giggled wildly as he was telling me that the rockets at the hamburger stands (like the golden arches at McDonalds) were real ICBMs and Cobra had figured out an ingenious way to deploy them all over America. I'm not sure what the first one I edited was, but it was probably Paul Dini's "Jungle Trap"—which, being written by Paul, it didn't really need editing—or maybe it was Roger Slifer's "The Germ." I also did Steve Mitchell's "Funhouse," and he was momentarily annoyed by some of the changes I made. And he might have had a point. I was pretty green. Somewhere in there, Steve and I jammed out the concept for his Smithfield two-parter. We were both *Prisoner* freaks (term we used in the day), so this was our homage.

G.I. Joe had a fascinating evolution. Ron Friedman wrote the pilot mini-series (*The Revenge of Cobra*) and the first five episodes. It is a testament to his versatility as a writer that he nailed the backbone of the series right off the bat. He wrote the "straight" (and I say that in a complimentary manner, because that's hard to do) episodes that Steve and later I could pivot off of for the wilder episodes. Ironically, the exact same Ron Friedman (who I learned much later wrote on *The Andy Griffith Show*, which is tied for my all-time favorite with *The Prisoner*) also turned in the insanely wild and imaginative first draft of *Transformers: The Movie*.

The first Sagard book had been written during a very cold period of the previous winter, and it was in deep editorial, waiting to be released with the rest, so Simon & Schuster was waiting until I got over the *Droids* hump that I never got over. Now I was back and writing like I had something to prove to the world.

Because I did.

This Sagard/*G.I. Joe* sub-era was one of those periods of my life that I idealize in my memory. I'm not sure whether I loved it as much then as I do now, but I think I did. The only bummer was that Gary was in and out of town, dealing with both various TSR issues and traveling (I think to Morocco) with Gail Carpenter, whom he would end up marrying and staying with until the end of his life, so I didn't interact with him as much as I would have liked.

Ernie and Luke ended up as great substitutes. They literally have this stuff in their blood. They'd been gaming and playing D&D as long they could remember and had gaming so internalized that it was second nature to them. I leeched off their knowledge and energy. When I think of LA clubs and metal and that whole exciting life, I think of Ernie. I very rarely went along on these adventures, but I heard about them and loved the fact that they existed. Ernie came complete with Peggy Wilkins at that point, and she was as close as anybody I'll ever know to an elegant rock 'n' roll dream girl.

For now, I had three books to write.

I hired Tracy Mann, who'd been a typist/coordinator at Ruby-Spears, to be my assistant for a few weeks. Tracy was grossly overqualified for what she was doing, but she was between jobs, available, and willing to do it. She'd meet Michael Charles Hill at a Sunday night Risk game. They would get married in a "sneak on" ceremony at Greystone Mansion (which I always thought of as Greystoke Mansion) and produce a child whom I'd intersect with at Fort Meade years later. But for that summer, she was just helping me with the book.

If *The Ice Dragon* was not-so-coincidentally written during a record cold spell in a converted stable with no heating or insulation amidst freezing rain, the next books—*The Green Hydra*, *The Crimson Sea*, and *The Fire Demon*— were written during a hot-as-hell summer and fall.

I remember sweating while I was writing and walking out of the dark stable and into a Death Valley heat so heavy it had weight. But I liked the atmosphere. I like the atmosphere in LA, and I especially like the fact that the places I like best aren't set up to deal with weather. They don't have insulation, heat, or air conditioning, and I can really feel the weather and the world.

The DDEC mansion was running full steam, and it functioned like a creative office. We had giant pieces of paper that we used as flow charts. Ernie helped me with the charts, and he, Tracy, Luke, and I would talk about upcoming story beats and what we needed.

The D&D compound was swarming with people in this period. Peggy, Penny, and Donna Yukevich would wander in and out at random moments. They were always entertaining. Master game designer Jim Ward would come in and talk games, play games, and generally embellish the place. Francoise Marcela-Froideval, now a famous game designer, would show up wearing a cape and saying things like, "I am Francoise. I am evil…" and leave. Gary's old friend Mike Megida came by and stayed.

Skip Town and his buddy from Jane's Bar came in and out of town. Joy McCloskey showed up from Lake Geneva to sort things out. It seemed like there was always somebody sticking their head in.

That was also the period when I was editing *G.I. Joe* and wrote "The Gamesmaster" and probably premised "Eau de Cobra" and "Skeletons in the Closet." It always seemed like there was a Chainmail game going on in the background. If the real player wasn't there, somebody subbed for him. We encouraged people to randomly show up beyond the Sunday night games. The game must go on. And it did—probably didn't stop for two years. There'd be new scenarios and riffs, but there was never an end.

So I'm spending most of my days and some nights up at the D&D mansion working on Sagard and then working on *G.I. Joe* with Steve. Sometimes Steve would come up for story meetings. He was never much of a gamer, but he was certainly intrigued by it.

The Death Procession of St. Bloodaxe

LET'S STOP AT THE sand table. In some ways, it was the creative heart of a very creative place. For those of you who don't know, a sand table is literally a sandbox on legs. The idea was that you sculpted terrain on the sand table—hills, roads, rivers, lakes—and then placed in foliage, castles, and miscellaneous buildings. The final thing was to place the armies, and the end result was quite beautiful. In this case, it was Gary's beautifully painted Elastolin miniatures, and his sand table was an impressive sixteen by seven feet.

The core game we were playing was written by Gary Gygax and Jeff Perren and was pretty much the launchpad for *Dungeons & Dragons*. In fact, the original *Dungeons & Dragons* was an insert for *Chainmail*.

Sometimes life blurs and blends together in surprising and interesting ways. *Chainmail* was pretty much the beginning of my real game design career. The Sagard books were a pick-a-path with a very simple combat system, but we were beginning to think far beyond that in our gameplay.

On the sand table, we were mixing role-playing back into miniatures games. At the beginning of scenarios, I'd write up brief descriptions of what each player was trying to do and what each player *thought* the other players were trying to do.

In one scenario I remember and will try to recreate, we had the Order of the Blood Eagle—a fanatical sect of Viking monks—trying to move the corpse of St. Bloodaxe from one end of the board to the other while avoiding attacks from bandits led by Bob the Hood (a dark version of Robin Hood), and fanatical Templars led by Peter ("Don't Call Me Simon") Templar, who wanted to seize the corpse and anoint it with holy water to neutralize the saint. And just to throw in some fun, we had a posse of elite bounty hunters led by Rasius DeBraug, who were hoping to capture Bob the Hood.

This was simple fun stuff. It didn't take itself all that seriously, was full of puns and hidden meanings. Rasius DeBraug was a name I came up with when I misunderstood the line "easiest to bribe" from *Butch Cassidy and the Sundance Kid*, when Butch asks Sundance who the best lawman is and the latter responds, "The best how? You mean toughest? Or easiest to bribe?" (Hey, theater sound systems in the seventies weren't always great.) At any rate, I kept wondering why I didn't see Rasius DeBraug in the movie. When I realized my mistake, I made him a character: the best lawman.

The thing that fascinated me, and does to this day, was the idea of competitive gaming in which there was "fog of intention," which meant each player didn't really know what the other players' true motives were. This was an effort to rekindle some of the thrill we got during Diplomacy games in my fraternity (which were far more interesting for the diplomacy, roommate information stealing, double dealing, treachery, etc. than for the actual movement).

Of course, there would always be an obvious goal, a true victory condition, but there were also the hidden relationships and agendas of the players. For instance, when we discovered that the lead Templar was Bob the Hood's brother and fellow crusader and that his robberies were funding the Templar sect, it told us something about where the game might go.

Likewise, when we learned that the mound near the far side of the board was a Viking burial mound that would erupt with Undead Zombie Viking Warriors determined to protect the corpse, this ensured a bloody finish and gave the Vikings a chance. Sometimes, we gave players hidden objectives that involved secret treasure to find on the board or betrayals and the like. Of course, that information would be distributed to other players, so no secret was safe. This was the first experimentation with uncertain agendas that would bloom fully in the diplomatic rules for A Line in the Sand in 1991.

But on top of this was a very straightforward battle, and different players approached it different ways. Some ignored all of the subtext and just tried to carry out their known mission. Others were wary and standoffish. Some played the information gathering game and acted like power brokers. And every turn, the corpse moved a little farther down the board.

The other interesting thing is that the "referee," who in most miniatures games really functions like a sports referee, kind of becomes a DM, trying to balance the game on the fly because these games were one-offs. These weren't products, and they only worked if the players were gaming for the sheer fun of it. Winning and losing were more or less subjective and relative. "No winner" gaming was radical at the time. A game with no board and no winner was not something the industry wanted to buy then—hence why Gary had to publish it himself. Sometimes, industry confirmation bias creates a whole new industry.

The irony of all this, which *was* lost on me at the time, was that I was working with Joe Bacal, who was the king of the Hasbro game commercial in which the kid yells "I win!" at the end of every commercial. That was the cognitive dissonance that's persisted in game world from the eighties to now. Are there winners? What is winning? As long as we wrestle with issues like this, the game business will be dynamic and exciting. But at the time, we didn't think we were doing some massive intellectual exercise; we were just throwing hotter peppers into the curry to see what would happen.

The games would go on till all hours, and everybody would throw their own habanero in. Ernie would decide that the Vikings could summon the power of Thor for a turn and presto, it would happen. Of course, you had to have balanced play. If the Vikings got their Thor spell, the Templars had to have a Lazarus spell, and all of a sudden all Christians would come back to life. This caused plenty of controversy, to be sure. There would be arguments and whining, and there was even a special award created, which we called "The Gyconi."

The Gyconi was a strange tribal headdress from Africa with super tall horns that just happened to be lying around the DDEC Mansion. I have no idea where it came from or how it made its way from somewhere in Africa to my DDEC office at the top of Beverly Hills. It might have been something left over from King Vidor, or it might have been something brought in by some interior decorator staging the mansion's hunting lodge motif. Doesn't matter. Some things just are.

Somebody, for some reason lost to time, moved it over to the creative office. But anyway, there it sat until Dave Marconi and Luke Gygax were bickering one night. As a penalty, the Gyconi (a contraction of Gygax and Marconi) was created. From then on, whoever argued got voted the Gyconi and had to wear it, though I'm not really sure it was wearable, it was more held up over the head for a few minutes as a dunce cap. And it should be noted that the only person who never wore the Gyconi was Ernie Gygax. I remember asking him one night why he never got upset. He said that he didn't care whether he won or lost. He said, "It's all about the joy of gaming." I've been processing that ever since. Not a bad way to approach life.

The point of all this is that this was our world of gaming in the eighties. It was partly stolen from how we thought rock bands jammed, it was partly gaming and partly laying a narrative over what was, essentially, math.

We were doing the same thing Gary was doing when he turned actuarial tables into character record sheets, and this kind of thinking, which was not limited to us by any means, has rippled through the culture ever since. Maybe it's just my imagination, but I don't think so; I've been watching *The Last Kingdom* on Netflix, and it feels like an extremely sophisticated and well-crafted version of the Death Procession of St. Bloodaxe.

And it is almost impossible to watch *Game of Thrones* and not see an extended game of *Dungeons & Dragons* whose plot is more determined by game rules and an extremely bloodthirsty Dungeon Master than the normal rules of franchise management or conventional television drama. Most show runners, networks, and corporations don't kill off their lead franchise characters. Only Dungeon Masters of the Gary Gygax variety do that.

At one point or another, everybody in our crowd showed up at the mansion. Frank didn't play, but he did smoke cigarettes, drink beers, and watch. Paul played. Buzz played. Gary would play sometimes, and other times he'd just kind of watch over the scenarios, throwing out comments and ideas. Steve Gerber tried his hand at it. And if somebody wasn't there to play their part of the scenario, somebody else would fill in. It could be anybody: Penny, Donna, Peggy...even John Beebe showed up. I remember Wally Burr (an ex-military guy) was fascinated by the pieces and rules.

It is not knowable how much this influenced the work of all these people later on, but take a look at the shared world aspects of the first three *Sin City* books, and you tell me if Frank didn't get shared universes and alternate timelines. Great stuff happens when people from wildly different disciplines hang out together in a shared world with purpose. Doesn't matter whether it is music or gaming. I wasn't there, but my guess is that our creative synergy wasn't all that different than what happened with musicians like CSNY, Jimi Hendrix, Jim Morrison, Frank Zappa, and on and on and on, two canyons over in Laurel Canyon about a decade earlier, or what happened down at the Garden of Allah or among the dealmakers at the Polo Lounge. There's something about the hills and canyons that is almost magical.

I seem to remember St. Bloodaxe returning to life as scourge and avenger and clearing the table. But maybe that's just my imagination.

Trophies and Talismans

BEFORE THE GYCONI GETS lost in this story the same way the real Gyconi got lost, it brings up an interesting thing. As is probably obvious by now, I'm fascinated by the overlap between fictional structure and reality. Why do we tell the same stories over and over, generation after generation? They're slightly modded, localized, and updated, but they are the same stories.

My theory, and I won't dwell on it, is that it's because dramatic structures, like Joseph Campbell's template, are modeled on real life, but amplified. Think of any story you tell about your life that comes out well. There's a call to adventure, a refusal of a call, you cross the threshold, there are gatekeepers, mentors, etc. Next time you find yourself telling a story, analyze it. I think you'll find it has all of the aspects of the heroic template.

I'm not Spider-Man, but if you lose the webs and the Green Goblin, my heroic stories are the same as his. And the real world is filled with all sorts of magical objects. We just don't think of them that way. Long before I arrived at Ruby-Spears, there was an award known as the SS *Eisenberg*. It was an old battleship named after Jerry Eisenberg, a writer at Ruby-Spears. The SS *Eisenberg* was a model of a World War II ship, about eighteen inches long, that sat on a shelf. It was awarded to the writer or artist who had done the most to destroy their own career. For some reason, I won the Eisenberg in 1983. It's not like there was a formal selection process; it was just presented to me. Seemed pretty unanimous. Truth is, I have no idea why. I left it in my office, or maybe gave it back to Buzz or Jack when I left Ruby-Spears for Lucasfilm, but that's the interesting thing: Magical situations create magic objects. Weird things that exist for no reason and are ritualistically passed around.

Another one at Ruby-Spears was "The OJ," which was my creation. When I was in sixth grade, I began the one and only collecting binge of my life. It was a contest Coca-Cola had. They printed pictures of the Chicago

Bears players on bottle caps, and if you collected five sets (along with logos of all of the NFL teams) and took them to a Coca-Cola distributor, you got a free football. It was an obsession. I went to every bar in town and sifted through the bar trash, and it was a really big day was when I got a Gayle Sayers or a Mike Ditka. The hardest cap to find was the one with the New York Jets logo, and my mother drove me halfway across the North Shore to get one from a guy named Howie Sinker, who found one in his lunch Coke.

So I got a football signed by O. J. Simpson when he was still a running back. Somehow, the OJ ball traveled with me from Chicago to Carmel to Los Angeles to Ruby-Spears, and chucking the OJ became a thing. What an odd journey, and what an odd thing in a group of people who were not jocks. Everybody seemed to like chucking the OJ. Somewhere along the line, the OJ disappeared, as magic objects are wont to do. I wish I had it now, but it looms large.

You get the idea. Magic times come with strange magical objects that seem to travel through space and time with a destiny all their own and then magically disappear. If I had any of these things, I'd mount them and display them, and people would wonder why.

The Gamesmaster

SOMEWHERE IN LATE FALL of 1984, Tom Griffin and Joe Bacal flew out to LA, and I met them for the first time. Almost immediately, Tom felt like an older version of myself, and Joe was the brilliant creative guy who could also be a stand-up comedian or poet by turns. In short, it didn't feel like I was meeting anyone new; it felt like I'd known them forever or in some past life. Even better, they seemed to think of me the same way.

They wanted to put me under contract and make me an associate producer. I asked what an associate producer was, as I'd missed the class in film school detailing producer credits. The salary was huge, as were the script commitments. They said I'd go on with my story editing functions, but I'd also start going to recording sessions and sweetening sessions, and I'd start going over storyboards. I told them I had the Sagard books to write and some other things in play in Hollywood. They didn't care.

At that exact moment, Griffin-Bacal was the fastest-growing ad agency in Manhattan. Tom and Joe had been at another major firm and left to start Griffin-Bacal. When Hasbro wanted to jump into the syndicated television industry (following Mattel with *Masters of the Universe*), they went to Griffin-Bacal, which spawned Sunbow—and I worked for Sunbow. It took me a long time to figure out that I was almost as much of an ad guy as a TV show producer, but for my purposes, the distinction didn't matter much, except when I was in New York or when I'd get a call from Jay or Carole asking if I could write some ad copy. Writing is writing, and I was fortunate to be young and arrogant enough not to know I couldn't do it. And Tom and Joe were great. They knew just how to pull the best out of their talent. In short, meeting Tom, Joe, and Jay was the beginning of a relationship that's still there thirty years later.

Day-to-day, my contact was still going to be Jay Bacal, who was Joe's twenty-three-year-old son. If Joe was the best creative guy in the advertising business at that moment, then Jay, who was just out of Harvard, was the best and most diligent creative director going. In fact, I've never met a better creative director than Jay Bacal.

That was his title, too—though it's not really a TV title, it's an ad agency title. Jay supervised all of our shows. That meant he went from story premise to final sweetening session on every episode. I have no idea how anybody tracks that much data all at the same time. And he wasn't just sort of there. He was right there. He knew my scripts as well as I did. He always had a solution. He kept things moving. Nothing ever got stuck. With 130 episodes of *G.I. Joe* and *Transformers* a season, getting blocked wasn't an option. We'd talk for a couple hours almost every day. There'd always be something else to go over. We'd be working on a couple outlines, approving a premise, going over a script, talking through a storyboard, putting together casting sheets, whatever. I can only remember one occasion in which we ever left anything undone.

More Spankings Back at the Mansion

ALL THE SIGNS OF a money scramble were present at DDEC, and some of them were amusing. 1985 was the heyday of the VHS tape, and adult films led the way. Liberated from the dirty movie theaters, all people had to do was endure the embarrassment of buying the tape in the first place, and for the first time in history, they could have dirty movies in their own homes. I'm avoiding the word "pornography," because this story is about what were called "hard R" films at the time. These films were Playboy or Penthouse Magazine octane, not what was called "hardcore."

At some point, somebody got the idea that DDEC (a.k.a. TSR West) should make some quick money making R-rated films. Given that TSR was in the business of making products for children, this seemed like a very bad idea to me. Nobody cared that I thought it was a bad idea.

One day I walked in during a meeting. I was introduced to Edy Williams and a couple other people. Edy was a strikingly beautiful woman who'd not only been in the TV shows I grew up with—*Batman, Twilight Zone, Lost in Space*—but she had also gone on to marry Russ Meyer, director of *The Valley of the Dolls* and other distinctly sixties and seventies films featuring large-breasted women, as well as healthy doses of camp and satire. Edy, however, was most famous to me for taking her clothes off at the Cannes Film Festival and jumping into fountains, or something like that. By this point in the eighties, she was appearing in movies like *The Happy Hooker Goes to Washington, Chained Heat*, and *Mankillers*.

Now here she was standing right in front of me. She looked good, and she seemed like a fun cross between businesswoman and sexy actress, which is exactly what she was.

There were scripts on the table, and they were talking story.

Later on, when the meeting was over, I sat down to have lunch and a script was still there. I started thumbing through it. As I said, it wasn't filth; it was just kind of eighties cheese with aspirations to be more. But it wasn't the script I found most entertaining. It was the notes: "More spankings" and "Good scene for a spanking." I don't know whose copy of the script I was reading. Not Gary's, because he'd been at the head of the table. But, yeah. Given that most of my career up to that point had been spent doing children's shows, "more spankings" was a whole new kind of note to see on a script.

The Reason the Title of This Book is *The Gamesmaster*

I MIGHT HAVE BEEN redeployed from *G.I. Joe* to *Transformers*, but I'd have my trips back to the Real American Hero now and again. One day, Jay Bacal called to say that a script had "fallen out" and that we needed to put something together fast. And it came with a challenge: "Let's do an episode that's different than all the episodes," he said. "No blowing up the headquarters. Let's see what the characters do in their personal lives. Let's get deeper into their relationships. And let's stick our toe into fantasy."

Thus was born "The Gamesmaster."

Given that *The Gamesmaster* is the title of this book, it's probably worth a minute to explain why. The reason is *not* that I consider myself to be a "gamesmaster." That's for somebody to decide after I die. It is because I wrote an episode of *G.I. Joe* with the same title that appears on a lot of favorite episode lists. When I crowd-sourced a title for this book on my Facebook page, somebody suggested it. I can't remember who, but maybe someday I'll learn how to find the thread, and I look forward to properly crediting whomever came up with it.

I liked it. I liked it partly because it seemed to tie together the themes of this book, and partly because "The Gamesmaster" was almost an exact outpouring of my subconscious at the very moment I wrote it, and I didn't even know it then. It was written very quickly—likely within forty-eight hours from concept to final in split sessions with the Sagard books. When the engine cooled on one project, it heated on the other. I was in the stable in the blazing heat of summer.

I'd assume that Steve Gerber and I talked about it at some lunch place like Jerry's Deli in Studio City, or Art's Deli, or the Smoke House. I knew that the basic idea of setting a story on a Candy Land–type island with *Prisoner* overtones would go right down the center of Steve's bowling alley. Everything about it played to our common sixties spy influences, with a healthy dose of the absurd. After all, Steve was the guy who created *Howard the Duck*.

As I was writing it at DDEC, I'm quite sure I bounced it off of Ernie and Luke and Tracy Mann. It was probably written during a period when Gary wasn't there. More than anything I've done before or since, it bubbled out of the Osterizer of my conscious and subconscious brain at the time and is the closest thing I've come to channeling a dream and turning it into product.

But let's talk about the story itself.

It opens with two holographic robots having a sword fight. One beats the other, and we discover that they were being controlled by a mysterious character known as the Gamesmaster and his clown buddy KoKo. The Gamesmaster—a giant, rotund, childish genius—is bored. He needs a bigger challenge.

Next thing we see is Flint, my *G.I. Joe* namesake, racing down the street in his red convertible on his way home, before being captured when his entire apartment elevator is snagged right out of the building by a helicopter piloted by KoKo the clown.

Cut to Lady Jaye in a dressing room at a fashion boutique, where she's trying on clothes. Next thing we know, a pair of giant animatronic robots close up the dressing room and cart it away as she's undressing.

The Baroness is relaxing in a hot tub with a sun lamp in her off-hours. The sun lamp comes down, trapping her, and carts her away. Three of our four characters are carted away without a fight or any ability to resist. As we only had twenty-two minutes in the show, there was no time for failed escape attempts.

So what would Cobra Commander be doing with an R&R day? Reviewing his troops, of course. This was an opportunity to show off our "featured vehicles" for the episode—Firebats, Eeles, Tele-Vipers, and HISS Tanks. Of course, Cobra Commander vanishes through a trap door and is snagged and replaced with a robotic dummy. When Destro taps him on the shoulder and his head springs off, we get a hint as to the very nature of his antagonist.

While Destro is ordering an investigation, Cobra Commander's missiles are spirited away by clown Cobra troopers. The Gamesmaster is as practical as he is comical. He knows he's going to need missiles if he's going to start a battle between G.I. Joe and Cobra. The guy might be mad and childlike, but he is not stupid.

Thus begin two parallel investigations. Noting that Flint and Lady Jaye are missing, Gung-Ho, Duke, and Scarlet initiate a hunt for them. Meanwhile, in typical treacherous Cobra fashion (contrasting the very nature of their groups), Zartan accuses Destro of a leadership coup. Zartan is, of course, trying to stage his own lame leadership coup, and that's the nature of villains. This would be reprised with Starscream and Megatron in *Transformers*, but the crazy guys (both played by Chris Latta) were flipped.

Finally, we see the Candy Land/toy store/mega-billionaire island, though we should stop to note that the real look of it came from artist Larry Houston, who had an incredible ability to read past my very sparse writing, penetrate my brain, and create stuff that looked a lot better than my vision. Uncanny synergy.

Flint, Lady Jaye, Cobra Commander, and the Baroness are startled by an extremely loud cuckoo clock (based on a clock I had when I was a kid). Everyone climbs out of an enormous crib filled with stuffed animals and listens to the unseen Gamesmaster, who initiates the simple game he has devised, wherein the winner is the one who finds the helicopter on the island and flies away.

"And what happens to the losers?" asks Flint.

"They die," replies the Gamesmaster, giggling like a kid.

Right here, just like the St. Bloodaxe scenario twenty feet away on the sand table, we have a lot of complexity layered on top of a clear objective: get to the helicopter and get out—or die.

Joe and Cobra are about to come to blows, until they realize that there is a third party involved (see: "prime target") and that they are de facto allies in an effort to find their leaders. And this gets to an interesting thing. While everybody else in the world thought of Duke as the leader of the Joe team, I decided Flint was the leader for obvious reasons. After all, Tom and Joe said, "We named a character after you, so you've got to take the job."[5]

Other than the obvious ego component of making Flint and Lady Jaye a counterpoint to Duke and Scarlett, it's also a smart franchise move. It adds depth, nuance, and variety. Duke and Scarlett tended (key word is *tended*) to star in the more conventional episodes, while Flint and Lady Jaye tended to be in the more bizarre episodes, as if they were some prototype Fox Mulder and Dana Scully in camo.

So the story alternates between sky strikers and tanks, and bonbon bushes, candy cane trees, and caramel pools. There is an undeniable cheesecake element to this episode. The Baroness is in a bikini for most of it, and the romantic overtones and jealousy issues are undeniable. (I'd hit this button harder in "Eau de Cobra.") Meanwhile, the Gamesmaster torments them with giant lawn mowers, robotic dragons, and fake funerals and pallbearers. I won't belabor the episode any longer or spoil the rest of it—you get the idea.

It is basically a game. In fact, it would be a great G.I. Joe/Candy Land crossover that takes *G.I. Joe* into a fantasy area with a backbeat of very familiar plane, tank, and gun battles. If the episode has made it onto a lot of "best of" lists, it's because it has followed the "hit" pattern: a little bit proven, a little bit deeper (personal lives and romance), and a little bit wildly new. It is the kind of episode that you can only do when a series is fully grounded, and it was a good time to follow Jay Bacal's instinct of "not blowing up another headquarters." As a franchise advances, you have to start kicking out crutches. (For instance, what if Bruce Wayne loses his money?)

And there's another "writer" lesson in this about how working fast and letting your own psychodrama out sometimes creates good work (as long

---

5   This may or may not be true. Probably a joke. But sometimes in life, it's best to believe what you want to believe. They were certainly aware of me, and Flint has turned out to be a great name. I recommend it.

as you follow the above guidance—give them what they expect, what they want, and something new).

Internally, "The Gamesmaster" represents the distillation and perhaps apex of this period for me. There's Flint, my fantasy alter ego, driving an optimized version of my red convertible (I had a Mustang). His real life is fun and he's about to step into a fantasy world filled with danger—really fun dangers—and he'll have problems, though they're really great problems to have. And, also, Lady Jaye or the Baroness? I think we all know the right answer. There were plenty of Lady Jayes and Baronesses in my life at that moment.

There were also multiple Gamesmasters. Whether the Gamesmaster in my subconscious was Gary or Hasbro or the world is open to debate, but certainly, I was living a fantasy, or multiple fantasies, that were really just a subset of much bigger games being played far above my pay grade.

We may think of these shows as a whole lot of fun, but they were big business. Transformers was the first billion-dollar toy line, and that was back when a billion dollars was a lot of money, back before millions turned into billions and money grew multiple zeroes on the end.[6]

So, in a very real sense, I was like the creative equivalent of Flint working on a Special Forces Team (Sunbow) on an assault against Cobra (all of the other toy shows). It was my job to create fantasy, and in order to do that, I had to live fantasy.

And just like Flint in "The Gamesmaster," there was no line between my personal life and my business life, and I was likely to be pulled out of elevators and into fantasy worlds at any moment. There was a strange blur between real people and their fantasy counterparts. Shipwreck was overtly Buzz Dixon, but lots of other characters in the work were based on real people, too. And I'd see real people embody them at Wally Burr recording sessions. Whether Chris Latta was Cobra Commander or whether Cobra Commander was a cartoon version of Chris Latta is open up for grabs. Whether the Baroness was some girlfriend or a manifestation of the various women parading around DDEC (with her hot tub perhaps being

---

6   The account of this battle, written like a spy thriller, can be found in Toy Wars by G. Wayne Miller.

the one in the mansion's backyard) is all the territory of some archeological psychoanalyst. But what is very clear is that I was writing a fantasy about a reality that was, in fact, a fantasy.

The world was very blurry, and the odd thing is that I find myself very comfortable in blurry worlds. So if Joe and Cobra were cooperating, that was also the world I was in. We might have been working on competing shows, and our writers might have also been writing competing shows, but I don't remember anybody caring. We were simultaneously competing and cooperating. That's how it is in a boom town. There were jobs and money all around, and thus there was little to fight over. There were endless fantasy worlds to explore.

And, in the delusion of any boom town, to the extent that we looked at the future at all, we believed it was never going to end.

At some point, I slowly morphed off of *G.I. Joe*. New characters came in that I didn't know, like Serpentor, and new places, like Cobra-La. I just didn't know the franchise anymore. The only thing I can compare the feeling to was when I was a kid and baseball was my life. Then, one spring, I was listening to a White Sox game and I didn't know who any of the players were. I never quite caught up.

But before we leave *Joe*, there were two more scripts that are worth some conversation: "Eau de Cobra" and "Skeletons in the Closet."

"Eau de Cobra" and "Skeletons in the Closet"

"The Gamesmaster" might be the title of this book and the episode most widely remembered by fans, but "Eau de Cobra" holds a special place in my heart. I don't remember what script fell out to create the hole I would fill with it—maybe we just got behind—but I'm quite sure that like "The Gamesmaster," it was conceived of and written very quickly. This is not a bad thing. When you have to work fast, your mind isn't cluttered by rethinking things.

The story is structured like all of my favorite films, in that a bunch of seemingly unrelated things happen as part of a larger plot: an ancient tablet is stolen from the British Museum (quite possibly my favorite place in the world), Cobra runs a covert operation to harvest a rare plant in Antarctica, and we discover that Cobra is trying to recreate an ancient "aphrodisiac."

Of course, you couldn't talk about aphrodisiacs on eighties television shows, so it is a "love potion," which despite the implications are totally acceptable fairytale story devices, and therefore nobody was going to get upset. In the period in which we now live, there would probably be all sorts of political interests upset about this for a variety of reasons, but this story was written in the fun eighties and not the somber/agitated times in which we now live. In fact, rewatching "Eau de Cobra" reminded me of why we want to escape back to the eighties—or at least why I do.

The rest of the story spins into territory more reminiscent of a romantic comedy, or maybe even an Edy Williams picture once Cobra's plot is revealed. It seems that they're recreating Cleopatra's love potion, which they then plan to use on an Aristotle Onassis–style shipping magnate to gain control of the world's largest shipping route.

Flint and Lady Jaye infiltrate the magnate's yacht with formalwear under their scuba suits and try to stop the Baroness from seducing the mark. Instead, the Baroness ends up "entrancing" Flint. After a brief struggle, the perfume is knocked overboard, and both Joe and Cobra divers race after the formula—which is stolen by a crab that vanishes into its sea floor lair.

The episode ends with Destro getting a big laugh at Cobra Commander's expense.

Looking back at the episode, what really stands out to me are the storytelling shortcuts we had to use to do a twenty-two-minute show, and thus it works as a sort of genre primer in the process. In the real world, Flint and Lady Jaye would likely just go over to the British Museum and ask for photographs of the tablet as opposed to breaking into Cobra's lair. And then, instead of Lady Jaye being able to translate hieroglyphics on the fly, they would take it down the hall to a resident Egyptologist, who would translate it for them. But that's the BBC procedural version of the story. In a *G.I. Joe* cartoon, we want to see our characters break into a secret headquarters and steal the tablet, thus giving us an action scene in an exciting environment.

Another thing this episode shows, probably more clearly than any other, is that Steve Gerber and I (and Jay Bacal, to a lesser extent) thought of *G.I. Joe* as a kind of James Bond show more than a military show. Or I guess it was more *Mission: Impossible*, really, as James Bond was growing a bit long in the tooth by then and people were trying to figure out what came next for the genre. Tom Clancy books, ignited by Ronald Reagan's interest in them (Reagan did the same thing for Tom Clancy that JFK did for Ian Fleming), introduced an American type of Bond character, and Robert Ludlum's Bourne books were yet another take in what felt to me like a do-over of *Coronet Blue*. My point is that everybody was trying to recrack that genre, and "Eau de Cobra" was the *G.I. Joe* attempt.

"Eau de Cobra" was also a way of making *G.I. Joe* about something more than guys in camo blowing things up. It was about elegance and boats and evening gowns and billionaires (back when that was rare). It expanded the world. And though the term didn't exist then, and what we were doing was more instinctual than conscious, it was about world building. We had to create a world in which Lady Jaye could read hieroglyphics and in which ancient aphrodisiacs really work and ancient plants could be found under the ice (probably left over from Atlantis) and semi-sentient crabs could steal vials and thus thwart even our most advanced commandos. We had to make that world because we only had twenty-two minutes, we had a lot of action toys to show, and our audience much preferred to see things blow up, as opposed to hearing long-winded explanations from archeologists in museums.

That having been said, I honestly believe you could rewrite "Eau de Cobra" as a story in a 2020 *Da Vinci Code*–style streaming series that involves tech moguls financing competing teams of ex-spec ops to find lost ancient knowledge. As a matter of fact, if I didn't have this book to finish, I'd probably start developing that.

Instead, let's talk about "Skeletons in the Closet." In what is probably more a reflection of the social world that I lived in during 1985 than anything else, it is another story that features romantic tension, ancient family castles (technically medieval), and contains a whiff of a whole new element that I could not have known would occupy my Sunbow life a year later: Lovecraft. Forget the execution, which looked kind of goofy; the idea that there was an *Inhumanoids* kind of character living in a well in the basement of Lady Jaye's ancestral castle was irresistible to me. The episode is an almost perfect representation of what was, and is still, living inside of my brain. It won't leave. Ancient dungeons, secret societies, ancestral blessings and curses, and lots of action.

This was also one of the few episodes to ever address the question that's asked in every screenwriting 101 template: "What does your character want?" For perhaps the only time in a *G.I. Joe* episode, we learn that Destro and the Baroness want out of the madness of Cobra. It would have been interesting to do an episode in which they actually did try to leave Cobra, but nobody would have thought of that back then.

Also, there's the revelation as to why Destro wears a metal mask and how it relates to the generations-old familial relationship between Destro and Lady Jaye. It made the story world deeper and presented possibilities for the future.

Of course, as a practical matter, the objective of this script was, as Jay had suggested, to have episodes that don't end with Cobra Headquarters du jour being blown up. This was a "stretch the franchise" kind of an episode. Obviously, it could have grown up to be *G.I. Joe* versus *Inhumanoids*, but as the idea of crossover was taboo, it never did happen.

Maybe it still could.

If we really wanted to expand the series, we'd have had Flint and Lady Jaye get secretly married in the stone chapel on the grounds and then have Marissa Fairbourne. But this is not the stuff of eighties cartoons.

The other thing that wasn't usually a feature of eighties cartoons was the political content of "Eau De Cobra." There are a couple of seemingly prescient elements to it. We have a political activist slipping and calling Americans "comrade," thus revealing sinister Russian interference in our politics, and we have Destro selling crap Cobra equipment to a group of rogue nations in a theme that would come back to haunt us decades later, during the War on Terror. What's interesting to note is that none of this would have been considered "partisan" back in the day, but it almost certainly would be now.

New Year's Eve, 1984

ALL OF THIS IS a setup for the lampshade incident, and I'll get to that in a moment. Memory is an interesting thing. In reconstructing events from thirty years ago, there are certain dates that are important. The DDEC New Year's Eve party is one of them. It's the pinnacle of a time. It was when the mansion was running on full tilt.

Anyway, on New Year's Eve 1984, they had a party up at the D&D mansion. It seemed like a bad idea. Summit Ridge Road, where DDEC was situated, is dangerous enough at noon when you're sober. The amusing thing about the guest list was that it had both children's TV executives and softcore adult film talent who were hoping to be in the "more spankings" film. I walked in with my girlfriend at the time, Vickie Shellin. She was elegant. Peggy and Donna thought she looked like Michelle Pfeiffer. She didn't spend a lot of time around DDEC, mostly because I was working there and she had an actual job, so this was a relatively rare occurrence. Besides, I think she thought the place was kind of sinister. I assured her it wasn't.

So we walked through the front door and straight into Edy Williams. She was wearing what can be best described as a doily dress with nothing under it. That didn't surprise me. What surprised me was what she did after she said, "Look." She took the lampshade off of the lamp, put the light on the floor, and stood over it. It was all meant in fun—probably to embarrass me, though I'm not all that easily embarrassed.

Vickie simply said, "I think it's time to leave."

We didn't stay long, but I did stay long enough to see Dennis Marx, D&D showrunner and one of the most prominent animation writers in the world at that moment, hiding in the kitchen in fear of a network executive who would be a major player in the final scene of this era. Her name was Judy Price, and I'd later come to understand why Dennis was hiding.

And that gets to a fascinating point about Hollywood. Often, when the mighty fall, they really fall. One week an executive is a titan deciding the fates of whole companies, careers, and what millions of people will watch—and then they get fired. They disappear, sometimes without a trace. It happened to several network executives of the animation era. Then there were others—the survivors, like Margaret Loesch—who had comeback after comeback. I'm not sure what determines who will vanish and who will survive, but I never cease to be amazed by the rapidity and finality of some of the vanishings.

So if the weather isn't good now, wait a beat. It will change. That also cuts the other way. Strike while the iron is hot, because you're going to blink and your exec will be gone, a company will have folded.

It's the fruit business.

So, Where Are We on the Hero's Journey?

I'VE CROSSED MULTIPLE THRESHOLDS and been on the road of trials. Some worked out, others not so well.

And now, a quick nod to contemporary culture. Next up for Campbell is "woman as temptress." I've been thinking of dodging this part, as it could trigger sexist rants from people close to me, maybe even claims of sexism. The reader should feel free to (and it's a good thought exercise, I think) translate Campbell's "woman as temptress" to any gender you want. The principles hold true. As I was born, through no fault of my own, I see the world from a certain perspective.

In the epics, this part of the journey deals in seductresses. Odysseus dealt with Sirens, Circe, whatever was hanging around with the Lotus

Eaters, and Calypso. It should be noted, though, that he also interacted with extremely powerful women, such as Athena, and had non-illicit relations with Helen, Nausicaa, and Arete. In fact, Buzz Dixon once told me that his theory of *The Odyssey* is that half the books are the story he told to his wife, Penelope, and the other half are the stories he told to his buddies.

Fascinating theory, but I wasn't there.

Before we fall too deeply into the *Odyssey* rabbit hole, suffice to say that there's a shockingly good balance of women in it given what is normally taught about the age in which it was written.

And let's take the taint off of seductresses and get to the point I'm trying to make. When you're on the hero's journey, you have to be focused. It's not a time for demanding relationships, spouses, kids, or any of that. Sorry, but that's just the truth. As a result, anyone that distracts you too much is a tempter.

As with any other rule, there are huge exceptions to this. If your spouse also happens to be your collaborator and turbos your powers (Lynn Varley comes to mind) or is your agent/manager/partner, then ignore this—that person is no longer a tempter.

In general, you need to be nimble. It is hard to be a freelancer when you have a big nut to cover every month. Campbell never talks about this, but he should have. Heroes on an epic quest tend to travel light and move fast. Odysseus had a ship and a crew, and not a lot more. Yeah, there was the palace back in Ithaca, but he didn't have a fleet or a luxury ship. Han Solo flew a low-end piece of crap around the galaxy (if Leia's opinion is accurate) and had a Wookie for a crew. There aren't four hundred people on the Millennium Falcon. The Hobbits were happy with a few cakes from the Shire and some smoking tobacco.

Point is, travel light.

A big mortgage, an expensive car payment, a drug habit—indulgences that sap your finances are extremely dangerous. You have to have your rainy-day fund, because there is always going to be a rainy day. Even in Los Angeles.

So, yeah. If you're on some creative quest, live simply. Your entire career is a one thousand to one shot, and there's no reason to run the odds against yourself higher. It's hard to sneak into the inmost cave with a brass band, baton twirlers, and a parade.

Not Sure If This Is Temptress or Muse or Just a Story I Want to Tell

Rewind to Winter 1980: Battle Beyond the Stars (Or, why I decided to be a writer and not work on sets)

As I NOTED IN THE chapter heading, this story is only thematically linked here, but it does answer a primary Hero's Journey question. When did I become a writer? When did I cross that threshold? I'd never really asked myself that question before writing this book, but somewhere in the process, I realized why. And fortunately, the best way to get to the story is with a temptress. Of course, she wasn't tempting me, but nevertheless, we're somewhere in mythological temptress/muse territory.

1980 was the rainiest winter I can remember, though maybe I remember it that way because I was outside for too much of it. I was working at Roger Corman's New World Pictures studio, which was really the ex-Hammond Lumber yard on Lincoln Boulevard in Venice. I was still finishing up at USC, but since I was in a writing phase, it seemed perfectly sensible to take a job that worked me eighteen hours every day. I was a PA, which is short for "production assistant." In other words, I was the low man on the totem pole. And, before somebody else says it, I was arguably the worst production assistant in the history of film. My first day, I backed a five-ton truck over some flats. The next day, I almost electrocuted myself vacuuming water off the set. And it only went downhill from there.

But there was one memorable moment.

One night, Sybil Danning came to me and said she wanted some Sudafed. Made sense. Everybody on the set was getting sick. But for some strange reason, I'd never heard of Sudafed. I'd heard of Contac, DayQuil, everything else, but never Sudafed. Or maybe I had heard of it and just didn't understand her accent. Either way, that was okay with Sybil, who said she'd ride with me to find it. (Apparently, George Peppard had been making advances on her. Or at least that was the story I'd heard.)

Now, the good news and the bad news was that she was in costume. So my job was to drive a valkyrie around Los Angeles at midnight in search of Sudafed. There is no straight guy in the world who wouldn't think that was the coolest thing. Or the scariest.

We started at the local 7-Eleven. We walked in. The arcade games were jammed with players popping quarters up on top of the stand-ups to get dibs on next play. Venice was not the gentrified Silicon Beach in those days. If you want to know what the antidote for video game addiction is, just have a valkyrie walk into the room. Everybody stopped playing to look. You could hear the Galaga and Defender ships dying. The guy behind the counter got a look of dread on his face. He was clearly also thinking, *"This could go bad, fast."*

Sybil didn't seem to notice anybody noticing her. She was focused on Sudafed. There was no Sudafed in the store. There were other cold medicines in the store, but no Sudafed. I'm not sure whether she was just fixated on Sudafed or whether I was an unwitting accomplice in a jailbreak from the set, but she wanted to go to a drugstore.

I had a book in those days called *Twenty-Four-Hour LA*, which I'd bought at Book Soup, a great bookstore and seemingly one of the few that is still around almost forty years later. I opened it up, and we headed off into the night. We didn't talk much, and I can't remember where we finally found Sudafed, but it was a journey that could have turned into one of those eighties movies where somebody heads off on a mundane errand and ends up on a wild adventure.

It didn't.

Sybil and I found the Sudafed and got back to Hammond Lumber alive. There wasn't some wild romance. George Peppard, who hadn't noticed me for any reason before that, gave me a dark look, and then the night went on. Still, I'll never forget the stories my brain was telling me while I was riding with the valkyrie.

There were some other interesting things about the *Battle Beyond the Stars* shoot, too. The art director was a brilliant, intense guy. People seemed intimidated by him, but I liked him. We spent a lot of time hastily putting sets together, gluing McDonald's boxes and egg cartons onto walls to create futuristic spaceship environments. Apparently, the original art director quit a week before the shoot started and hadn't done anything, so this was all on the fly. Not to worry—James Cameron did such a stellar job that Roger Corman let him direct his next movie, *Piranha 2*. In hindsight, I can honestly say this: he was one of those people who you knew was going to be a star. As they said in *Apocalypse Now*, he had that weird light around him.

Switch to Transformers

Winter 1985

"Bruce Springsteen, Madonna
Way before Nirvana
There was U2 and Blondie
And music still on MTV"

—Bowling for Soup, "1985"

THE ONE THING I CAN'T put a date on is exactly when I moved from *G.I. Joe* to *Transformers*. It had to be pretty early on—I'm guessing December or January of '84/'85. The thing I do remember is the pitch Tom and Joe gave me. "We need you to bring some 'edge' to *Transformers*—kind of like what you did with *G.I. Joe*." At the time, I'd never heard the word used that way, though it would become a ubiquitous buzzword in the nineties. People still use terms like "edgy," but as of that day, I'd never heard it before. I figured out pretty quickly what it meant.

I'd mostly ignored *Transformers* up to that point. It was Doug Booth's show. He was going to stay on it, but he was also tasked with developing *Robotix*, and unlike me, had long relationships with Marvel and the people already working on *Transformers*. That meant I had to learn about the other show we were doing, which I'd only seen out of the corner of my eye.

And I'd have to learn real fast. I knew that it was a sales phenomenon, but I hadn't given two thoughts as to why.

It didn't take long to figure it out.

From the toy perspective, *Transformers* filled three "play pattern" categories all in one. Every Transformer was a vehicle, an action figure, and a puzzle. You got an action figure, a car or plane (or gun or boom box), and a Rubik's Cube all in one toy. This led to an unprecedented amount of play value.

They also hit the market at the exact moment when computers were showing up in the home and office. Transformers and computers would be among the first things that children could master and leave their Baby Boomer parents behind. Just stop for a moment to imagine the neck-snapping impact of this: for the first time in history, children were more adapted to deal with the technical world than their parents.

While parents were being shipped off by their employers to take dreaded computer classes, their kids were effortlessly picking up the skills. Their children were their tutors, protecting them from obsolescence. And atop the indignity of that, the kids were playing with toys that they could effortlessly transform, which created nothing but awe and frustration for their parents. It was a whole new world.

In every other era of human history, there's a sharp line between childhood and adulthood, but the eighties began an era, which continues, that blurs the line between childhood and adulthood. If you don't believe me, attend Comic-Con.

And there's another component to this story. In the eighties, Japan—vanquished by Grandpa in places like Iwo Jima, Guadalcanal, and Okinawa—had risen to be an industrial titan. The Japanese were buying everything. When I was a kid, "Made in Japan" was a slur long before it wasn't. Along with a fear of Japan came a kind of fascination. Ninjas were everywhere, and after we grokked that *Star Wars* was influenced by Kurosawa, we all went to film festivals to watch black and white movies in other languages, and many of us pretended to learn a lot from them. (In fairness, some actually did.)

The version of the Transformers origin story I heard went something like this. Transforming robots had been around in Japan for a long time.

Usually, they had a pilot that went into the cockpit of the planes, and the robot was a vehicle with a face—it wasn't its own personality. Hasbro figured that they could save money not making the human figures or the various hinges to open cockpits and the like if the robot *was* the character! Who needed the human? This seems normal to us now, but at the time, that was a breakthrough necessitated by both business and creative needs. There's a certain high harmony when show and business meet in show business. And it hammered on the one thing America did—and still does—well: intellectual property.

The ability to look at something and see something else is where Sunbow comes in. You're importing these toys, you've ditched the little figure that piloted Starscream, but what do you call these characters? Tonka did a similar thing and called them "Go-Bots." The "go" was probably vestigial, as that's a word Japanese seem to like (Niantic is doing Pokémon Go as I write this), and "bots" was the name you used for robots when you didn't want to get sued for using "droids." The name made sense, but it sounded kind of kiddy. And in the mid-eighties, "kiddy" was just becoming passé.

During the process of transforming these obscure puzzle robots from a Japanese franchise into an American one, they toyed with a number of names. They liked "Convertibles," but it sounded too much like a ragtop. Eventually Jay Bacal came up with the name "Transformers." At this point, Joe's prodigy son was fresh out of Harvard, and the suggestion was not met with applause. People thought it sounded too much like electrical stations or something. But apparently it stayed on the list, and over time, people warmed to it. Jay would later say something, not in this context, that bears repeating here: "Never underestimate the power of being the first idea in somebody's head."

Now, it's obvious that the thing you do is divide the Transformers into good guys and bad guys. But it wasn't obvious how you'd do it, exactly. If somebody had asked me how to divide nearly a hundred characters into good guys and bad guys, I probably would have defaulted to sports and suggested to match them up, paint the good guys blue and the bad guys red (or vice versa), and be done with it.

That would have left the franchise looking pretty binary and wouldn't have had the richness Transformers eventually gained.

So how did they do it?

Legend has it that Joe Bacal was on the way to LaGuardia and had to make the decision about how to divide up the product line. He decided that weapons and planes were bad and that cars were good. It was just that simple. And you can slice it any way you want or argue the point, but three decades and billions of dollars later, I'd argue the decision was about as good as decisions get.

There was an underlying genius to it. The Decepticons were individually more powerful than their corresponding Autobot, so the good guys would have to be a strong team to win. The overpowered bad guys would be overconfident and squabble with each other the way bad guys do and tear themselves apart—hence all of the fun we'd have with the treacherous Starscream and Megatron.

Returning to the "golden age" theory, for a moment, there are a few other components to what makes for a golden age: exposure to new influences (Japan), a need (your economy is getting eaten alive), and a social disruption (computers). All of these things generate a certain amount of fear. That's the bad news. The good news is that they engender creativity and an environment where people are willing to do new things, but there's a lot more to a golden age than that.

One Long Argument

THIS IS PROBABLY THE best point to introduce the fact that my arrival on *Transformers* was like one long argument. At the height of my problems, Jay explained to me that one of the reasons they picked me for the job is that I am generally good with people. You wouldn't have known it from my first few months on *Transformers*. No small part of the problem was that I had no idea whatsoever what I was doing. The other part was that Sunbow was wittingly and unwittingly disrupting an old way of doing things at a number of levels. Our saving grace was that they had a lot of money, paid well, and provided a lot of work to a lot of people.

In film school, we were taught that (as Raza Ahmad would put it decades later) you write a film three times: once in script, again in production, and finally in editorial. The animation business didn't see it that way. For them, once a storyboard was delivered for recording, it was "locked." I had never heard the term before, as nothing was ever locked in film school until the final had to be delivered. We grew up with an auteur mentality, which in and of itself was a non-business idea. We were now in an industry that wanted to work like a factory. When you went in to record, the only changes the Marvel producers expected to make were in areas where there were typos or maybe the shading of a line. This was not compatible with my feeling that if a better line came to mind when I was actually hearing an actor's voice, I ought to be able to change it.

At first, the line producers were patient with this, but eventually they became frustrated and angry and started complaining. Much to Joe and Tom's credit, they backed me up every time. From Marvel's point of view, the input of a green Sunbow associate producer was disruptive and expensive. They wanted it to stop. From Sunbow's POV, we were the client, and if we thought we were making the product better, we were making the product better. It should be noted here, and I've never really thought about it this way before, that Joe and Tom kept the business invisible to me. They were always about making the show the best we could.

Different sessions worked different ways, depending on how tight the schedule was and whether we were doing pickups. The beginning of the session was tech time—levels were adjusted, tapes were changed, clerical stuff was handled, stools were rearranged—but more and more we'd begun using that time to have the actors do a read-through. Voice actors are a rambunctious lot, and they like to have fun. The Saturday morning animation community felt like a close-knit group who'd done a lot of shows together. They all seemed to know and be comfortable with each other. Like athletes or musicians, they needed to warm up—or perhaps they just liked to. They'd read through the script with no recording on. They'd mess around with the lines, adding serious raunch and comedy. Once the real recording started, the fun disappeared, and it was all business. These guys were pros.

Nevertheless, in the mess-around periods, they'd come up with good stuff and remember their characters. When I'm writing or editing a script, of course I'm thinking about the characters and dialogue, but more than that, I'm moving them through the story like chess pieces. The actor who plays a particular character sees the story from the point of view of that character. They added little tweaks in there that were often better than the dialogue on the page. Once you've got an actor inhabiting a character, the character really comes to life. So I'd take the mess-around lines and want to record them. On one hand this slows everything down and disrupts the order of the session, and on the other hand, it makes it incrementally better and more unique and more authentic.

My feeling was that we'd paid everybody for a half day often for twenty minutes of work, but if pressed, we expected a half day of work. It's a pretty good argument. The thing I didn't know was that often these guys were double-booked, and in friendly arrangement with Wally Burr (our voice director) or Marvel or somebody, they would try and get people out early. I was slow to pick up on this. I didn't have a half-day rate. With me, Sunbow bought the "all you can eat" plan, and there was no clear line between work and pleasure in my life, anyway. In fact, there was no line in my mind between what I was doing for Sunbow and what I was doing with DDEC. Life was just one massive project.

I came out of film school in the auteur era and was taught things like "pain only lasts a minute, but film lasts forever." Even when I was working on Roger Corman films, it had that ethos. This was auteur meets low budget, which was always the case. Watch *The Other Side of the Wind* and you'll see how that worked. However, once I got into animation, I found myself leaving auteur world and entering into union world. I'm now a long-term member of the WGA, and I totally understand the need and importance of guilds and unions, but at the time they just seemed like a painus-in-the-anus.

At this point, the irony of my situation is obvious, so let me just state it here.

After the *Droids* debacle, I never wanted to see a robot ever again—except there I was a year later, working on *Transformers*, and Joe and Tom wanted me to give it some "edge." I'm sure some part of me wanted to beat *Droids*. The competitive part of me wanted to knock off *Go-Bots*. I'd like to believe that I had a serious and rigorous methodology for immersing myself in *Transformers*, but I didn't. I just kind of stumbled around it.

Jay briefed me, and I watched the early episodes. I liked the clicky sound effect of them transforming. I liked the flipping Autobot/Decepticon shields. I liked a Walther PPK turning into a giant robot, turning into a high-powered rifle to be fired by another character.

Then I watched about five minutes of *Go-Bots* and knew everything I needed to know. It was a kiddie show.

Game on.

In the eighties, animated shows were a disreputable business. Saturday morning, and by extension syndicated animation, were the bottom of the entertainment food chain. Only comics were lower, and that's because they didn't pay as well. We look at the world as I'm writing this, and A Movies are the kinds of things you could only do in animation back in the 1980s.

Animation, at the beginning of that era, was a children's medium. My feeling is that by the end of the era, it wasn't just children watching, and the children who were watching didn't stop being interested in the things they liked when they were kids. And there's another factor that must be borne in mind. There was a recession. I remember Tom Griffin telling me, "You know what the difference between a recession and a depression is?"

"Not really." I wasn't sure if this was an economics question or not. I had a working answer, but not one I wanted to put out there.

"It's a depression if *you* don't have a job."

Point was, it was a recession if it didn't affect you and a depression if it did. True enough.

Well, there was a recession going on when I was working on *G.I. Joe* and *Transformers*, and I remember thinking that I was doing a show that a dad, who was at home, could watch with his kids while he waited for another job to turn up. It was a sad image then, but now, I'll bet a lot of those dads remember those afternoons very fondly. And a lot of those kids, who might have been the last generation of post-War toy kids, never did see a reason to stop collecting.

The generation of kids that grew up playing cowboys and Indians fueled Westerns for decades. Kids playing cops and robbers fueled gangster movies for a long time. And what starts out being crapola turns into art, eventually. *The Godfather* comes to mind.

Of course, part of the shift is digital technology. Finally, superhero movies could actually look good. Things that only Jack Kirby could draw in 1960 could be realized—literally realized—in the *Avengers* movies.

Before *Star Wars* (or maybe *Jaws*), you had to put on your "B-Movie" glasses to watch this stuff. You had to sort of not see the strings in the George Reeves *Superman* or the slight belly on Adam West's Batman. (In fact, my brain worked extra hard to take that one seriously.)

In fact, I remember the first rave review of *Star Wars* I heard from a frat brother when it came out on finals week of my senior year. He said, "Man, the effects were so good that I didn't have to be stoned to watch it."

The algorithm was simple in 1985. Younger kids will watch older shows. Older kids will not watch younger shows, though moms might. Girls will sometimes watch boy shows. Boys will not watch girl shows. Dad will happily watch boy shows with his kids if there's something in it for them and he's not embarrassed. Mom will sometimes watch boy shows. Dad will never watch girl shows.

And there was an irony staring me in the face, and I couldn't even see it. Think of all those episodes where Optimus was leading the Autobots down some lonely, mesa-filled desert rolls, usually kicked off with "Autobots, transform and roll out." It was a cavalry show. Two generations earlier, the line would have been "Saddle up and let's ride." The actor would have been John Wayne, and John Ford would have been directing.

I was once again doing the same thing I'd failed to do a year earlier.

This time, though, the results would be different.

Actually, let's interrupt *Transformers* production and ride with the topic of unions for a moment, because unions are extremely relevant to entertainment production and people rarely talk about them. Think of unions as a semi-hidden layer to the story of most linear entertainment products. (I'm making a distinction because there aren't really unions in the games business.)

There is the belief that it's unfair that animation writing doesn't get residuals like live action does, that there's no arbitration, and that despite the fact that writers are part of the animation union, they are more captives there than welcome collaborators. Let's start here: An animation script is exactly like a live-action script, and possibly more rigorous because you have to describe everything, and they are, in theory, twice as long (two pages per minute rather than one). However, there are no residuals, no separated rights, and no arbitration. The producer decides who gets the writing credit—something that would cut both ways for me in later years.

Why is this?

Well, back in exactly this period, America was reeling from losing the auto industry to Japan and didn't want animation to go the same way. As TV—live-action or animated—is basically a writers' medium, the National Labor Relations Board decided to keep writers in the animation union to prevent runaway animation. Of course, everybody got around it, but it is understandable that animation writers felt like sacrificial lambs to a bunch of ingrates in the animation union who didn't, at the time, see why there even were animation writers.

One good thing about not being offered residuals, in my mind, was that it made animation writing less attractive to slumming, big-time TV writers, and as a result, that left an opening for beginners—which is exactly what I was at that point. Writing animation was a great training ground. The issues with animation are a lot like the issues with games, and that would help much later in my career. And, frankly, the last thing I was worried about were residuals and pensions. I was young and didn't worry about health insurance (though I always seemed to have it), and retirement was a lifetime away, and it didn't occur to me that anybody would ever, under any circumstances, want to rewatch our stuff, so this issue didn't mean much to me.

And, quite frankly, I never expected to be in animation very long anyway. I had no idea where I was going to be, but I figured animation was just a side trip on whatever my career was going to be. We can discuss the pros and cons of living in the moment and long-term planning, but at the time, I wasn't thinking past the next day.

It was a very "mindful" period of living in the moment.

My first mindful moment with the animation union was about two weeks in at Ruby-Spears, when I received a letter I didn't understand that basically said I had to send them a wad of money to join the union or I'd never work in this town again. Everybody told me to send the cash, join, and it would be fine. I sent the wad and realized I belonged to the AFL-CIO (or some other huge and intimidating sounding union). After that, I never really dealt much with the animation union other than sending them checks and attending a couple meetings in some rundown building somewhere in Burbank. (It might not have actually been in Burbank, but in my mind it was in Burbank.) I was part of it, but it wasn't part of me.

So that was my experience with my own union. I crashed into whatever union the voice actors were in those days and didn't even know it, but oddly enough, I was technically right. When you pay for a half day's work, you're supposed to get a half day's work.

There were other rules. I only vaguely remember what they were, but they were stipulations along the lines of "an actor who had a half day and a full day and could only do three voices," and there was some kind of a breakdown between what was a major and a minor role, and so on.

Of course, nothing works in the real world like it works in concept, and often actors would do more minor voices or favors like free pickups in exchange for working fewer hours or various other things. Rules are meant to be subverted. And this is where the premise of guilds runs into reality.

On one level, the member is supposed to be loyal to the unions and guilds (to this day, I only vaguely know the difference). However, producers didn't have to hire an actor who they saw as "difficult," so it was a constant push-pull between following the rules and gaining employment.

And when you live in a shadowy world like that, individual actors have to make formal and informal deals. In this particular instance, I was the unwitting dupe caught in the middle of a game I didn't understand and which nobody had much interest in explaining to me because I was ALSO the "client"—otherwise known as the person actually paying for the production.

Being a noob, I didn't fully understand the implications of that. I was utterly unaware of the fact that in the normal world, I was the most powerful person in the room simply because I represented the people who were writing the check. I didn't think about it that way. In fact, I didn't think of the money at all. Thinking about money doesn't come naturally to me, and that's a good way to be when you're the creative person.

The fact that I was also a writer, and at that moment every show I'd worked on had been a hit, brought another whole wrinkle to it. When I ran into opposition, I tended to take it personally. As I said, I was young, but I'm not sure I've ever grown out of that mistake. The advice here is to try and be cognizant of the power dynamic in which you're functioning. Sometimes it's not personal or artistic. Sometimes it is business. Usually it is a complex combat matrix of all of the above.

But for the purposes of our discussion on voice sessions, I was confused when actors who seemed to so joyfully experiment with the characters and dialogue when the mics weren't running were suddenly annoyed when I wanted to get an extra take or change the script—even if the change was stimulated by one of their ad libs. My thought was that we wanted to always get a usable version of the scripted line and then get the better alt, then we'd figure out which to use later when we listened to the session tapes.

In theory, I was right on both counts: we had paid for the time *and* my job was to deliver the best show I could. But that's theory. In the real world, I had entered a very complex ecology that I didn't understand. In film school, I'd been trained that production was part of the creation process, and therefore I expected to be able to create during production. In the real world, Wally had made a deal with the voice actor that let him run off to do *The Smurfs* inside the half day in return for free retakes and doing more than the union-sanctioned number of voices.

I was cracking the favor piggy bank that I, and my employers, benefitted from. And everybody but me knew that the real bank in this world was the favor bank. In the case of Wally, this was pretty benign, but what I did not have the perspective to understand was that shows came and went, but relationships endured. Clients came and went, but the internal relationships between the actors and the voice directors continued on.

So maybe I was "right," but it didn't mean that I wasn't annoying and disruptive. Of course, as time went on and all of our shows were either number one in their category or second only to another one of our shows, it was hard to argue with the scoreboard. Arguments were had in the sessions and off-screen between New York and LA that I was only vaguely aware of, but over time, the format of the sessions became looser and more open-ended, and I had less resistance. Part of this was that we tended to get more offbeat actors who weren't part of the system, and part of it was that everybody got used to it. I remember that by the time we got to later *Transformers, Inhumanoids*, and *Visionaries*, it was pretty explicit that I only wanted to audition actors who would be there the whole time. Everybody knew the rules of engagement heading in.

When you approach any creative project, watch the balance between order and chaos very carefully—especially in the digital world. Too much order, and you lose an intangible human element; too much chaos, and you have a mess. Compare, say, music from the sixties and seventies with modern studio music. A recording session in which band members have to all get it right at the same time produces a very different product than an album where the musicians aren't even in the same room on the same day when the song is assembled. They might be playing the same notes and singing the same lyrics, but it's different. When you're in a medium that is by its very nature constrained, like animation or games, you want to create a sense of chaos and spontaneity to counteract that, and in a medium that is chaotic, like improv theater, you want to create rules and structure to rein it in. But I'm also aware that there are opposite and equally valid opinions. You always get something and lose something.

And I've touched on this elsewhere, but Sunbow also introduced a kind of chaos into the system that the cozy world of Saturday morning animation hadn't quite seen. This was offbeat actors. Joe Bacal discovered Chris Latta in some comedy joint in Greenwich Village. He saw an extraordinarily talented guy who was raw, careening out of control down the highway of life with a unique voice. Injecting that into a room of polished, disciplined pros created a unique dynamic. Out of it came Starscream, Cobra Commander, D'Compose, and numerous other characters. And Chris was far from the only rogue element Sunbow introduced—he was simply the most extreme.

In an alternate universe where some scholars analyzed animated shows of the period, I'm sure they'd find that something changed then. Shows just sounded different. They may have been toy shows financed by Hasbro as twenty-two-minute commercials, but there was a sense of creative freedom and adventure that I've rarely seen in my career, and I think it shows in the final results. Corporate work isn't necessarily less creative than art work, no matter what some old hippie tells you.

I think in all of this analysis, I might have missed a fundamental truth. Recording sessions were fun. I always liked going to them. They were sometimes tough and contentious, but they were always fun. And the world is a dynamic place. There were bumps in the beginning, but everybody began to understand everybody else, and accommodations were made for their legitimate issues. Ultimately, though we rarely talked about it, we were proud of both the product we were creating and the ratings we were getting.

The next phase was post-production. I am not an editor, a sound effects guy, a composer, or anything technical, but I had to approve everything all the way through the sweetening session. Sean Sullivan came in to do the telecine and really technical stuff that all seemed like voodoo to me, and Joe and Tom rapidly figured out that the exact reckless, ADD qualities that made me valuable at the front end of production probably made me worthless at the back end. They didn't try to make me something I wasn't, they just sent in support: Eric Early, Steven Heth, Michael Charles Hill, Sean Sullivan. That's the thing about great creative teams. You build around each other based not only on strengths, but on weaknesses. I am most effective when I have detail-oriented people around me, people who plug the holes. Capitalize on strong points and cover weak points. That's not to say I was always pleasant about it when people pestered me about what I considered to be minutiae.

All I knew to do in post-production was look at stuff and listen to instincts. *What if we turn down the music here? We're in a cave, can the guns sound echoey? What if we intercut faster?* Whether my suggestions were valuable or garbage, they created an environment where the guys who actually did know what they were doing could experiment, could do things a little differently, could do the non-obvious take. That works everywhere. And the big key to instinct for me was when my mind started wandering or I was getting bored or I felt like everything seemed too predictable. *What's the bump we can throw in? What's the better question to ask? What's the cliché to challenge? What happens if we don't have wall-to-wall sound? What happens if we don't use the loud music during the battle?*

If the disruption of the recording process was a hurdle, it was nothing like what happened when we went in and started giving edge to the show in the story editor room. Bryce Malek and Dick Robbins were the story editors of *Transformers*. They were polished professionals who were delivering a highly rated show. Why would they be thrilled when suddenly the Sunbow operatives showed up and decided that the show needed to be changed? What needed changing? What does "give the show some edge" mean?

What are you guys doing?

When I was moved from *Joe* to *Transformers*, Doug Booth, who'd been associate producer on *Transformers*, moved over to *Joe* and started developing other shows like *Robotix*. He was my twin and equal employee; however, he was far more experienced. Take a look at his IMDb page. He worked on everything. I think he's one of the few people who wrote both a *Transformers* and a *G.I. Joe* episode. Like Jay, he was a Harvard guy. Incredibly smart. He was a beat older than we were but looked like he was still in high school.

Doug also knew the Marvel guys well and came from their world. It was a different animation world than I'd come from. I'd come from the Ruby-Spears world, and because of Steve, Buzz, and Hildy's presence, Sunbow was a heavily Ruby-Spears accented shop. So my arrival at Marvel to work on story represented a number of bad developments in the Sunbow/Marvel relationship far beyond whatever my personal obnoxiousness might have been.

To Marvel, it was the first step in Sunbow taking over the story editing on *Transformers*. Sunbow had always controlled *G.I. Joe*, but *Transformers* was different. It also represented a different network invading and a change in direction. One of the basic things I've noticed about human nature is that people love the concept of change and "shaking things up" and "keeping things fresh" and "going to the next level"—they just don't much like the reality of it. Change creates uncertainty and friction. And if I were in Dick and Bryce's position, I would have been stunned and offended. Where was this desire for change coming from? The show was a hit, neck and neck (from what I was told, I never saw ratings) with *Go-Bots*.

If *G.I. Joe* was effortless for me, *Transformers* was the opposite. Two years earlier, when I was at Ruby-Spears, we'd taken a lunch trip to Japantown. I bought my first transforming robot there. I had never seen anything like it. It was a small corvette-looking car that turned into a robot. Bought a plane, too. We did a show called *Turbo Teen*, which I had little or nothing to do with, that was about a flesh-and-blood kid that turned into a car, but that was all I knew about transforming things. One thing I'm not and have never been is what Malcolm Gladwell calls a "maven." That's a person who becomes an expert in things and collects information for the sake of having information. I only know about what either a) interests me, b) is placed directly in my path, or c) a maven tells me about. That's it.

I got the basics easily enough: Optimus Prime was part semi and part John Wayne (more or less), and Megatron was a nasty cartoon bad guy. There was a human kid (Spike) in the middle of the story and the VW Bug was kind of his friend. Things started getting interesting for me when I discovered the whack characters.

As toys, I kind of liked the things that looked like regular objects that turned into robots. I have a theory that there are about four kinds of boy play patterns: trucks, dinosaurs, robots, and toy soldiers. I was definitely a toy soldier kid. And, oh yeah, there are trains. I was a bit of a train kid and designed my first war games with miniature lead soldiers on a train board. Dinosaurs and robots existed to fight with my toy soldiers. I had an endless army of Britains (mostly British soldiers) and semi-HO scale Civil War soldiers, and they'd fight robots on my playroom floor and always win. I even had rules—not unlike I would later learn with Chainmail, but infinitely less complex.

A few years ago, when I was interviewed for the *Transformers* and *G.I. Joe* box sets, I went back to figure out exactly how far along *Transformers* was when I started. The answer is complex. As I came on as a producer and shows were already in process, I was doing post-production (sweetening, editing) for some very early episodes (like "The Golden Lagoon"), storyboards for episodes right behind that, recording sessions for other episodes, writing scripts for upcoming episodes, and then muscling in on premises.

The animation production cycle, from the perspective of the associate producer, goes something like this:

1. Premise: We started asking for three premises based on a loose springboard. (*G.I. Joe* worked like this, and I brought this into *Transformers.*) The premises only had to be a paragraph or page at most. The idea was that we got three takes on the idea. The first take would always be the obvious one, the second one would usually be a variant or a slightly less obvious one. By the third take, the writer (sometimes us) was out of obvious ideas, so you got something wild. My experience is that each one prevailed about a third of the time.

2. Outline: We'd bought the premise, now the writer went to outline, which ranged in length from ten to twenty pages, depending on the writer. We later substituted the beat chart, based on the one I snagged from George Lucas, and it featured twenty-one beats of the story. One beat per minute. The thing that was great about beat charts is that they pinned the story to time. Our stories were twenty-one minutes and our commercial timings were precise. You could look at the beat chart and know how well the script laid out, which saved a lot of trouble later on.

    So what about the extra beat? After all, the show is twenty-two minutes and we only had twenty-one minutes of beats, so where's the other beat go? The answer: anywhere. Maybe you spread it around the script, maybe you made the middle act a minute longer, maybe you had more setup or added something to the ending. My theory at the time was that leaving the discretionary beat in there meant something about the script had to be unique. It had to feel different than any other episode. Formula works, but if you follow the formula, you will end up with mediocre. You have to build in something odd. Something with discomfort.

3. Script: The writer then turned in the script. We usually expected them in two weeks. Typically, the writer would do a draft, we'd send some notes, they'd respond, and then the story editor would take it over. The story editor's job was twofold: 1) make the script work, and 2) sync it to the series. We had a lot of writers from a variety of disciplines. We could not expect them to be experts on the world of *Transformers* or know what we were doing in other scripts or how we'd been playing each of the characters. Some writers knew the series really well. Some didn't. Part of the magic of our stuff was that we had so many different types of writers working on the show that they brought wonderful and unexpected things. Sometimes, however, they weren't wonderful and were horribly unexpected. For instance, one writer didn't understand that each of the *Transformers* had a specific thing they transformed into and figured they could turn into anything they wanted at any time, like Plastic Man or something. So this writer had a character go into Glove Mode. Obviously, a serious rewrite was necessary.

If there's a writer lesson here, it's pretty obvious. If you're going to write a show, even if you're being brought in for your "out-of-the-box" prowess, you should still know the general location and shape of the box.

The story editor would go over the script with Jay, and/or other story editors if the rewrite had been extensive and they'd lost objectivity, and from there the script was approved to go to storyboard. (Sometimes, when we were really crunched, they'd go to voice recording, but typically, they went to storyboard.)

4. Storyboard: We had some of the best storyboard artists in the world. By the time we were deep in, I'd pretty much developed a thirty-six-page script length as opposed to the previous forty-four-page script. The difference was that I didn't call every shot or detail everything in the script. After all, a good storyboard artist was at least as good at visually representing the story as I was. They weren't pinned to

every shot like they were in the old Ruby-Spears days. By and large, the artists liked the freedom, and the best of them liked to put their signature on the episode. Who wouldn't? I think the explanation for the old system was that TV animation came from a television model where the writer is king. In movies, you don't call shots—or at least that's what I'd been taught in film school—and it was considered amateur hour to do so. Take a look at nearly any screenplay. In TV animation, it was different.

Storyboard was also where the show was timed. If it was over length, they either cut things or suggested cuts. I never knew exactly what directors did in animation, but Steve Gerber told me they were the guys with the stopwatches. Timing is not trivial in animation. You don't shoot coverage. It's not like live action. Ideally, nothing is wasted. Digital production brought a lot of animation techniques to live-action films. Of course, as digital gets more fluid, there will probably be more opportunities for alternative shots. And if people get serious about doing animation on advanced game engines, it might become very easy to do animated films in real time.

Another reason that Sunbow shows felt different than other shows of the time was that we didn't do "perfect pause," which was a trick used in animation to leave a second between every line of dialogue. The theory was that the viewer wouldn't notice and that if there were sixty lines of dialogue in every script, the studio would save a minute of animation. This is significant. In many ways, I lived a charmed life in animation. I never really had to time, I never had perfect pause, and I never worked with the stock system[7].

5. Voice recording: We recorded the sessions at Wally Burr Studios on Hollywood Way in Burbank. It was a strange old Tudor-esque building right down the street from the now-deceased Last Grenadier game store and the thriving Allied Train store. Wally had been a tanker during World War II, and that's probably why the studio was

---

7   The way it has been explained to me, writers had to write to certain "stock moves." For instance, you had a small number of preanimated motions, like swinging a sword, and you had to select one from the book and put it in the script.

done in barracks chic. The lobby had a crap green couch and a dying white chair and the classic *G.I. Joe* and *Transformers* posters on the wall. There was probably a bowl with gratuitous candy, and I seem to remember there was somewhere to get hours-old caramelized coffee, but that might be my imagination. I'd later learn what posh recording studios looked like, but this wasn't one of those. There weren't any models bringing you gourmet chocolate chip cookies or gimlets at happy hour with hors d'oeuvres. This was to the bone.

Beyond the lobby/green room was a straightforward recording studio. The studio was fully loaded, but it wasn't one of those cushy places for rock stars; it was down to business and had everything we needed to produce highly stylized soundtracks. Most of the voices for *Transformers* passed through a thing that added subtle sound effects beneath the voices of the characters. For instance, an Insecticon used to have buzzing insect sounds in its sound bed. Unless, of course, it was Frank Welker, who seemed to have insects living in his voice box. I have no idea whether vocoders still exist or they're now a setting on Pro Tools, but at the time, they were the far edge of tech.

For anybody who hasn't been in a voice recording studio (it works in a similar way with music), recording studios are divided into two parts. There is the studio room (or control room), which features a large mixing board, various tape decks, a central seat for the director, and a seat for the tech. Ours also had a swivel chair at the front for the producer and a couch and a couple chairs for the various other attendees. I was a various other attendee.

Armed with a script and a microphone, with which he communicated with the actors through two-way soundproof glass, Wally sat in the director's chair. The actors worked in a fully soundproofed room. As I recall, there was enough space in the room for five actors, their mics and stools, and not much else.

A lot of magic happened in Wally Burr's studio. Wally, in 1985, was a tall, graying, slightly dapper, slightly crusty guy who was charged not only with wrangling a wild and chaotic cast of actors, but also with wrangling rogue producers, keeping to a deadline, interpreting bizarre dialogue and explaining it to the actors, and keeping the show going. In short, he was one of the greats.

The thing that everybody knew but nobody talked about or even cared about was that even then, maybe from being inside a tank and too close to artillery, he was hard of hearing. I sort of figured that if Michelangelo could paint the Sistine Chapel when he was blind and Beethoven could compose the Ninth when he was deaf, Wally could still direct voices.

Recording sessions had all shapes and sizes. Most often, it was a revolving door of actors, usually five at a time. The goal was to read the script more or less in order, but if an actor only had a few lines and they were in different parts of the script, they'd get all of the actor's lines so he could get out and another could come in. Sometimes we'd do retakes and pickups from previous episodes, sometimes we'd record random stuff, like lines for commercials or a "knowing is half the battle" public service announcement (PSA).

(Speaking of which, if you want to have a fun experience, look at the "Knowing is Half the Battle" parodies online. The PSAs weren't new to *G.I. Joe* and *Transformers*. Even back in the *Mister T* days, we were doing some with the tagline "The More You Know." Nobody got excited about writing these things, and they always seemed to come out of nowhere. Carole Weitzman was well aware that they were kind of the KP of Sunbow. Sometimes we'd sit around the Sunbow conference table and write them together. The dialogue was pretty similar to the parodies. We understood they were tribute to the various pressure groups, and we delivered. Even now, they're an interesting cultural artifact.)

I usually worked from two scripts during recording sessions. One was the actor's script, which only had dialogue, and the other was either the script or the storyboard of the episode. Typically, it was the storyboard. Sometimes I'd look at the storyboard and hear the line and want to change it. If I didn't do this too many times, it was accommodated. If I went over the producer's subjective limit or we were spending too much time getting the new line, there would be friction.

A "line reading" is when the voice director reads the line to the actor. In general, actors don't particularly like being given line readings, but these guys were pros, and the material we recorded was sometimes exotic, so if Wally felt like the line was complex or sarcastic or the actor just wasn't getting the nuance, he'd give them a line reading and they were mostly good-natured about it. A lot of times I felt the problem wasn't the actor but the line, so I'd change it. Sometimes this was a hero move, and sometimes it was annoying. I had to pick my moments.

Thinking about it now, I realize how complex Wally's job was. At one level, he had to make the trains run on time. At another level, he had a lot of professional pride and wanted to do a great show, and he had to deal with this every session. There was always a period of screwing around at the beginning when we were reading through the scenes and "rehearsing." (This didn't happen in all sessions.) Voice actors are extremely verbal. You probably wouldn't do the job if you weren't verbal. That comes with the turf. They were also often witty and nearly always amusing people, and so they'd read through the scripts and throw in their ad libs. The vast majority of the ad libs are things that would not make it through any broadcaster's standards, but they were a way of loosening up. I thought of the beginning of the sessions as kind of like musicians tuning up or athletes stretching. They were getting their voices ready and they were getting into character. Often, the lines they came up with were better than what we had in the script.

At some point, Wally would halt the circus, and we'd get down to work. He'd try and keep the balance of what was usually an up mood in the room and getting the session done on time. He was a great cat herder. And the actors figured out the drill. By the way, if you want to know what all of this looked like to a voice actor, read Dan Gilvezan's book *My Life as a Transformer*. He played Bumblebee, and he talks about the recording sessions from the inside. He's a great guy and has gone on to do a ton of stuff. And if you really want to dive deep, check out Neil Ross's *Vocal Recall: A Life in Radio and Voice Overs*.

I was too close to it at the time, but if I'd taken a moment of introspection, I'd realize that it was less than a year earlier that I'd vowed not to do any more robots and I'd had quite enough of John Wayne cavalry westerns. But there it was, right in front of my eyes. Optimus Prime, who always was John Wayne, leading a convoy of Autobots across a John Ford desert. And even now, I wonder if the disaster of *Droids* paved the way for the success of *Transformers*.

Let's stop for a moment to talk about the business of the business. This is not my field of either interest or expertise, so I'll make it quick. It will inform a lot of the decisions and motivations around issues that fans ask about.

When you're looking at the credits for any movie, it's very hard to parse what they mean and who did what. Here's how it worked at Sunbow, though there are a lot of asterisks here. For instance, we did *Visionaries* with TMS (Tokyo Movie Shimsha) and not Marvel. There are formal and informal roles (sometimes people had multiple functions and did things outside of their title), so what follows is the general rule of thumb.

Hasbro controlled all of the properties we did in that period. Hasbro paid for the shows and Hollywood follows the "golden rule": he who has the gold rules. However, Hasbro effectively turned creative control over to their advertising agency, Griffin-Bacal, because from their point of view, the shows were twenty-two-minute commercials. Griffin-Bacal created Sunbow as their production arm. Joe Bacal is all about rainbows, but he's way too cool to call a company "rainbow," so he made it Sunbow. Sunbow subcontracted to Marvel Productions, which at the time was an animation studio.

Marvel had a robust staff and subcontracted to other specialists like Wally Burr, composers, etc. (It is possible that Sunbow subcontracted them, I just don't know, and it doesn't make a lot of difference for this discussion.) Suffice to say that the producers, storyboard artists, editors, etc. were most often Marvel, who subcontracted the animation overseas to companies like Toei.

The final, but very important, component was distribution. That was handled by John Claster and his company, Claster. He was the guy who made the deals to actually get the shows on the air. I don't know how distribution works, so I don't have much to say about this one. In an organizational chart, Claster had a dotted-line relationship to Sunbow. Top to bottom, it was Hasbro, Sunbow, Marvel, and the contractors branching off of Marvel and Sunbow.

Lee Gunther and Margaret Loesch ran Marvel. I liked both of them and went on to work with Margaret on several occasions later. I rarely saw Lee and Margaret during day-to-day. Probably the closest parallel to me was

Jim Graziano. The first few times we crossed paths, it wasn't pretty, but we sorted it out, and I actually got to like Jim and his wife Stephanie (who was the Marvel producer on *Inhumaniods*) a great deal. They went on to form GRAZ entertainment and are still vital in the industry to this day.

On a day-to-day basis, I dealt with the producers: John Walker, Gerald Moller, and George Singer. I think by the time I got into *Transformers* sessions, they were used to us and the new rules of engagement were in place. That's just speculation. Also, I should mention that the sessions weren't all that different. There was a lot of cast and crew overlap, and Wally was, of course, ubiquitous.

There was one very weird incident that should be mentioned. It was early on in my *Transformers* experience. I went over for a meeting with story editors Dick and Bryce, though there might have been others. As I said before, this was not all that welcome to Marvel. It wasn't so much a conflict of people as a conflict of missions, though in practice, conflict is conflict in a meeting. *Transformers* was a hit, and Sunbow wanted a bigger hit, or at least they wanted an edgier one.

The weirdest incident involved a report that I had somehow broken into the vault room where prints were stored and taken something out. We will probably never know whether this was a complete fabrication or whether prints really were misplaced, but nobody believed it. Pretty much everybody involved knew I had enough trouble finding the studio and the room I was supposed to be meeting in that there was near zero chance I was going to suddenly turn into Alexander Mundy[8] and start stealing whatever they thought I was stealing. Once this was laughed off, I had the kind of immunity that only a false accusation gives you.

In Joseph Campbell terms, this was entering the "Belly of the Beast." I was on Marvel's turf and, from their perspective, this was an alien invasion. And by the worst kind of alien: the client. As the client, or the client's representative, I had the right to be there, but I wasn't really welcome. To them, I was kind of like an Internal Affairs investigator at a police station.

---

8   Robert Wagner's character in *It Takes a Thief*. I even remember his prison number: 131425. When I'm amazed by fandom, all I have to do is remember that I remember this from 1968.

In theory I'm on their team, but I was perceived as a bad guy. This would eventually change, however.

I probably lost more than I won. I was doing this for the first time, and they had done it hundreds of times. You don't have to be much of a gamer to know who'd win. There were all sorts of reasons not to make changes, and they were often coupled with the usual threats to quit or take some other big action.

In retrospect, it would have been bizarre if there weren't problems. Not only was this about making changes to scripts, but it was fundamentally changing the power structure and putting a face on it—mine, in this case.

It all worked out well enough. We worked fairly harmoniously with both Marvel and Sunbow story editors for most of the second season, and Sunbow took over all of the story editing for season three. And this is important, because there is one unchanging rule in the media business: "He who controls the script controls the show." As often as not, creative control means script control.

As to Bryce and Dick, Dick passed on a few years later, and I ran into Bryce much later in a completely different context. We talked about the stress days. No harm, no foul. He seemed to be having a very good and successful life. Work is like that. You struggle with people for a time, but then years later, you realize that you have more in common with them than with most other people in your life. It's like the NFL Hall of Fame inductions. Guys who were supposed to be archnemeses on the football field a decade earlier were highly amused to tell stories on themselves and each other later on. Life keeps moving. As long as you play cleanly and honestly, the people who are your archenemies this time might well be your teammates the next.

Buzz Dixon came on board and replaced me as *G.I. Joe* story editor when I went over to *Transformers*. Buzz was the third stooge to me and Steve. In a room full of wild imaginations, Buzz had the wildest. He had been in the army in Korea, where he met his wife, Soon-Ok. He was born under a lucky star. It took me six years to break into Hollywood; Buzz got out of Korea, went to Filmation in his first month in Los Angeles, and Lou Schiemer hired him. Steve once said that Ruby-Spears started declining when Joe stopped listening to Buzz's third idea. You can't blame Joe for this, as Buzz's first two ideas were usually so appalling that it would take a lot of discipline to listen to another one.

Back in the day, Buzz was known for the outrageous. Buzz was uninhibited. Buzz was always an incredible warehouse of information—some of it useful, and some of it so obscure that you'd wonder how he or anybody else had come to know it. He was also a really fast writer, and his stuff played extremely well on screen. He had a natural sense of pacing and cinema. And he was his own brand of scholarly.

The strangest thing about Buzz is that he had the most normal life of any of us. He lived in a house in the suburbs with his wife and two children. I was unmarried and would remain that way through this entire period and beyond. Dini was the same way. Steve was divorced. Donna and Gordon were married, but they didn't have kids. Doug got married in this period, and his wedding was almost a Sunbow event. Jay Bacal got married near the end of this period. But for a lot of us, it was a very long, extended adolescence.

Meanwhile, Back at the DDEC Mansion

WHILE ALL OF THIS was going on, I was still splitting my time at the Dungeons & Dragons mansion, and it was not all work. Sometimes we'd actually play Dungeons & Dragons, and those were some of the best game sessions I've ever had. I can't speak for Gary, but my particular favorite style of role-playing involves almost nothing. I can see the necessity of maps and dice and figures, but I'm not that big a fan of books and rules. To me, anything that gets in the way of the shared mental vision of the world is an obstacle.

One day, we were up at the D&D mansion at the huge dinner table, which doubled as a conference table. Gary might have had a DM screen up. (The official Gary-Con T-shirt that I bought reads, "The DM only rolls the dice because he likes the sound they make.") The implication of this is that the DM, in this case Gary Gygax, views himself as a storyteller and tour guide through an adventure more than he views himself as a referee. I don't blame him. Who wants to be a referee? Nobody ever shouts, "Kill the storyteller."

Anyway, our adventure team, which included a combo plate of noobs and extreme high-end gamers[9]—Jim Ward, Luke and Ernie Gygax, Donna and Penny Yukavich, Joey Thompson, maybe Jim Johnson, and me—had entered a strange city I'd later use in Sagard, and we were in search of a character known as the Sultoon Jazeer. Our mission was either to overthrow or kill him. We played through the afternoon and past dinner. The interesting thing was that there wasn't a single fight in the experience, and there wasn't a map. Gary put us in a bazaar that was part real Middle Eastern and part fantasy. I can still remember what it looked like (oddly enough, it's kind of like the bazaar in *Uncharted 3*, though there is no cross-pollination).

Anyway, Gary's NPC was a sleaze monkey of a mercenary local who was doing his absolute best to tip everybody we ran into to the fact that we were a team of foreign insurgents attempting to kill Sultoon Jazeer. He'd say stuff like, "My friends are mercenary assass—uh, I mean, distinguished travelers from distant lands," and we'd think this was hilarious. As a matter of fact, I remember laughing all the way through. At least that's what I remember of the real world part of the game. The real wonder is that my memory of the Sultoon's bazaar is all set in the world, and it is as real as any memory I have of anything else in that era that actually happened to me. That's the magic of old school paper role-playing.

The point is that my favorite day of D&D had nothing to do with battles or rule books (of course, TSR paid the bills by selling rule books, and I totally see their value) or even die rolls. It was the shared experience of a fantasy journey. Over the years, I've tried to bring this into film, TV, and

---

9   Let me, one last time, insert the disclaimer that this might not have been the actual group. Some people mentioned might not have been there on exactly this day, and people might have been there whom I've forgotten. We played a lot of games, and all of them were there at one point or another, or at least plausibly there.

game development. People will try it out, but curiously, it's very hard to get them to do it, even though they enjoy it and understand the value of it. I've never been able to figure out why.

One of those projects I've thought about doing for years and never, in fact, done would be a narrative and character-building role-playing game. In my present DARPA project, we call it "generative gaming." Don't you love the buzz terms? I don't remember who coined the term—it could very well be my own term I'm making sport of here—but the idea is that the game itself generates a product.

221B Stark Tower

CAROLE WEITZMAN CAME INTO town to set up an office. Since Joe and Tom stayed at the Westgate in Westwood (now the W, originally built as a UCLA dorm), they decided that Westwood was a good place to have an office. And they were right. It was freeway-centric, and that's what mattered in LA in the eighties. Our meetings were all over town, from Beverly Hills to the deep valley, so the freeways mattered, and Westwood remains one of the few places in LA where you can walk. I thought it was great.

Carole found a second-story office you entered from an innocuous door on Westwood Boulevard above a Mrs. Fields. It was hidden in plain sight, like I imagined a quality spy agency would be. It was more 221B Baker Street than Stark Tower. More like Abbey Road studios than Universal. It was kind of perfect for us. Nobody walking by would know that Cobra Commander and Jazz lived there.

So we've come to that part of the Hero's Journey where we talk about the thing nobody talks about: Innermost Caves (a.k.a. Hidden Fortress or Secret Lair). Epic stories have great secret lairs, a.k.a. interesting places to hang out. My theory is that very few people do their best work in an airless corporate office. At least, creatives don't tend to.

The hidden lair is the place you operate out of. It is the place you feel safe.

- Batman has his Batcave—his hidden place to research, think, invent, heal, plan, and store his stuff.
- Superman has the Fortress of Solitude. If you're Superman, you don't have or need a lot of stuff, but you do need a shrine that reminds you of who you are and what your purpose is. Batman lives in his slain parents' home. Portraits over fireplaces remind him every day.
- James Bond has MI6 headquarters. He doesn't own it because he's a civil servant, unlike Bruce Wayne, and he doesn't have the money. However, he does have M and Q, and they give him all of the stuff he needs to live like Bruce Wayne. As a matter of fact, he gets to go to a lot more exotic resorts than Bruce Wayne ever does.
- And don't get me started with villain lairs. Suffice to say, you need a sanctus sanctorum, and it's good to have a lot of safe houses stashed around.

The most basic requirement is privacy. You need a place where you can go and not be bothered. In the old days, that just meant a room with a door and a lock if necessary. Beyond that, you have to have your tools. It's also not a bad thing if it has a way of obscuring the passage of time, like a casino or post-production facility. But maybe that's just me. I want a sense that there's a world outside, but I don't want it to intrude.

But it is your sanctus sanctorum.

This changed a little bit with laptops and portables, and some people like hiding in plain sight, at coffee shops and the like, but you do have to have a 24/7 secret lair. If an impulse strikes you at 3 a.m., you have to be able to follow it, because creativity is nothing if not inconvenient.

The more interesting hidden lairs in the day weren't really all that hidden, but they were only open to select people. By the time I got to Lucasfilm, George Lucas was building the ultimate secret lair, but while I got to see the promised land, I wasn't there long enough to really experience it in its heyday.

However, Paul Dini and I did get an office in the super-secret and super-mysterious Egg Company in Los Angeles. The Egg Company was, as I understand it, a small building that Lucasfilm rehabbed for their Los Angeles work. It was located where the Universal City Metro Station now is, and if you rolled down out of the high street that leads to City Walk and the tours, you could crash through the Egg Company. It was a dark, quiet retreat from the sun-baked expanse of the San Fernando Valley and a cool refuge from the molten concrete.

And there was the DDEC office. Best ever. I've already described the converted stable office at DDEC, and if I had to pick a favorite secret lair, that would probably be it. But its greatest asset was also its greatest liability. It was almost completely open to the outside world. We'd have lizards and snakes wander in now and again, and when I opened my computer to install a card, I found it was a whole spider ecology. But I never got bit, stung, or lizarded, and I've always loved feeling the world around me. It was an inside space that was also an outside space, kind of the opposite of what I. M. Pei was probably designing for Michael Ovitz and CAA at that exact moment.

"Prime Target"

Dealing with Fall-Out

JAY CALLED ONE DAY to tell me that a script had "fallen out." I don't remember what script fell out or why. Maybe one of the writers had a personal crisis or a conflict, or maybe it was the script from one of the writers who didn't read the bible very carefully and thought that Transformers could turn into anything. Anyway, we needed something fast. I'd had an idea rolling around in my head for a while. I wanted to figure out what would happen if somebody decided to hunt or trap Transformers for sport or reward. It was just an impulse. If cars and planes and boom boxes could transform, why couldn't buildings or streets or air hangars?

In fact, characters like Omega Supreme and Megaplex are kind of buildings—but what if they looked like Earth-based buildings? Okay, Megaplex is a city and not a building, and Omega Supreme (whom we knew as Tuna Supreme) is a base, but you get the idea. Why couldn't cities transform?

In fact, most traps are transformers themselves. They look like one thing and become something else when triggered. It was a new possible dimension for *Transformers*. In my mind, I imagined a whole line of Transformers who were really trap playsets. The Eiffel Tower lures planes in and then somehow springs when they come near, like a giant nineteenth-century Venus fly trap. The Golden Gate Bridge turns into a net that catches things that sail, fly, or drive near it.

Or on a smaller scale, what if a car wash was a trap? What if manholes or street grates suddenly opened up? Tunnels closed. Bascule bridges (the hinged bridges over rivers that go up to let boats pass and down to let cars over) became traps.

This is the kind of idea you get when you come to this from games. Games are all about the environment. Terrain matters. In game design, it's called PVE (player versus environment). We didn't use environment in *Transformers* much, so it was fun to take the idea for a drive.

That having been said, I was well aware of a potential can of worms. These traps couldn't be sentient, or I'd be breaking the rules of the show and committing a sin that wasn't all that much different than "Glove Mode." But I liked this idea, and I began to merge it with "The Most Dangerous Game," which is one of those stories that lives in my brain.

The question was: how would I get the script done in twenty-four hours and keep the schedule intact?

The answer was much shorter: Buzz.

The exact same Buzz Dixon I was partnered with on my first, somewhat disastrous day in the animation business. You know the old saw: "If you want something done, go to the busiest person you know"? At that exact moment, Buzz was story editing *G.I. Joe*, but I knew he had time. Buzz always had time. For all of the crazy stories and rumors, Buzz never blew deadlines, was extremely fast, and always had time.

Buzz was an idea machine with a very strong sense of structure. He got it immediately and even had a character for the big game hunter: Chumley. We started with a Russian jet called Oktober Guard being suddenly speared by a submarine under the ice. The pilot, who may or may not have been a crossover character from *G.I. Joe,* gets away, and we learn that the plane was not shot down by the Americans but bagged by Chumley, who then tells his manservant, Dinsmoore, that he really only needs one more thing to complete his collection: the head of Optimus Prime.

Of course, the Russians don't know this, so they threaten to go to war and we have a "Stop the War" B-story. Remember, it was the eighties. Reagan was president, and the Cold War was still very much on. At the time, Reagan was touting SDI, or the "Star Wars" defense. Fiction and fact were meeting in the real world. Anyway, the Transformers would have to figure out what was going on and stop World War III.

And then of course Chumley ends up working with the Decepticons, and of course Starscream doesn't miss the opportunity to point out that Chumley has accomplished more in two days than Megatron has accomplished in two years, and of course, since Buzz and I wrote the script, there was a surprise crossover cameo from Hektor (Hector) Ramirez.

"Prime Target" was delivered on time and ended up a fun, slightly whimsical episode. Where else do you get lines like:

"Decepticons! Trust them to spoil the hunt."
"Yes, sir. Just like the Humane Society, in a way."

—Chumley and Dinsmoore

Or the sci-fi whiff that Chumley might be some kind of an immortal:

"She's a lovely specimen, Lord Chumley, but there's a frightful international row brewing over it."
"Ahhh. These things blow over. Remember the Boer War?"
"Painfully, sir."
"Oh, yes, well. Everybody else has forgotten it."

—Dinsmoore and Chumley

Or even Optimus, who's not known for gag lines, getting funny:

"Amazing. A booby trap that actually catches boobies."

—Optimus when the Decepticons get ensnared

"Prime Target" was one of the few *Transformers* scripts I share a writing credit on for season two. Looking back, it's not an epic episode that rewrites the mythology of *Transformers* or a tense, serious episode. It doesn't go anywhere. We never see Chumley or Dinsmoore again, but it is kind of a fascinating bridge episode that combines the lightness of the first season, the growing relevance and reference to contemporary real-world events of season two, and even hints at *Inhumanoids* (the Soviet jet and Hector Ramirez). And the fact that he's looking for the head of Optimus Prime indicates to me that I was probably working on this around the time I was starting rewrites on *Transformers: The Movie*, in which the head of Unicron would play a prominent role.

Or maybe I'm remembering too much into it. But it's an episode I remember fondly, and I wish we'd done more PVE.

The Battle for TSR

AND AS I WAS EDITING Sagard in winter 1985, the storm looking over TSR and DDEC began.

I'd originally planned on dodging the issue of the collapse of DDEC, the takeover of TSR, and the end of the mansion, but as I ended the first draft of this book, I realized that it left too much of a hole. I've got to deal with it, but I've got to deal with it my own way. There is a small industry of books on Gary; my sister, Lorraine Williams; and the battle for TSR, and any of them is more factual than anything I have the will and ability to research. I'm not a lawyer or really even a business guy, and thus a forensic autopsy of a hostile takeover is not really in my range.

For over thirty years, I've avoided talking about it in various interviews, because it's negative and what's the point? And, as I write this, I'm trying to find a way into this section of the book, and more importantly, a way out. Also, one other caution. I tend to forget the negative. It's something my wife often finds unnerving and annoying. Even now, I'll tell her I'm going to a meeting with somebody and she'll say, "Don't you remember what happened last time you worked with that guy?"

The sad thing is that I usually don't. Or I'll remember some of the facts, but the emotional charge is gone. I could argue either way whether this is a good thing or not, but I can't deny that I have a bad memory for things I don't want to remember.

So here goes.

There was always a sense, in Gary's time in Los Angeles, that things weren't going well in Lake Geneva and that he was fighting with his partners, the Blumes. There were whispers of financial problems, and every once in a while, Gary would fly back for some kind of a showdown or a meeting with a group of business consultants who had a name like ABC (that wasn't it, but it was something like that). I'd also seen the cover of *Entrepreneur* or maybe *INC Magazine* naming TSR as the fastest-growing privately held company in America lying on a table in Gary's master suite. I tried not to notice that the issue was a couple of years old and tried to suspend my disbelief for most of what I read in magazines. I'm not sure I've ever seen a story (like a trade article) I was involved in that was totally accurate. The numbers always seem to have an extra zero on them, and relationships are often garbled.

From the beginning of the DDEC expansion to Los Angeles, there was a sense that something was wrong at TSR. And when Gary would talk to the consultant, he'd come back with ideas that didn't seem real to me. When I'd hear that if the company kept growing at its current rate, it would be bigger than the US government by 2000, I didn't take it very seriously. At this point, I'd seen enough of the entertainment industry to know that things change very quickly.

But none of this mattered or was particularly apparent when I'd see Gary buying $1,500 jeans after a Beverly Hills shopping spree or brochures for Excalibur cars on his desk. Gary, like Ray Bradbury, didn't drive. I've heard conflicting stories about why, but the story he told me, and which I completely believe, is that he did drive for a time but he'd find that he couldn't remember how he got to places, and it unnerved him. Gary's the kind of guy who shouldn't drive. I'd say the same of Frank Miller. Riding around with him in a supercharged Mach I was a terrifying experience. But I digress, because I'm trying to avoid writing this section.

Soldiering on.

So there was a general sense that, while we were in a mansion so high in the hills that we could see both the Valley and LA, all was not well. But whatever the problem was, it was lost somewhere in the smog on the far side of the horizon. That having been said, there didn't seem to be much of an urgency to make deals.

One morning, I remember walking in really early. It was still dark. I'd entered the sunken bar, which was the scene of many crimes and wasn't really sunken, but had a view of LA and the Hollywood Hills looking toward Blue Jay Way as the predawn sun tried to cut through the fog.

I was looking for a cup of coffee, but what I found was Ernie with a look of shock on his face. It stopped me in my tracks. Something was very wrong.

"What's up?" I asked.

"The bank just pulled TSR's line of credit," he responded flatly. "Pop flew back to Lake Geneva." Ernie referred to Gary as "Pop" sometimes.

"So what are they going to do?"

He shrugged.

Not long after that, Gary was back. He was talking about how TSR needed a shot in the arm. He was sort of hinting about borrowing money from my family or getting us to invest. My response was something that would change the history of TSR. We can debate whether it was for good or for bad, but it changed the course of the company.

I said, "You might want to talk to my sister—she's done some turnarounds."

There's a lot of backstory here. Feel free to skip it. I won't be offended. In fact, I won't even know. I'd skip it if I could. As I analyze that moment, my guess is that I was just trying to dodge the issue of me or my family lending him money. First off, I didn't have that kind of money (though I did end up lending some to Lorraine later on). I had a ridiculous amount of money for a kid who was just upgrading from living like a college student to an actual adult and who had no kids or expenses and had avoided obligations other than rent and trivial car payments. However, I did not have "keep a company alive money," and I sure as hell wouldn't have invested in that if I did.

Lorraine, on the other hand, was a business type. I knew no details, but I thought she had been working to turn around a hospital, and she'd led me to believe that she'd helped Dad prep his company to sell it. I also knew she'd left Easter seals, where her husband worked, and was looking for something to do. I had no idea whether she'd really turned around hospitals and Easter seals, or whether my dad really benefited from her help, but I did know that she was smart, so I made the connection and went about my business.

The thing that kind of surprised me was that Gary took me up on it. He called her, and they met. I'd assume that it happened in Lake Geneva or Chicago, but I can't remember—it happened quickly.

The next thing I knew, a number of things were happening. Gary had returned to TSR, exercised some option, and was now running the company again, with Lorraine as his second. The Blumes were on the sidelines.

Meanwhile, in LA, it seemed like there were a number of deals that were represented as maddeningly close to closing but which never seemed to close. John Beebe, and to a lesser extent Joey Thompson, had been my source of these stories. This became my first experience with executive smog. I attended a couple of meetings, and when I'd scan the company reports on the desks, I'd see that the reports of these meetings were a lot more optimistic than I was. And I might note here that it wasn't like I was really snooping in on these reports. Occasionally things would show up CC'd on my desk. I had no idea why anybody was including me. I wasn't an executive or even an employee.

The vibe in the mansion had changed. Donna and Penny were still there, but in a completely different capacity. Gail Carpenter had moved into first position as Gary's girlfriend. And this would be permanent. She would become Gail Gygax. So the shift in tone that was also probably about budget cuts came to me as a general sense of the depowering of the mansion.

For my part, I was doing everything I could to get things to happen. At one point, we were trying to turn *The Sceptre of Seven Souls* into a TV show. John Beebe told me it was too expensive. I figured it depended on how it was shot. If you broke the show down, it was a western, a detective story, and a sword and sorcery set piece. Take a drive on Universal's backlot, and they had all of those things right there.

"Where did you get experience in budgeting films?" John said tersely.

"I saw what Roger Corman did for not a lot of money, and he had above-the-line stars—granted, he got them on a budget either at the beginning or the end of their careers. And, yes, we're mixing genres, but what that really means is that they have to walk a hundred yards from Spartacus Square to Universal Gulch to New York Street," I said.

He wasn't buying it, but I still think I was right. I remember having this gross feeling that he wasn't really trying to win but instead trying to make it look like he was on the verge of a breakthrough in order to get another check and preserve his job. This might be an utterly unfair assessment, but that's what it felt like. Of course, I only dimly perceived this, because the money layer of things is something that I had to train myself to look for. For many, it is THE layer. For me, it's mostly an inconvenience. And I don't say this with any pride or smug superiority; it's just something I don't perceive as quickly as I should. John had been around for a long time and was at the end of a career. He probably knew the ship was sinking and just wanted to keep it afloat for one more month.

I liked John Beebe; I just found myself frustrated by him. This is the natural battle between youthful naiveté and elder experience, and a lot of great stuff can happen in the junction. Nothing other than Sagard specifically came out of it, but John was the font of a lot of good advice, and occasionally he could be challenging. I'd go in with some rant, wondering why so many of Gary's girlfriends were on the payroll. He responded that these were very innocent, non-predatory people and whoever replaced them might well be worse. Years and a lot of experience later, I realize the wisdom of what he was saying.

Once he asked me why I held Gary innocent in all of the chaos that was going on. I didn't have a good answer. If I was trying to construct one now, it was probably that I perceived Gary as being a lot like me, except he found himself running a company.

Gary was caught in a strange place. He was a creative guru who was, depending on how you look at it, either having a midlife crisis or catching up after years of toil, poverty, humiliation, parenting, and strict adherence to the Jehovah's Witness faith. From a theological point of view, his years in LA were his backslider period, but what an epic backslide it was.

Actually, let's digress inside the digression, and I'll avoid talking about the business stuff for another beat and answer the question that I'm really asked most frequently about that period: "Was it as debauched as I've heard?" I mean, nobody actually uses the word "debauched," but that's the question all the same.

Did I see piles of cocaine, prostitutes, spank-movie actresses, bikers, and people who may or may not have been psychotic? Yes. All present. But there is always an asterisk to any scene—with the exception of probably Andy Warhol's Factory—in that ninety-nine percent of the time it feels different when you're actually moving through it. I was simultaneously present and absent, a place that I often seem to inhabit. I was afraid of drugs, so I kind of topped out at nicotine. And even though I kind of looked like a biker when my hair wasn't cut and I was dressing in homeless chic, that world never held any appeal for me. Beyond that, I find psychos downright terrifying.

However, the theater of it all was endlessly fascinating. If I were a different kind of writer, I could do wonderful character sketches of the people you might find at the mansion on any given night, but I didn't get that gift. In some ways, I was like an older Luke, and I watched the passing freak show as a kind of street theater. We shared a fascination with the motivations of the people involved and a fleeting interest in figuring them out, but this stuff was way beyond any fourteen-year-old's ability to process. Truth is, I was literally twice his age and I didn't get it. Yes, I understood it, but not really, because once you were actually in the environment, these weren't cartoon characters, these were real people—complex and interesting ones, too. Some of them were even very talented.

While I only know where some of the stories ended up, most of them went to normal places. People grew up, went on to normal lives, maybe slightly fearful that some of this would come out. Maybe a wince now and then when a too-vivid memory comes back, like a combat flashback, but this was a pre-digital world. Almost nothing was recorded. Memories fade. Time passes. Social networks disintegrate. Politicians, old buildings, and prostitutes become reputable with age. Not so in our current world, but that's how it used to work. I have no idea what our world leads to, but fortunately, that's outside the purview of this book.

So back to the TSR wars. The next report I got from the battlefront, and this was confirmed on all sides, was that Lorraine had "shored up" the company. I believe that to be true. Anybody who knows me well enough knows that Lorraine and I have our difficulties, but this isn't the time or place to go into them. I'm going to call this one as straight as I can and be done with it.

In short order, the company was off the ledge. At some point, Lorraine shed dozens of employees named Blume and others viewed as nonessential. Gary told me he thought she was doing a great job. My response came out of my mouth unfiltered. "Yeah, and you're going to think that right up until she figures out that *this*," I indicated the mansion around us, "is the problem."

Gary didn't take offense. He just lit up a cigarette, and we started talking about something else. I'd made my point.

Not that it did any good for anyone.

Transformers: The Movie

The Secret of Cybertron

I DON'T KNOW WHEN I first heard about *Transformers: The Movie*. I'm sure there was talk drifting around, but I'm also quite sure that I paid little attention to it. I had too much on my own plate with the show, and this seemed like a "never trouble trouble" situation. I figured that sooner or later it would surface—or maybe not. A lot of movies are talked about and never happen. I'd learned that in my snipe-hunt phase.

In fact, probably ninety percent of the moves you hear about never happen. So I figured if *Transformers: The Movie* ever happened, it would just be a glorified episode of the show in limited release. I was utterly unaware of how grand the plan was.

I knew a theater movie would work. Once, after a sweetening session where they'd projected the TV show on a theatrical screen on the lot at Paramount, Doug Booth pointed out that "if you got all of the shots right and maybe buffed the animation a little bit, these could be movies. They're not bad to watch."

I agreed. The episodes on big screen weren't *Snow White*, but they were eminently watchable.

You have to remember that this was before Disney came out with their run that started with *The Little Mermaid*, and in this period, animated movies were both extremely rare and very low quality. The Disney classics like *Fantasia* and *Pinocchio* were rarely screened except, maybe, now and then at revival houses or on TV or limited VHS releases. So most animated movies were either weird art and foreign films played at art houses or unwatchable things for kids. Maybe I'm being a little harsh, but only a little. Ralph Bakshi movies (*Lord of the Rings* and *Heavy Metal*) are a hard watch.

Anyway, at one point, Jay told me that Ron Friedman's script for *Transformers: The Movie* had come in. That "The Movie" part of the title was an eighties way of saying that something you thought of as a TV show or play or record album had been turned into a movie. I think *Star Trek* might have started the "The Movie" trend.

I asked how it was, and he said something to the effect that there was a lot of good stuff in it, but that it needed a lot of work. Jay and I read the script aloud together like bad actors, which has always been (in my estimation) the best way to really get a script. Everybody experiences it at the same time. You know right where the shining moments are and where the problems are.

Indeed, Ron's first draft was a warehouse of amazing ideas and images, but it was very hard to follow. That was not his fault, though. It was a first draft and read like a loosely assembled laundry list of really cool stuff strung together, but not really a movie. There was plenty of stunning dialogue and incredible visuals, and it was impossible to read it and not want to see it made. That's why Ron got the big bucks. He tried to get everybody's stuff in there and make it fly, knowing there would be a hundred more drafts to get it right.

Since then, I've had people send things from the Internet purporting to be the first draft of *Transformers: The Movie*, but I don't think any of them were the draft from that first day. They seem to be either later drafts (Ron was rewriting in parallel for a while) or composite drafts that were edited later.

There would be so many drafts that it's hard for me to remember any individual one. I'd later try to use some of the outtake scenes in "The Five Faces of Darkness"—not literally as cut and paste, but the ideas of the scenes. As odd as it seems, I'm always kind of surprised to find what's actually in the movie, because I remember hundreds of versions of it, all of them just as clearly if not more so than the one that actually got made.

Jay came out to LA, and we had a couple meetings trying to figure out what we'd do for a rewrite. Eventually we settled on a strategy of starting fresh and putting in good stuff from the script in a new context. We didn't have a digital file of the script, because then, even if Ron had turned over a disc, it was unlikely to be compatible with my word processor. And besides, it's always better to start a second draft with a blank page, anyway. While word processors brought a lot of efficiency, they also made it too easy to leave stuff in. There was something about the old typewriter days when you had to retype everything that forced the writer to confront every scene and line of dialogue afresh. I remember Professor Jim Boyle at USC saying that it was best to retype when you were tired and crabby—that it made it more likely that you wouldn't reinsert the crap.

I can't remember exactly when we decided that we were going to write a whole script, but at some point Jay took up residence on the couch in my Westwood apartment and we started hammering away. Day and night. Obsessive. Maybe we took breaks to attend recording sessions, but basically it was all movie, all the time.

A week later, we had a draft called "The Secret of Cybertron." It was an intense experience. We knew most of the characters in the beginning of the movie but didn't know the stars (Hot Rod, Galvatron, Kup, or Unicron at all). Behind the idea of making a movie was the business reality of introducing a whole new year's product line while "discontinuing" several of the stars from the first two seasons.

When Jay and I got done, we thought we had the best script ever written by anybody for any reason. The overall premise, as I recall, was that Unicron was coming to destroy Cybertron and he was sort of acting in league with the Decepticons, or they were acting in his interests. The Autobots were determined to stop this, but they had no idea how. Finally, they realized that the Autobot Matrix had a secret power: It could transform Cybertron. The problem was that it had to be inserted at the very center of Cybertron, and the Decepticons had holed up in there and set numerous traps to stop the Autobots from succeeding. At one point, every Autobot we've ever known screams into Cybertron in something like the *Transformers* equivalent of the Charge of the Light Brigade to install the key. Or at least, that's how I remember the story, and remember, memory is a very tricky thing. In any case, in one charge we wiped out ninety percent of the 1985 Transformers product line.

I think one of my models was Sam Peckinpah's *The Wild Bunch*, which was probably the most violent movie I saw in my entire childhood. Not exactly children's fare, and now I can only imagine the trauma that would have been caused if kids had seen their entire product line slaughtered.

Joe and Tom didn't share our feeling that this was the greatest script ever, and thus ended the short, ugly life of "The Secret of Cybertron." The only people who ever read it were Tom and Joe, Jay, and Roger Slifer, to the best of my knowledge. Nelson might have gotten one, too. Maybe Hildy and Carole had copies at one point.

For that reason, nobody has a copy of it. I've asked around and... nothing.

I still have my Mac disks from that period somewhere, but I have no idea what could read them. I probably wrote it on the DecMate, but I don't know where those discs are. I have a fantasy that somewhere in some box, deep in storage, I have a copy of it. I'm enough of a hoarder for that, but my wife isn't, and it well could have been tossed at some point. It is sort of the missing link in the *Transformers: The Movie* story.

We started over again from scratch, but the exercise had some value in that Jay and I synced up on our vision of *Transformers,* and not only did it influence the movie and season three (ideas kept sneaking back into the movie script), but it forced us to figure out the mythology of the Transformers world in a way that I don't think anybody had really done before. To that point, our endless bibles were really just character bios with little setup and very brief explanations of backstory and character relationships. The transmedia concept of a deep, deep world didn't really exist back then in TV or comics, as I recall.

Shortly after "The Secret of Cybertron," Nelson Shin presented us with an entire draft of the movie. I don't think I ever saw it. I'm also sure that it had a lasting influence on the movie, though I don't think anything directly came out of it. So that would be the other missing puzzle piece.

A Low Grade of Flint

In GEOLOGY, CHERT IS a low grade of flint. In *At Moonset Blackcat Comes: A Tale of Gord of Greyhawk* by Gary Gygax, published in issue #100 of *Dragon* magazine, Chert is a Barbarian who is actually a slightly higher grade of me, but I'm quibbling.

> *"Chert, my friend, tonight we visit the Foreign Quarter! Why there? Chert demanded. There's more action and prettier women just nearby! he exclaimed, waving one of his massive arms vaguely toward the flaring torches, which illuminated the elegance of the establishments of Fortune Street and the other byways of the fashionable upper portion of New Town. But last night you nearly killed that snot-nosed rake Lord Fradel's*

scion, as I recall when you caught him cheating at dice. If we are seen in these parts again soon, do you think that some band of his henchmen won't fall upon us with murderous intent? So? Such twits as Fradel's whelp can muster will be no threat to us! shot back the lately sophisticated barbarian.

Considering Chert's towering, six-foot, six-inch frame, bulging muscles, and weapons skill, his claim was unquestionably true even without the commensurate sword and dagger work of his comrade to support his contention. Gord looked fondly at his friend again, measuring him from the top of his curly, light brown head of hair, already showing signs of its usual disarray, down to his thick legs encased in leather boots of the latest design popular with the elite of Greyhawk. You appear civilized, Chert, but it is only a veneer! We must be regarded as boon companions and moneyed sports, not brawling killers. You'd soon have us on the wrong side of society, rightly or not. How then would we practice our livelihood?"

—Gary Gygax, 1985

So I'm only 6'5" and not 6'6", and I'm not sure I went to the gym enough to have bulging muscles, but compared to the rest of our crowd, I looked like I belonged in the NFL. Gary was quite amused with himself when he showed this to me. Okay, it's amusing. I think it was the hair in disarray. In that period, I considered putting a comb in my hair to be some kind of submission. And maybe you could argue it was light brown, but there was already gray coming into it, even in my late twenties. In my own way, I suppose I was a barbarian, but a pretty benign one. And as to whether my civilization is only a veneer, well, others can judge. I don't think so, but it's a lot more fun to imagine it is.

I've never seen a drawing of Chert, but I imagine he'd be a barbarian version of me from that era. And, of course, it was flattering as hell. It always is when somebody puts you into their fiction. In fact, my fictional life is far more interesting than my real life, but I guess that's always going to be true. The truth is, the fact that people like Gary Gygax, Frank Miller, Thomas Greanias, and Joe and Tom (whether or not I'm really Flint in G.I.

Joe) think I'm worthy of being a fictional character is probably the most flattering thing about my life. Even having Steven Spielberg make me "a dumb guy named Flint" in a *Tiny Toons* episode still feels tremendously cool.

I'll take it. So I'm not really a barbarian or a Spartan soldier or a duplicitous arms dealer or a Special Forces officer (though the jury is still out on "dumb guy"); the whole idea that I'm interesting enough for people of this character to memorialize me in fiction is probably the biggest trophy I have in creative life.

Mom Does My Taxes

SINCE I WAS STILL LIVING like a college student, despite being twenty-nine, my mother used to do my taxes. She'd come every year around tax time, and it was usually a pretty uneventful experience. Yeah, she'd seen the numbers go up since 1983, but nobody had been keeping track of how much I'd been making. I had no reason to. I had direct deposit for my regular paychecks, and script fees came in regular checks in $3,000 increments (Sunbow paid $6,000 a script), and then there'd been the Sagard checks. I can't remember what Gary and I got as an advance for that, but for some reason I remember $40,000, and there were various other things. Point is, I was making a lot of money and spending like I was a college student, and this had been going on for a couple years, so money was piling up in my checking account.

My mother had a business degree from the University of Chicago that she used during the war running accounting for the Electromotive Department of General Motors (or something like that). She was also pushed into service occasionally at National Newspaper Syndicate (Dad's company), so I think she found it kind of fun to do my taxes now and again. At that point in her life, friends told me that she reminded them of a beautiful Margaret Thatcher, and I can kind of see that. She had a blessed life.

This time the numbers were different. "Do you realize you have $315,000 in your checking account?"

"No, I haven't balanced it. I knew I had enough in there to pay my bills." This was a little untrue. I knew there was a lot, I just didn't know how much. I've never been much of a money guy. That is not a good thing. Money is a very real issue, and you have to stay on top of it. I do not recommend this kind of ignorance.

"Well, you're going to get killed in taxes. You have to buy some real estate."

Her point was good. While I might have thought it was cool to be an "I don't care about money" guy, the IRS cares quite a bit about money and has created a very elaborate game to take as much money away from you as they can.

The deeper point is that once you have money, you become a target for all sorts of predators. Know this and believe it. We've all heard stories about athletes, stars, etc. who get ripped off by managers, keelhauled by the IRS, or snookered by lawyers, spouses, family members, and friends.

So I went out and made a couple of one-bun (a polite way of saying half-assed) hunts for a house. I thought I wanted something high tech. Everybody else knew I wasn't going to end up with something high tech. Sometimes your family and friends know you better than you know yourself. The real house hunt lasted one day, and I wasn't even there. My mother and sister went out, found a place, and said, "It's perfect for you."

I went over to look at it the next day. It was in Westwood on Strathmore, right near UCLA's fraternity row. It was within walking distance of Sunbow. I'd lived in Westwood the entire time I'd lived in LA and had no desire to move. At that point, Westwood was a cool place, a town of movie theaters, restaurants, and bookstores.

My "house" was actually a townhouse that had been built as professor housing in the twenties, when Westwood and UCLA were being developed, and then turned into condominiums in the seventies. The place I was looking at was the unit the developer lived in. It overlooked the pool, UCLA, and Westwood, but most of the view was obscured by tall hedges, which was just fine with me. It was the courtyard that sold me. You walked through the gate, and next thing you knew, you were in a garden.

At the time, the place was being rented to the Australian Film Commission or some such. In order to drive off prospective buyers, they had a severed head from *Friday the 13th: Part III* on a stick in the living room. I'm not making this up. Stuffed in a refrigerator in the movie, in real life it was on a stake in my front hall. They thought this would scare me away.

Wrong client.

The place had been on the market for a while. It was way too weird for most people. Every room was done in some bizarre wallpaper. The most normal was leopard print. That should tell you something. But the rest of it was perfect for me. Spiral staircase. Stained-glass window. Loft office. Four-poster bed that they left because they couldn't figure out how to move it. It even came complete with a Bombay trunk.

We bought the Strathmore place that day, and I've lived there ever since. I added a basement room and a laundry room a decade later.

The night I moved in, I took Jay Bacal and Roger Slifer over to see it. From the backyard, I saw people moving upstairs—or thought I did. Didn't think much of it. The next day, I walked in and realized I'd been robbed, or rather we'd walked in on a robbery. I suspect it was some dodgy movers we'd hired, but I will never know. They didn't get much—a walkman and some coins. A bust of Dante was on the floor, looking at me. Maybe they were planning on taking him.

Before the moment passes, I do have one serious piece of advice for writers and creative types. While it is kind of amusing that I had a ton of money in my checking account and barely knew it, that is no way to run a financial life.

Pay attention.

Life is long, and compound interest is a thing.

Your freedom is tied to living below your means and limiting your vulnerability. The fastest way to see your career vanish is to get into financial trouble and either start taking jobs you shouldn't take or to have to get out of the business altogether. You are going to have good times and bad times. Highs and lows. Plan for it. When you understand that you can make a million dollars and it's really $300,000, you understand the odd math of money. People who don't get picked apart by scavengers.

Take the time to learn the basics of finance. Your whole career is a huge risk. You do not need to compound it.

And this goes for other life decisions, too. Be careful about flashy cars, getting married, buying houses, having kids, or doing anything that puts you at risk and in debt. I'm not saying not to do these things, just think long and hard before you do them and wait for the right time and circumstances. As my grandmother used to put it, "Marry in haste and repent in leisure." You can take your chances with the tactical stuff, but strategic decisions matter.

What followed was painters and, if you can believe this, an interior decorator—Craig Rand. He was a friend of Doug Booth's and even wrote a *Transformers* episode. He was also a minister. He had an uncanny knack for picking out things I would like. So the house was painted and furnished, and thus was the first "adult" place I'd lived in. Gary and Gail stopped by to inspect it. It is a pure Gary place, an LA reflection of Stone Manor. Of particular interest to him was a castle sculpture. It came with the place; I just had it painted and plastered into the wall. And of course there was the mysterious Bombay chest.

Spring bled into summer. Life was more stable. Rhythmic. I'm quite sure I went to Gen Con that year, but if there was a bad vibe anywhere, I don't remember it. I guess it's remotely possible that I didn't and I was in New York, though, because that overlaps with the period in which I was writing *Transformers: The Movie*.

The Voltronic Galaxiter

BACK IN THE WINTER/SPRING of 1985, in the thick of it with *Transformers* and still juggling Joe (which is how we tended to refer to *G.I. Joe*), we came upon the "Voltronic Galaxiter." In a testimony to false memory, I remembered cutting the Voltronic Galaxiter out of a script, but after I published this section on my Facebook page, a number of fans immediately pointed out that the Voltranic Galaxiter made it into the show multiple times. I know it is in "Blaster Blues" and then a Buzz Dixon episode, but I doubt Buzz invented it. It is far more likely that Buzz knew how ridiculous I thought the VG was, so he snuck it in just for kicks. This, remember, is the same Buzz Dixon who almost had the Joes do an offscreen BA ("bare ass"—eighties concept) in one episode, and was only foiled because Jay had gone to Harvard and actually read and visualized the description of the characters reacting to nudity—which even offscreen was not going to make it into the show. He was kind of proud of himself for having caught it and thought it was hilarious. You hire Buzz Dixon, you better know you're going to get a truly disruptive force. That's his brilliance.

Anyway, I honestly believed that the object in question never got used. I was wrong.

The Voltronic Galaxiter is simultaneously one of the stupidest and most important objects in *Transformers* history. Jay and I were reviewing a script we'd received from a writer (mercifully, I've forgotten which one). It wasn't going well. Then we came upon a line from some character—probably a Decepticon—claiming that they would defeat the Autobots once and for all with the Voltronic Galaxiter.

"Oh, no. We've got a Voltronic Galaxiter," I said.

Jay started laughing, saying something about a Voltronic Galaxative.

What were we laughing about? Surely, with all of the bogus science and improbable devices we inserted into *G.I. Joe* and *Transformers*, what's one Voltronic Galaxiter matter? But it matters, because we'd hit a tipping point, or, for lack of a better term, jumped a shark. The Voltronic Galaxiter made us stop and pause.

Were we really doing a show that was so vapid that we could create a phone or device that would solve all of our problems? Yeah. Maybe you could have gotten away with that on a children's show three years earlier. Maybe it could have been in a pulp thirty years earlier—followed by three paragraphs on exactly what a VG was and how and why it worked—but here, we were skipping the science, skipping the explanation, and going straight to a bogus plot device. Literally, a device to solve our problems.

Some observations about the Voltronic Galaxiter in no particular order:

1.   If you're a writer and you ever throw a Voltronic Galaxiter into a story, for any reason, you have to revisit why you're telling this story, and perhaps why you're a storyteller.

2.   I would submit that any plot that can be solved by a bogus device is a bogus plot.

3.   It's interesting to speculate on a plot where a Voltronic Galaxiter could work.

Thought experiment: What if Hasbro had sent a sheet that said, "New Product: Voltronic Galaxiter" without explanation. What would we have done with it? We would have had to make it extremely important, and it would have to be something with the power to change the dynamic of the battle between the Autobots and Decepticons. It could be featured in a trilogy. And suppose it drew endless Energon from Earth's atmosphere.

First episode, the Decepticons have it and the Autobots get it back.

Second episode, the Autobots have it and the Decepticons get it back.

Third episode, we find out that it is destroying the Earth. The Decepticons, except maybe one (think of who), don't care. The Autobots realize that it must be destroyed. They destroy the Voltronic Galaxiter. Trilogy over.

Or maybe they try to destroy it, but they only damage it and it starts creating toxic Energon.

The humans destroy it.

The Transformers are sick and retreat to recover.

Or maybe it made Energon that was like heroin and it was created by somebody who wanted to dominate the Transformers. The Quintessons are my favorite villains in this scenario, but a mad human scientist is always a possibility.

Point is, the Voltronic Galaxiter could get three or four episodes—enough exposure for any toy. From there, they could sell it until they discontinued it. Or until the follow-up, where somebody else makes Voltronic Galaxiter 2.0.

4. The Voltronic Galaxiter was an important thing for us. It tested our limits. We knew we had to evolve. The early days were over. We had to tell stories that grew out of our characters. The deeper you get into a series, the more the plot comes from characters…

5. …until reset episodes. Sometimes the character story gets too ingrown and you have to start doing plot stories. The *X-Files* had to do a Loch Ness Monster story every few episodes because the conspiracy became too complex to understand. *Person of Interest* is another example. There came a point where there were so many weird characters with so many weird agendas, I had no idea what was going on. Which, don't get me wrong, is great for bingeing— but not a steady diet.

6. We also had to consider that maybe we were wrong. Maybe our core audience just wanted to see Voltronic Galaxiter stories. The first season had a lot of them. Maybe series don't have to advance, and that push forward is what wrecks them. Certainly, season three was extremely controversial for a number of reasons. Old favorite characters were gone, and the episodes tended to leave Earth. (The animation deteriorated, but that's another discussion.) Maybe television series are about doing the same thing over and over again and ignoring the writer's desire to advance the meta story. Certainly, *Moonlighting* and *Castle* and *The Andy Griffith Show* didn't improve when their main characters got into long-term committed relationships.

7. Related to the above, one thing I had to reconcile was that I kept growing and advancing, but the audience remained eight.

8. Maybe it was just the name. Had it been called the "Vortex Device" (or pick your own name that sounds less ridiculous than Voltronic Galaxiter), maybe it would have worked and we would have blown past it without comment. When we started calling it the Voltronic Galaxitive, it was game over. What's in a name? Sometimes a lot.

9. At some point or another, a Voltronic Galaxiter must have worked, or something at least that ridiculous. My immediate thought was

the *Maltese Falcon*, but that was plausible. There really were Knights of Malta and jewels and motives to conceal them.

10. I have a theory that the best funky gadgets in movies have very little effect on the story. If you think about James Bond's Aston Martin, probably my favorite gadget ever, it had almost no plot function in *Goldfinger* that couldn't have been achieved any other way. Bond could have simply sideswiped Tilly Masterson on the alpine road and the story wouldn't have changed much. His exciting drive in Goldfinger's complex ended much as it began when he ran into the mirror. Take the sequence out, and you have a far less interesting movie, but the story doesn't change much. In some ways, the Aston Martin defined James Bond. He's the only spy in any movie up to the time who drove a car as expensive as a house. Maybe our problem was that we didn't want to be defined by the Voltronic Galaxiter.

11. To our credit, Jay and I cared about the material. If we didn't, we wouldn't have noticed the Voltronic Galaxiter. We may or may not have been right in our assessment, but at least we were making assessments.

So why do I remember the Voltronic Galaxiter thirty years later? My feeling is that it's kind of a career landmark. It's just kind of sitting there as a fork in the road or a branch in a pick-a-path novel:

1. If you want to head down the road to pure hackdom and embrace the Voltronic Galaxiter, go to the next page.
2. If you want to want to become that famous literary author you said you wanted to be and who's read and respected by seven people, turn left and don't look back.
3. If you don't like either of the other paths, stop and think about what you're doing and why you're doing it. Make your own path.

And on the flipside of all this is another cautionary concept. Can you count on your audience to grow and evolve with you? I remember Ian Anderson of Jethro Tull talking about how he was hoping his fans would evolve with him. I don't know how it worked out, but I still listen to his new albums. The flipside, though, when you're making children's shows is that children, by definition, remain children.

But were we making children's shows anymore?

Do people grow up the same way they used to?

We knew that no small part of our audience was fathers who were out of work in the recession. We were also writing for them. So, without anybody talking much about it, we were writing children's shows that also had to appeal to adults (frankly, the people who were buying the toys)—so who was our audience? Did this mean we were writing something for the children who grow up and watch it with their children? And who keep watching it as adults, partly for the nostalgia and partly for all the stuff they didn't see the first time?

We didn't invent this. Listen to the actual dialogue of any vintage Bugs/ Daffy cartoon and tell me if it's really for children. Not what you remember the dialogue being, but what it actually was. I transcribed "Duck Wabbit Duck" and realized it was totally different than I thought it was. When I was seven, I didn't hear all of the stuff about endangered "fricasseeing wabbits" and the need for hunting licenses. In fact, I'm not even sure now what fricasseeing is. Didn't matter to me then and doesn't matter to me now. It's there, and it's funny—even if I don't know what it means.

Which gets me to another thing. If you want to know what something really is (not just the surface) and you're a writer, transcribe a sample scene—word for word, shot for shot. You'll see layers and nuance you didn't see before. You realize that most things don't work the way you thought they did. Don't debate me, just try it. Pick a three-minute scene you like and write it up in screenplay form, complete with instructions to the actors.

At any rate, the thing we have to highlight in any discussion of Sunbow in that era is the sheer volume of work done by a very small team. We did sixty-five episodes of *Transformers* and *G.I. Joe* in one year. We were developing other shows—*Inhumanoids, Visionaries, Robotix, Jem, Muscle Machines*—and, of course, a lot of the company's attention was spent on *My Little Pony*. Things moved fast.

It felt sleazy, but as Jay put it, working on those shows at that velocity was like being on an assembly line with cars rolling through too quickly to do anything but minor fixes. You missed a mirror or a windshield wiper here and there. The fans were mostly good with it. They understood.

But there was a strategy behind it. We were a "fix on the run" operation. That means every step of the way—from concept, to beats, to outline, to script, to storyboard, to voice recording, to editorial, to post—we could fix things as we went. We never got stuck in preset. There's a certain raw energy and spontaneity in projects produced this quickly. You tend to take more chances... You don't second-guess yourself. When you have several dozen episodes, you tend to think you can try out risky ideas. That's what's always fun about a franchise. You get to take characters out more than one time. You don't have to get everything into one script.

More time doesn't necessarily lead to better product, however. The problem with a lot of feature films is that they get stuck in script. Endless writers are brought on to fix the script, and often as not it doesn't get better— just different, or worse. Except in cases where a script was unusable, we had to make things work. (When scripts were unusable, it usually led to the story editors writing a script.) We'd eat the cost or send it back to the writers, and we'd write one. It wouldn't surprise me if all of my *G.I. Joe* scripts were written under those circumstances. I know that "The Gamesmaster" was, and given that I have no recollection of writing "Skeletons in the Closet," I'm suspecting it was, too.

Also, scripts don't age well. Buzz Dixon's compared it to the chicken joke. It's really funny the first time, amusing the second time, and the fifth time it's not funny at all. It's hard to remember that the viewer isn't sick of the line. Time is not always on your side.

Assembly line iterative work only works if you have a good team and everybody is willing to fill holes. Thirty years later, I still remember Sunbow being as good of a team as I've ever played on, and I've played on some great teams. The interesting thing about the Sunbow team was that I don't remember anybody referring to it as a "family." They were too honest for that. Companies aren't families. In boom times, it's easy to get that impression, but when things go bust, it's all business. That said, thirty years later, I'm still in touch with most everybody from the core team who's still alive. That tells you all you need to know.

Movie Rewrites

Summer 1985

I WENT OUT TO New York around July of 1985 and stayed for weeks at Donald Trump's Grand Hyatt, which was near the new Sunbow office. It was a fun time. I actually felt a little bit like a New Yorker. To get a sense of context, Sunbow was a subsidiary of Griffin-Bacal, which in the summer of 1985 was listed as the fastest-growing ad agency in Manhattan. It was Hasbro's ad agency, and Hasbro was in the middle of the opposite of a perfect storm. They had three phenomena going at the same time: *G.I. Joe, Transformers,* and *My Little Pony.* Along with the new status came a new Manhattan office.

If I ever saw the old office, I don't remember it, but I did spend a lot of time in the new one. It was a very cool warren of staircases and offices and open conference rooms and activity. That's what I remember most: the activity. People going in every direction, working on the TV shows, on ads, and so on. I'd get roped into meetings regarding copy and campaigns, and my memory of that time is of being a dazed guy from LA caught in a Madison Avenue whirlwind and being blown wherever it took me. I love those memories. There was something different every day. There was excitement, but very little stress—mostly because I didn't know enough to be stressed.

The real "Belly of the Beast," however, was when I'd go out for lunch with Tom Griffin or Joe Bacal—my only true firsthand experiences with Madison Avenue. Tom and Joe were in their mid-to-late forties and had lived through the golden age of advertising. They would have been the young guys in Don Draper's office in a *Mad Men* episode, back when Madison Avenue was the cultural engine of America.

TV might have been the medium of the day, but commercials ran TV.

There was always a fascinating and exotic collection of old guys who talked to me like I understood what they were talking about, and I raced to keep up. They were a type of person that I knew existed—I'd seen a lot of them on TV—but that's different than when a guy who seems more fictional than real is talking to you across the table. Joe and Tom were so normal that it only drew these characters further into relief. I mean, not that they're not characters in and of themselves, but they were incredibly solid, stable ambassadors to a crazy world.

Living on this edge of advertising and TV was a fascinating place to be. Madison Avenue meets Hollywood Boulevard. And the cultures met in an interesting way, too. Today, you look like an alcoholic if you drink at lunch, but back in 1985, it was standard op. In Los Angeles, people went to what I called "white places," restaurants where the walls were painted white and the menu was something called California cuisine, which seemed to boil down to "lite" Italian food with chicken and vegetables. And there was always the glass or two of white wine (or rosé) at lunch.

When I went to New York, though, it was completely different.

In New York, restaurants really matter, and Carole Weitzman always knew the best and the latest. We went to Tavern on the Green, Smith & Wollensky, the Russian Tea Room, and a million other places I don't remember. Lunch would usually be at places that seemed to have been around since the fifties, and you didn't drink some wiener glass of White Zinfandel or Chardonnay—you'd drink real man cocktails. Those places came from a time when people actually had their drink. My dad had the old fashioned without sugar (he was diabetic), my grandmother had a John Collins, my grandfather drank martinis with extra olives. It was a form of branding. It defined them. It wasn't about who the maker of the alcohol was—that was a product of advertising—it was about whether you were bourbon, scotch, gin, vodka, or rum.

I never had a specific drink, but I usually defaulted to bourbon as I didn't like it much, so I didn't end up getting wasted. At the time, the three-martini lunch was a political issue. It was about corporate taxes. The funny thing is that I never saw anybody get drunk at lunch, and they all went back to the office and got work done.

From 1984 for about a decade, I'd spend every Valentine's Day at Toy Fair. Toy Fair defined the winter for me in much the same way that Comic-Con defined the summer. It was a magical view of Manhattan. We'd stay in swank hotels like the Plaza, the Ritz Carlton, Le Parker Meridien, and make the trek to the Toy Center at 200 Fifth Avenue, which, in fact, was its own little urban network of buildings connected by bridges. Hasbro had their own building not far away, which was a hyper-real version of an old-time toystore. It was filled with dioramas displaying action figures, dolls, plushies, toy guns, arts and crafts, games—you name it.

In the main building, you'd see toys you'd never see again. It was marvelous and wondrous. It was every fantasy Christmas in America spilled out into one building. It was Santa's workshop in full swing, but it only existed for one week a year. I would often wonder what it was like in the Toy Center the rest of the year, and I never figured out why they didn't keep it open all year long.

I rarely had much actual business at Toy Fair, but both TSR and Sunbow thought it was worth flying me out and putting me up. Basically, it was about getting the gestalt of the toy and game worlds. Every year, there'd be the big things people were talking about. Sometimes it would pan out, sometimes it wouldn't. It was the eighties, and people used the phrase "buzz" the way people in the 2010s used "trending." Some things got the buzz, others didn't. Everybody wanted it.

For me, it was mostly about seeing people. I'd always get together with Bob Prupis, head of boys' toys at Hasbro, and of course Joe and Tom. Sometimes I'd hang out at the Griffin-Bacal office pretending to be an ad executive (which is what I technically was), and sometimes I'd be at TSR.

In any case, at twenty-nine, I had a whole alternate life in New York. John Phillips, Patty, and Wendy were there, along with a smattering of other folks. A lot of LA people were there. Dini and I never let a trip pass without a visit to Trader Vic's in the basement of the Plaza. I never *didn't* have something to do.

I learned to function in an alien city. As the song of the day said, "Nobody walks in LA," but you walk a lot in New York. I'd take cabs when I was lazy or it was a long way, and I'd take the subway when I had a native with me. The background sound bed was honking horns and guys yelling. In the winter there'd be steam rising from the grates, and in the summer there'd be a million different smells from street-cooked food mixed with exhaust.

From the moment I arrived at the airport (usually LaGuardia), I'd get chop blocked by some gypsy cabbie who'd try to lead me to his car three parking garages away. I fell for it once. Then it would be bump and grind as I stared in amazement at the skyline. I'd grown up in Chicago, so I appreciated skyscrapers. My favorite thing was the lonely globe in the park where the 1964 World's Fair had been held and which had been immortalized in DC Comics.

The other great thing about New York is that everything is right there. You're walking down the street and oh, there's the Empire State Building, or the New York Public Library or the Met. So much history, iconography, excitement, and energy all compressed into such a small place.

At one point, Sunbow was trying to do something with Radio City and the Rockettes. It was called "Rookie Rockette." I had never heard of a Rockette and only vaguely knew about Radio City Music Hall, but the name had a great whiff of the thirties. Maybe it was then that I started incubating *Agent 13*. We did a tour of Radio City trying to think of a story. We went backstage, onto catwalks, into boxes, into a vast labyrinthine warren of props and costumes and dressing rooms. Try as I might, I couldn't think of anything other than murders and weird conspiracies. None of my ideas were very helpful, but being there was like a vacation to a different life in a different time. The interesting thing was that it was the first sign that Sunbow was thinking beyond kids' entertainment.

A Word from Our Sponsors

THIS ISN'T WHAT FANS want to hear, but it's important to talk about. We were in the business of selling toys. From a Hasbro corporate point of view, the TV shows existed for no other reason than to sell toys. They were twenty-two-minute commercials. The genius of the shows is that they turned a profit, and competing companies had to advertise in the middle of a Sunbow commercial.

Let that sink in for a moment. If Mattel wanted to sell Barbie, they had to buy ads in their competitor's show (we didn't have Barbie commercials, but you get my point). Their ads paid for Hasbro's ads and, unlike regular commercials, the television shows were evergreen products. People are still watching the commercials thirty-five years later. Not only does that bring in revenue, but it also keeps the franchise alive for generations. This is a very big deal.

What this meant was that there had to be a lot of churn. Hasbro wanted to advertise expensive toys and cheap toys. Seaspray and Omega Supreme were very different price points, and both were extremely important. Most of the main characters—Prime, Megatron, Starscream, Bumblebee—were mid-price products. Products were released all year, and when they felt they had sold as many as they were going to sell of a particular toy, they discontinued it.

When a product was discontinued, either another was announced or it was decided that they would push a current product. They would say something like, "Ashtray has been discontinued, please substitute Dipstick," and so we would do that. It was mostly invisible to the audience, because we didn't kill off Ashtray, we just stopped using Ashtray and started using Dipstick. At the same time, if we liked Ashtray, there were no rules against using him. Hasbro understood that we had to make a show and keep core characters alive.

There's the fascinating case of Jetfire (a.k.a. Skyfire), who was one of the few, if not only, Transformers who died in an episode. The interesting thing is that I'm thinking of him all this time later, and fans still ask us about him. It turns out he got the big bump-off not because he was discontinued, but because there was some rights/legal issue around him. Somebody tried to explain the problem to me, but it had too many threads and companies, and I couldn't follow the explanation. I was too busy trying to make episodes; legal wrangling wasn't in my lane.

I know I've said this before, but it bears repeating—at least it does pretty much every time I do a talk at TF conventions. The marketing purpose of the movie was to introduce the 1986 product line. What was unique was that it was a movie and thus we could—in fact, had to—do things we couldn't do on TV.

That meant killing characters. It also meant bringing new ones in.

The big wrinkle—and it was a creative decision made in Pawtucket, Rhode Island, not Los Angeles or New York—was the difference in the nature of the *Transformers* characters. The new characters were less and less Earthly. While early Transformers looked like real cars, planes, and boom boxes, the next characters were much more abstract. Springer didn't look like anything I'd seen on Earth. He was supposed to be a helicopter, but he was a triple changer, who, the joke was, turned from a "Huh?" into a "What?" and then into a "Whazzit?" There was nothing in the American or Soviet air force, for that matter, that looked anything like Cyclonus and the Sweeps. So the reality of the product, to some extent, dictated the fiction of the show.

We were prepping the movie from about halfway through season two. We knew massive changes were coming, and both consciously and subconsciously, we wanted to set the stage for them. We kept the old favorite characters in there, but there was a lot of new. A lot of things foreshadowed the coming abrupt shift in the show.

A lot of my favorite episodes are in the back half of season two. At that point, we were a lot more worried about continuity and mythology. Characters like Alpha Trion, who had a very short life span in the series, have gone on to be very important to future iterations of Transformers, especially in the comics.

Comic-Con When It Was Comic-Con

When I first started going, Comic-Con was held at the old convention center. Everybody who was anybody stayed at the Westgate, and it was a fascinating place in that it seemed to be done in a Habsburg Monarchy motif. I stayed at a place in Vienna years later called the Hotel Sacher, which felt like it was a model for the Westgate. The lobby was impeccable, ornate, and gilt. There was an epic Sunday brunch, and sitting in the small, dark lobby bar was like being inside an antique music box. Comic-Con was small and friendly, and I'd run into somebody I wanted to see in every aisle—and the aisles weren't that crowded.

I spent the first few years at Comic-Con either a) rebuying my childhood, b) buying my friends' stuff, or c) buying pulps. To this day, I regret not buying a model of the Flying Sub from *Voyage to the Bottom of the Sea*. It wasn't silly expensive, but I just couldn't take the plunge.

By 1985, I wasn't exactly a vet, but I wasn't a noob. Frank Miller and I had bonded back in the spring, and I found myself hanging out with him. We both smoked and we could talk endlessly, anywhere. Hanging out with Frank was like having a backstage all-access pass to meeting everybody. It is interesting to note in passing that Frank was kind of a bridge character between the old masters and the young hotshots. He'd earned the possessive title—"Frank Miller's *Daredevil*"—from his friend and mentor, who created *The Spirit*, which Frank would turn into a movie years later.

Stan Lee made a cameo in the bar, just like he would later do in the Marvel movies.[10] He clearly had a lot of respect for Frank. At one point he referred to himself as a phony and Frank as the real deal. Stan definitely wasn't a phony—but also, he definitely wasn't wrong about Frank.

There was a lot going on politically with comics in those years, but it mostly blew past me like smoke. The real-life characters involved were just as wild as the fictional characters. Sometimes they even stimulated them. If Howard the Duck was a metaphorical Steve Gerber, take a look at Destroyer Duck. There's a guy named Liebowitz in *Sin City* who's not nearly as colorful as the real Bill Liebowitz, who owned Golden Apple Comics in Hollywood. You'd get the old school ACLU civil liberties types, who from what I could

---

10   In my first draft, the verb was present tense, "does." In the course of writing this book, Stan turned to past tense—except I guess, technically, he still does appear in the Marvel movies. In any case, it is a perfect metaphor for what I'm trying to get to. Everything is in a constant state of change.

tell walked the edge between comics, seditious politics, and spanky books, and they were somehow involved in the Comic Book Legal Defense Fund. They were a perfect mix of ex–1960s intelligentsia activists who were still kind of young and kind of greasy guys whose office couches you wouldn't want to sit on without a black light test. What they had in common, though, was that they were against a rating system.

I didn't have much of an opinion but tended to think it wasn't a bad idea and that it worked for movies. Frank would explain to me that a rating system had a chilling effect on the content creators. He felt that the content of the books should be clearly labeled, but he didn't want to see an arbitrary system that put it in a box. It was a subtle but important distinction that never stuck in my head, so Frank had to patiently reexplain it a lot. To create the rating system was, by its very nature, restricting a nascent art form—and Frank took comics very seriously as an art form. I'm not sure he created the graphic novel, but he took no small part in its ascendency. He had literary capabilities that match his artistic skills, which is a rarity.

It's unusual that I don't see nuances in political positions, but the issue of a ratings system just didn't fit in any box I'd learned in the Berkeley rhetoric department, and it was utterly alien to me while working in kids' animation. The thing that's fascinating to me from a political/censorship point of view is how differently print and film/animation media are treated. Animation was always perceived as a children's medium and carried a Disney glow of innocence. Comics were also for children, in part, but cartooning also had a political edge dating back to the nineteenth century, and as the medium came of age during WWII, a certain amount of death and violence were expected. Which is to say you could be doing Captain America in both mediums at the same time but handling two entirely different sets of baggage.

And then, of course, there was the whole underground "Furry Freak Brothers" era of comic books. This was literature for stoners, and before Adult Swim there was no real competition in the animation department—Ralph Bakshi being the contemporary mainstream exception. And again, on top of that, there was the creator's rights battle going on, which was linked—in spirit if not legally—to Jack Kirby's fight to get his artwork returned.

But perhaps the most interesting thing about the politics of comics in the eighties is that they were fascinatingly conflicted. The battle lines hadn't formed.

Yet.

So here's one of those interesting things about human memory. I'm writing this sentence in June of 2019. You will be reading it sometime as early as 2020, God willing, if not many years later. At any rate, as of this writing, I have been to Comic-Con thirty-four of the last thirty-six years. Figuring that I've spent an average of three and a half days either coming to, being at, or leaving Comic-Con, that means that I've spent 119 days at Comic-Con.

That is almost four months of my life at and around Comic-Con over four decades.

If I'd taken ten minutes of footage every year at Comic-Con—I am imagining it right now and really regretting that I didn't—those 340 minutes could edit down to a great ninety-minute documentary. And what would my documentary look like? I'd appear from age twenty-seven to sixty-three. I'd see Comic-Con go from a frumpy fan event with luminaries like Jack Kirby, Will Eisner, and Stan Lee to a mega event, though, year by year, faces would disappear as people died. Batman would be there every year. Adam West or Super Friends Batman would get shoved out of the way by Frank's Dark Knight, which would give way to Michael Keaton, then Year 1, then Val Kilmer, George Clooney, lots of cool animation, classic Dini/ Timm, *Batman: The Brave and the Bold*, then Christian Bale and Ben Affleck. But there would always be Batman. There'd be Roger Moore to Timothy Dalton to Pierce Brosnan to Daniel Craig, but always Bond. Don't get me started with *Star Trek*. In addition to the mega venue change, there'd be people that popped in for a minute or so and disappeared, and then people who'd be in there pretty much every year, like Paul Dini.

I'd be there as an animation writer, comic writer, book writer, game designer, film producer, game company exec, comic company guy, presenter, and even a union pitch man for the WGA Transmedia Basic Agreement.

I'd be there on years when I looked forward to it and celebrated. I'd be there in years when I wanted to slink in and out, like after the demise of

TSR West. I'd be there with Niantic to launch Ingress, on a Buck Rogers panel with Erin Grey and Gil Gerard, and I'd be there when our next game, *Pokémon Go,* would lead to a forty-thousand-person PokéCrawl in the Gaslamp Quarter. Through triumph and tragedy, there was always Comic-Con.

I'd actually talk to Van Williams, who played the Green Hornet, for an hour while he was in a booth and hear some great stories about working on shows in the fifties—especially all the drinking backstage. (I get the impression that half the actors on TV were looped, and maybe that was part of the charm.) I'd almost get run over by Thor (the real one) and be at a *Sin City* party with Frank Miller and Robert Rodriguez and my then eleven-year-old daughter as we all realized that the film's producer—you guessed it, Harvey Weinstein—thought it was appropriate to have strippers at a Comic-Con party. Nearly three decades after the *Transformers* TV show, Chris Metzen and Livio Ramondelli and I would sign the Autocracy Trilogy, and Metzen and I would sign Diablo Sourcebooks.

Without some huge defining event, thirty-four Comic-Cons all blur into one thing. Four months of my life spread over thirty-four years is its own alternate world: Comic-Con world.

Discovering Pulps at Comic-Con

AND ALL OF THIS is to explain why I can't remember whether I discovered pulps in 1984 at Comic-Con. A few of the vendors had boxes of pulps. As incredible as it seemed, I had only vaguely heard of pulp. I'd explored, a little bit, Tony Goodstone's book about pulps, which was released by Chelsea House in 1970, about the same time that my dad released *The Collected Works of Buck Rogers,* but I hadn't really dug in. If I had, it would have either stunted my career or put it on fast forward, but things happen the way they happen.

Pulp stories are an incredible moment in literary history. They were written first by people from other mediums before spawning geniuses of their own. It happened with jazz and it happened with movies. People who learned their skills in an older, more formal form suddenly brought their talents to something new. The odd thing is that they seemed to get it right very quickly. Pulp writers were, in many cases, slumming it, often under pseudonyms because they didn't want to be disparaged by their more pretentious friends.

Pulps were written fast. They were to the point and they had to fit a formula. They paid badly and by the word, and sometimes the checks were very long in coming. But look at who you can find there: Ray Bradbury, Robert Heinlein, Raymond Chandler, Dashiell Hammett, Robert E. Howard, H. P. Lovecraft, and on and on and on. Pulps served as a place for these guys to not only do some of their best work but to cut their teeth. Oddly enough, I felt that cartoons and comics of the eighties were a very similar place. There's no way to overstate how disreputable it was to be working on a *Transformers* cartoon at the time. Thirty years later, there might be millions or billions of fans of these things, but at the time, nobody was impressed. I remember when being briefed for my first Amblin Entertainment meeting, I was told not to mention *Transformers*. Of course, Spielberg would be producing the movies thirty years later, but that's how much the world changes if you hang around.

In any case, when I discovered *Secret Agent X-9*, *Secret Service Operator #5*, and *The Phantom Detective*, I had found my mainspring. And, of course, the whole sub-genre of Lost World stories and the Cthulhu stories would utterly change my perception of the universe. And this wasn't even getting to the pirate stories and historical adventures. Oddly enough, given my *Buck Rogers* legacy, I was least interested in what were known as the "bug-eyed monster" stories at the time. That would come later. The other interesting thing was that I didn't make the connection to the Conan books I'd read earlier; I had little idea that Robert E. Howard had ever done anything other than *Conan, Kull,* and *Red Sonja*.

Pulps were cheap. They were something somebody found in Grandpa's house and sold at a yard sale before that buyer sold them to exhibitors, who then sold them to me. So I bought a bushel of them at whatever year's Comic-Con. I took the pulps back to Strathmore and spread them out on the floor. Dave Marconi was couch-surfing at my place, not because he was broke, but because he was in between research trips. He was working on *The Blonde Hurricane*, which is kind of a sad and interesting Hollywood story that powered the dreams of a generation of screenwriters. It was the second script by Diane Thomas, who became famous as "the Malibu waitress who sold a million-dollar script" (*Romancing the Stone*). *The Blonde Hurricane* was her much-anticipated sophomore script, but she was killed in a car accident on Highway 1 in Malibu before she completed it. Somehow Dave, who was a hot writer, inherited it, and it got him studio trips to places like Morocco and Paris, where he had an uncanny knack for meeting models and supermodels. I remember lamenting that because I was working on animation nobody sent me anywhere.

Some people are cool, and some aren't. Marconi was and still is. He's a wild guy with wild long curly hair and interesting ideas about flying saucers and government conspiracies, and he'd be mostly regarded as a nut if he hadn't also written a number of notable scripts: *Enemy of the State*, *Live Free or Die Hard*, *The Harvest*, and *Intersection* (both of which he directed), as well as *The Foreigner* (starring Jackie Chan and Pierce Brosnan, and directed by Martin Campbell of *Casino Royale* fame). Marconi is the guy you take with you if you want to buy the cool stereo or if you want to go to the cool club that doesn't have a sign on the door and only lets you in if you know the special knock. My point is, if Marconi thought the pulps were cool, they were cool as far as I was concerned.

We spent a couple days reading through my trove and came up with the bare bones of *Agent 13*. Marconi said we should take *Agent 13* out as a movie pitch as James Bond "meets" Indiana Jones, because that's the way "Hollywood talks." The story we forged was a mix of tropes from different kinds of pulps. We had the lost tombs and talking skulls of the horror and adventure pulps, the secret societies of the crime pulps, the aerial adventures of the *Flying Aces* kind of pulps, the elaborate disguises of *Fantomas*, and the Lost World monsters. There were even secret passages in gothic mansions. We had it all, except for maybe spaceships and cowboys—though if we ever write another, I'm sure they'll be in there too.

The thing is, if you mix enough ingredients together and stir them well enough, you end up with something original. *Star Wars* is the perfect example of this. Yeah, you can figure what's in the stew, but it's its own thing. Put in a bigger and more general sense, nothing is totally original. Everything we do is preceded by thousands of years of civilization. We are all captives of our own childhoods. Civilization is captive of its childhood.

And things change and morph. The original Green Arrow might well have been inspired by Errol Flynn's *Robin Hood*, but can you really see Sherwood Forest in Emerald city? Well, maybe a little. It's hard to escape your own DNA. It's hard to escape cultural DNA. And sometimes the sources of things aren't as obvious as they might appear. It's easy to look at *Uncharted* and see Indiana Jones, and it's unlikely that *Uncharted* would have ever existed without Indiana Jones, but when we were developing it, we were deeply immersed in the pulps of the thirties and forties and the serials—the exact same things that Lucas and Spielberg breathed inspiration from.

We cobbled together a treatment, and somebody—probably Candy or Dave's agent—connected us with Kevin McCormack, who at the time was working at Nelvana, which had been the animation house on *Droids*. They were expanding their profile and wanted to do live-action feature films. Kevin McCormack had done things like *Saturday Night Fever* and would go on to be a major executive at Warner and Fox. He helped us hone the story and set up meetings at studios. This was my first real experience with a studio pitch.

Marconi was a vet at that point, so he trained me up by imitating a rude studio executive. As I pitched, he'd cut me off, bring up irrelevant topics, and make phone calls in the middle of the practice pitch with the expectation that I had to keep going without losing my cool.

Marconi was particularly good at playing the self-absorbed eighties executive. We even practiced the pre-pitch talk, which was usually a brief introduction of us and some banter about people we didn't know. It was great training for the ridiculous collection of people we were going to meet.

Agent 13 was my first serious foray into the larger belly of the Hollywood beast, and Kevin McCormack and Dave Marconi were like my dual guides. It's all a blur now, but we met with executives at Universal, Fox, Columbia, MGM, Warner Brothers, and maybe Disney, though I wouldn't bet on the latter. And maybe we met with some major production companies.

The most important thing I learned was the ritual of the Hollywood meeting. It works like this. You show up. Somebody offers water or coffee or something. You go with it. You wait on a comfortable couch reading *Variety* or talking to the other people going to the meeting. Now I'm sure everybody is staring at their phone, but at the time, there were no cell phones. There'd be posters on the wall of movies that the executive was, or wished they were, involved in. Eventually, you'd hear something like, "Scott is ready for you."

The next part of the ritual was the producer chit-chatting with the executive. I used to think of this as kind of superfluous and awkward, but I was missing the point. This was brain-priming for the meeting. It was a beat where the executive could focus on right now and forget whatever maddening phone call they'd just slammed off of.

Usually the gossip was soft stuff. A mutual friend who'd either had a break or a misfortune, some scandal involving the studio or Hollywood in general. At some mysterious moment, the meeting would turn to the business at hand. This really means it was about Dave, because he was actually in the business and his reputation preceded him. The producer would then introduce me. Nobody much cared that I was working on *Transformers* and *G.I. Joe*, and, frankly, it was a little embarrassing. *Dungeons & Dragons* was just kind of nerdy, but every once in a while there was a secret geek who thought it was cool.

Dave and I would then pitch our story. Every once in a while, they'd really be paying attention and guess at the high moments. I didn't know whether it was good or bad that they already knew when the mask was pulled off it was China White and not Maggie Darr. Nevertheless, it showed that they were paying attention.

Often as not, there'd be a minor executive in the room. They all either seemed to be named Claire or Geoff with a "G." That might be my

THE GAMESMASTER

imagination, though. Whatever their names, there was always a very Ivy League feel to them, and they'd usually ask the hard questions.

I don't know exactly when this process happened, but I do remember that McCormack was at my thirtieth birthday party—a ragged affair at Dar Maghreb, the Moroccan restaurant where *Raiders of the Lost Ark* was shot— which would mean he was in the picture in November of 1985. And to this day, I don't know if it was a blow-off or a sincere request, but in any case, we eventually hit the "we're running out of studios" conversation. The relationship with McCormack and Nelvana never officially ended. These things never do. It just kind of drifted away.

Which left us with a great movie idea and nothing to do with it.

Nothing, until one night, before all of the chaos started, I told the *Agent 13* story to Gary Gygax up at the mansion. He really liked it. We agreed it would be a good three-novel set and a good pulp offshoot of the *Top Secret* game franchise. After writing the Sagard "fight-a-path" books, I had no real fear of writing a novel, despite the fact that my fraternity house murder mystery, *Fratricide*, had been rejected by a huge stack of publishers.

This was a different era.

The Board Meeting

BACK AT THE MANSION on the hill, things had taken a turn for the ominous. There was friction between Gary and Lorraine. Neither of them said much to me about it, but I felt it. Gary and Gail were heading back to Lake Geneva to make some major business moves. They weren't specific, but I could tell by the peculiarly grown-up way they were acting that it was something big. However, I shrugged away those thoughts. TSR was hardly at the top of my mind. Marconi and I were brewing up *Agent 13*, and I was busy furnishing my house and cranking out *Transformers* and *Inhumanoids,* so this became just static on my mental radio.

Turns out the reason everybody was acting adult was that they were heading to a showdown. I heard about the showdown secondhand from Joey Thompson, and my best recollection is that I was out of town when it all went down.

The bottom line was that Gary had shown up at a board meeting with the intention of firing Lorraine and replacing the board with family members and Gail. Lorraine had a little surprise of her own. She had bought the Blumes' stock. She had control of the company.

And the thing I'll say right here, right now, is that I had no idea it was happening. I was not part of it. I'd take a polygraph on that. Exactly who filed suit and when or what the legal points were—most of it is unknown to me, and none of it really interests me. At the time, I had a different objective in mind. The solution seemed incredibly obvious. Gary was the prophet of TSR. My thinking was that he should remain with a good salary, doing silver bullet projects, spreading goodwill, and doing whatever he wanted to do. Gary was to TSR what Stan Lee was to Marvel or Walt Disney was to Disney or George Lucas was to Lucasfilm. At one point, it seems like I faxed a letter to Lorraine to this effect, and it was certainly the subject of many discussions, but obviously, it didn't work out that way.

Let's take the personalities out of it for a moment.

TSR was at an inflection point. It was back from the brink. There were plenty of problems and lawsuits, but it was whole and standing, and nobody had an interest in it going down. Everybody involved wanted to turn it into the next Disney (which was just beginning to experience its own renaissance with animated movies). In fact, we can look at Disney as what happens when an inflection point goes well. They would emerge from theirs not as a dying business but, arguably, as the most important entertainment enterprise in history.

There is a world in which TSR became Electronic Arts, Activision, and Blizzard all put together. There is a world in which D&D grew up to become *World of Warcraft*, Buck Rogers grew up to become *Starcraft*, and *Ravensloft* became *Diablo*, and SPI/SSI (two companies TSR owned or worked with that did military-themed games) became *Call of Duty* and *Civilization*. It didn't happen that way in the real world, or at least in the universe we happen to be living in—though I'd be interested in checking in with some alternate timelines.

Viewed one way, TSR was perfectly positioned to fill those holes.

Then again, TSR could have vanished into oblivion at that point, like ninety percent of the other game companies of the day and almost all of the computer makers (Wang, DEC, Osbourne, Kaypro, etc.).

I could argue that decisions made in November/December of 1985 had implications far beyond TSR, but suffice to say, this was a decision point in the corporate pick-a-path of the company.

The good might-have-been: stop the fights. Stabilize. Keep Gary as the soul of the company, and I would argue that keeping the TSR bookstore in Lake Geneva would have been a way of keeping the shrine extant.

The middle path might have been what anybody facing a divorce should do, and that is to try to split their stuff and cut the lawyers out, because the usual formula is a third for the wife, a third for the husband, and a third for the lawyers.

Of course, they took option three: get into a bloody court battle.

Let me say it once: the result was not one way or the other. It was a mixed bag (a phrase from the sixties I kind of like using here), as opposed to a Decisive Victory or Decisive Defeat Scenario (as SPI Games would have described it).

In the time from when Lorraine purchased the stock options to the moment when a judge's gavel came down in October of 1985, the moment was ripe for TSR to either heal or splinter. In all honesty, I believe that had Lorraine and Gail been different people, a peace—maybe an uncomfortable peace—could have been forged. Gary would have been king of TSR both ceremonially and creatively, and Lorraine could have run the company. I could have taken all I'd learned from Sunbow and television and developing shows and intellectual properties, and the company could have platformed games and books (they had a number of bestsellers at this point: *Dragonlance, Forgotten Realms*, etc.) into comics and movies and video games in an environment that wasn't constantly stressed and financially drained by legal battles. Gary could keep his money and it wouldn't go to lawyers. TSR could keep its money and put it into product.

But it didn't happen that way.

It got personal. And some of the personal aspects were uncanny. During the lawsuit and post-lawsuit period, Lorraine and Gail both had children. Lorraine named her daughter Alexis; Gary and Gail named their son Alexander. Trust me, they didn't collude on the names, but it serves as a metaphor for how similar the two warring sides ultimately were. The good news, too, is that viewed from thirty years later, both kids turned out extremely well.

At a practical level—and this is probably what I said in the aforementioned memo—Gary and Lorraine didn't have a natural issue. Lorraine, though actually quite creative and possessing excellent aesthetic sense, had no desire for creative control and did not meddle, as far as I could tell, into the creative aspects of TSR, except when it intersected with business. And, it should be noted, she was probably the only person at the company with an actual degree in Medieval history (UC Berkeley, 1969). And while I expend very little effort defending Lorraine, I do have to speak the truth: the rumor that she looked down on gamers is not something I ever witnessed or experienced. She wasn't a gamer, but she loved mysteries and puzzles. In a strange way, she was a benevolent custodian of TSR.

Gary, on the other hand, might have started a great company, but there was nothing in Gary that indicated to me that he wanted to deal with the day-to-day minutiae of running it. This guy was a creative genius who changed the world. Using that outlier talent to figure out exactly how many square feet of office a level-two executive should get was the ultimate waste of his time. Sure, he probably could have gotten off by speculating on how an office was a benign dungeon, as that was exactly the kind of thing we'd talk about on occasion, but him working as a day-to-day executive would probably be the greatest waste of talent in the history of business.

Frankly, I still view myself as the most failed person in the whole scenario. I was the only person who had access to both of them in ways that mattered. Maybe I did a bad job. Maybe not all battles are winnable, and maybe not all deals are makeable, but it still seems like one could have been made.

There's a global power simulation game called *Guns or Butter*. I don't remember how the rules work, but the dilemma is that you are trying to build up your country, and you can pick guns or butter. The winner is the player with the most butter. However, at any time, either player can declare war, and the side with more guns gets all the other team's butter. Of course, in the real world, things are far more complex than this, but the simulation forces a fascinating mental choice. Gary and Lorraine were playing a corporate game of *Guns or Butter*. In the end, they went for guns.

In the coming decades, Gary would start companies, write novels, design games, become the elder legend of gaming, and get obituaries that talked about how he created the world that we all now live in—and I agree with those obituaries. In my opinion, he's up there with Jobs and Gates and the Beatles when it comes to shaping the late twentieth century and building the framework for the twenty-first.

If you visited TSR corporate headquarters in the wake of the lawsuit, you'd see a company in disarray. A legal staff fighting battles that would drain their focus and their wallets. A creative department churning out D&D but also doing *Rocky and Bullwinkle* and *All My Children* board games. Not a lot of focus there. And while there is a lot of value in using other people's intellectual properties—you can buttress your company and sometimes have breakthroughs—in the end, creative enterprises and companies are defined by what they bring into the world.

Over in accounting, they were dealing with both incoming and outgoing late pays, and life was such a day-to-day existential struggle that nobody was looking to the horizon and seeing the problem that would ultimately kill TSR.

I was at my new roll-top desk in my new home office on Strathmore (later to be the inspiration for Strathmore Castle in *Dragonstrike*) when somebody called to say that Lorraine had won every point in the lawsuit and it was over. I was happy for Lorraine, but I was unhappy that Gary had lost. For me, there was no win in this. Gary and I were alienated because he was convinced I knew about Lorraine's takeover, even though I was as blindsided as he was. I felt horrible for him. You don't have to have much imagination to empathize with his sense of injustice as his company was taken away from him. And in a creative, moral, and spiritual way, he was right. We can play corporate coroner all day long and rationalize the fact that, yes, Dave Arnison cocreated D&D, and that, yes, the Blumes were investors and without their investment the company never would have happened, and that, yes, Gary made decisions that put him in the position he was in, and so on. But the one thing you can't do, if you have an ounce of compassion, is not feel his sense of loss and theft, because every other component of the origin is fungible. It could have been somebody other than the Blumes and Arneson and the other motley cast of characters who made it work, but TSR never would have happened without Gary.

And that's just the plain truth.

Thus, if you put yourself in his position, you can easily see the world as a network of parasites and scavengers: lawyers, businesspeople, and others spotting vulnerability and enriching themselves by stealing his company. And, in a way, he's right. The law of nature and the cycle of life dictate that by creating a company and creating value, you've entered the food chain, and like everything else in nature, you're eventually going to get devoured by the scavengers, maggots, and bacteria until there's nothing left but bones and fossils.

It's life. Life is not fair. We all know it.

All of that having been said, had there been no Lorraine, it's quite possible that TSR would have shut its doors in 1985 and maybe been sold for scrap to some company that also would have gone facedown, and D&D would be a nostalgic memory and some moldering boxes in closets and attics and game stores, with all the rights trapped in some attorney's file cabinet until the requisite gold was delivered. Instead, TSR had another ten years and survived to be passed on to Wizards of the Coast, then Hasbro. A couple of months ago, I was standing on a Hollywood cosplay/live-action role-playing stage of Waterdeep while watching a podshow of celebrities playing D&D and spreading the religion to a whole new generation and reawakening backsliders. D&D in particular, and role-playing in general, is having a huge revival. That's due mostly to Gary Gygax changing the world with a game, and in part due to Lorraine preserving the company.

So given that this all started with a pulled line of credit and Chapter 10.5, it could have been a lot worse.

But it could have been a lot better, too.

The Magic Potions

In any hero's journey, at some point or the other, there are magic potions. Since drug taking was very rare or almost invisible in the geek eighties (whereas it was all over the real eighties), and nicotine and alcohol were common (the Trader Vic's navy grog was my pick), the biggest one we had was Napalm Hot Curry. We got this from a place called Canard de Bombay, run by a fellow named Saad Ghazi and his wife Karen and daughter Saaren.

Canard was right near my first agent's office on San Vicente Boulevard near the black hole where it crosses La Cienega. Think swinging London meets rock-era LA in a place named after some pun I never understood. Dark, moody, smelling of exotic spices, and as much shrine as restaurant—you get the idea. Canard offered the hottest curry in the world, according to a *Los Angeles Magazine* article framed on the wall. Saad classified his curry with a star system from one through ten. One star was oatmeal; anybody could eat it. Three stars was as hot as anything you could order in a normal restaurant, and noncombatants were warned away from it. At four, you were entering uncharted territory. Saad said it doubled every two stars above that. For reasons only known to Saad, after four stars came six, eight, and ten—there were no odd numbers past three.

Saad was into the health effects of his curry—the gastronomic mayhem was not unsubstantial—and for years I would show up when I got sick and walk out healthy. That's my testimonial, anyway, and I would pass a polygraph on it.

Saad put plaques on the wall for everybody who ate double the number of meals as the number of stars. For instance, if you ate eight separate four-star meals, you got a plaque. If you ate a dozen of the six-star meals, you got a plaque. And you could not go straight to ten. You had to collect plaques for four, six, and eight first. This meant that to get a ten-star plaque, you would need to eat at least fifty-six meals there. Most of the people who had plaques were somehow associated with drugs or rock and roll or both. I remember Tony Iommi of Black Sabbath had one. Timothy Leary, who used to have dinner with Gordon Liddy there, had one. I think Elizabeth Montgomery did, as well as Brooke Shields. Christine McVie of Fleetwood Mac had one, too. And there were others.

At one point or another, pretty much every major figure in this story went there. Not everybody used it as an opportunity to blow out their taste buds, but everybody showed up. My goal was to get a ten-star plaque, and I eventually did. Frank Miller got a four-star plaque. Dave Marconi might have made his ten-star; he's a competitive guy. Gary smoked Camels and drank Taj Mahal through a four, I think Paul Dini might have earned his four-star, and Buzz and Steve lit themselves up on numerous occasions. If there was a shrine in this world, Canard was it.

Creative people have suspected for a long time that spice triggers dreams and the imagination in general. I fully believe this. And nobody could question that a four-star at least triggered endorphins. You'd always walk out of there with a rush I'm not sure I've really achieved since.

It was also my first and only experience with gamified eating.

MOV'S Unfairly Named Porno House

ONE OF THE UNINTENDED consequences of the glut of toy shows was that they caused a gold rush of sorts in California. Sunbow was the gold standard. They paid $6,000 a script. Carole Weitzman cut a check for half of the script fee on the day the premise was approved, and they paid the other half the day the script was submitted. No money chase. No fuss, no muss. This was a welcome change for animation writers used to working with DIC Entertainment, who felt that they were being DIC-ked around, thanks to the company's notorious reputation for making people wait on their checks. Sunbow didn't make people wait, and they were, I'm sure, repaid many times over in loyalty and extra effort.

A word on that. Sunbow had a great reputation, and it started with their business practices. I think I heard that Joe Bacal asked around and got numbers for what the cheapies paid and then what the highest script fee was. I think he concluded that the cheapest was $3,000 and Jeff Scott got $9,000, so he settled in the center. That was a lot more money in 1985 than it is now. Write five scripts, and you could get by. Write more, and you were happy. I got paid not only for scripts but a salary, and I think maybe a story editing fee, so I had an ultra-great deal. And they also understood that I did other things and were good with it. They realized that the cross-pollination between games and animation and comics (in the case of others) was creating a valuable synergy. Just as Joe Bacal found actors like Chris Latta doing stand-up comedy, Steve Gerber was bringing in crème-de-la-crème writers.

Two of the superstars he brought into the fold were Marv Wolfman and Len Wein. They wrote some early scripts, and then I believe he gave them a multi-script deal that facilitated the move to Los Angeles. I'm not sure whether Len came out at the same time, but I very clearly remember Marv's moving-in party. Marv and Len were already comics legends.

I remember being flattered to be invited. It was a great chance to hang out with the cool comic guys. At that point, I was kind of in awe of them. Maybe we got paid more than most, but they got their names in big bold letters on the top of the comic. Frank was there, and so was Howard Chaykin. He was in the middle of a big run of *American Flagg*—which was one-third of the comics trifecta lighting up the world at that point, alongside *Dark Knight* and *Watchmen*. I was sucked into all of them.

At least as interesting as the guys at the party were the women. When I met Lynn Varley (at the time Frank's girlfriend, but later his wife), she had dyed her hair black because she didn't feel that blondes were taken seriously. At least that's what somebody told me. I didn't entirely buy it, because I can't conceive of how stupid somebody would have to be to think for even one minute that she was a dumb blonde. She was smart as hell, and maybe a little bit pissed—at what, I don't know, but it was bolstered by the pack-a-day voice rasp she rocked without having to do the whole pack-a-day thing.

Lynn also happened to be quite possibly the best colorist in comics. She's the only person in the world I could talk to about orange for an hour and a half and find it an interesting conversation—which is exactly the conversation that happened when Frank and Lynn and Terrie and I were on a National Trust Academic Cruise of the Greek Islands, researching an Odyssey video game I was doing and the graphic novel that would grow up to be *300*. On that cruise, she was looking for the colors of antiquity. She found them.

Then there was Christy Marx. She was working on *The Sisterhood of Steel*, and she was just like one of her characters. She lived in a cabin in the Sierra Madres (not exactly a cabin, but close enough), and I went shooting there with her and her husband, Peter. In fact, I remember when *Crocodile Dundee* came out it reminded me of them—especially as he was Australian, and especially as she was like a female Crocodile Dundee.

Meg McLaughlin was also there that night, I think. Even if she wasn't, she deserves a mention in this section. She was kind of the kid sister at Ruby-Spears. She was very quiet and very, very bright. She just hid it. Her sister Stacy was Joe's secretary and was the authority figure at Ruby-Spears. Meg did all sorts of stuff, but I don't think she ever wrote anything there, though she did at Sunbow. In fact, probably the biggest botch I had as a story editor was on her script. But back to Marv's party.

The real star of the whole show was Marv's house itself. It was one of those *Boogie Nights* places in the Valley that reeked of swingers' parties in the sixties and probably porn shoots in the seventies and eighties. I have no support for that suspicion, but from the way the pool was laid out and the look of the place, everything about the house suggested that if the walls could talk, they'd have to be bleeped.

We didn't have any porn stars, but we had comics legends blown up by the Hell's Kitchen mythology I'd been hearing about for the last couple years. I loved watching all of these legendary characters interact. A decade earlier, they were playing volleyball together in Hell's Kitchen and trying to break into comics. I'd pay a lot of money for a video of that. This wasn't what you'd immediately think of as an athletic crowd (though Frank is actually a surprisingly good athlete); volleyball with cigarettes is what I imagine.

I'm not sure who the oldest of the crowd was. Maybe Marv. He's had a career ever since, morphing from one industry to another—comics to animation to video games. Marv, along with Steve and Roger, seemed like the quintessential New Yorker. I'll throw Howard Chaykin into that box, too. Len, interestingly, never seemed as New York. There was a pattern in the New Yorkers who moved to LA. They'd show up and think it was really cool for a few weeks and then they'd realize that they weren't in New York and they'd be talking about some deli on the Lower North Side (yes, I know there isn't a Lower North Side, but that's what it sounded like to a Californian) and all the stuff they missed. Then, inevitably, they'd go back for a couple weeks, and when they returned, they didn't talk about the deli anymore, or even New York.

Everything about Marv was all pro. In fact, he might be the most all pro of all of us. He got his stuff done correctly and on time. The interesting thing about him is that he's as much student as master. When he showed up to do animation, he'd actually asked me how to do stuff. That was one of the first indications I had that I wasn't a full-on noob anymore. The real Marv Wolfman was actually asking me how to do stuff. He might have been the grand old man of comics, but he didn't rest on his laurels—which he could have. And if you have any doubts about just how deep into the mainstream he is, read *The Amazing Adventures of Kavalier and Clay* and realize that he is one of the people acknowledged in it. He's seen more stuff and more generations than any of us and created an amazing array of stuff.

At Sunbow, Hildy had inboxes for us. Marv's said "Mov" because that's the way he pronounced his name. Decades later, Marv mastered game writing, and in 2006 we'd work on the Bryan Singer *Superman* game together. The funny thing was that he started as the DC approval guy. That doesn't mean he was the guy who matched the script to the bible; it means that he *was* the bible. He knew all of the continuities, and if Mov said it was the continuity, it was the continuity.

I'm just guessing, but Frank was probably the youngest of the crowd. He's almost a year younger than I am. But if you told me it was Roger, I'd believe that, too. This stuff is all knowable, but it doesn't matter. The overall feeling that night at Marv's was that everybody was still young. Maybe at the end of being young, but still young. Some of us were married, but nobody had little kids. There were no strollers or playpens. Everybody dressed like they were single, going to a hipster party. I'd been playing out the post-college era of my life for a long time, and there was still a lot of time to come. It would be almost a decade before I'd get married and adopt any real responsibilities.

But there was something big going on, and I think we all could feel it. Comic books were breaking through. For just a minute, people were taking them seriously. You could read about them in *Time* and *Newsweek*. There was news that a Batman movie was in the works (helped by *The Dark Knight*, no doubt). *Rolling Stone* wrote about comics. They were culture and counterculture. People were noticing.

In a few short years, Comic-Con would begin its morph from frumpy gathering of fans to Pop-Culture Con. There would be the "collector craze" and there would be bouncers and security teams for Image Comics, but this was the little moment before the world blew up.

Out there, in 1986, at Marv's unfairly named porno house on an LA night that was cool enough that the New Yorkers could wear their leather jackets and hot enough that the LA guys could be in Hawaiian shirts and cargo shorts—I'd be wearing my blazer, jeans, and button-down (I can be sure of it, as I rarely wear anything else)—we felt cool for the first time.

On that night, I felt like I did when I went to my first frat party and saw my first trashcan zombie and met my first Chi Alpha. All of us liked where we were, and all of us felt like we were heading off on some adventure. Of course, we had no idea where it was going to take us, but we knew it was going to be good.

Writing Process

ONE THING THAT WAS fascinating, but rarely discussed, was the writing process. Steve Gerber and I were very similar in the sense that we tended to smoke a lot of cigarettes and type. The primary difference was that I tried to make it look easy and was fanatical about hitting deadlines because I knew that was the one legitimate complaint a client could have. If they didn't like your script, they didn't like it, but if it is was late, that was tangible. I don't remember blowing a fixed deadline without a good reason and an agreement, verbally, that we both knew it was going to be late and why. More often than not, it was because we'd decided to go a different direction with the story and it was going to take more time. Still, it was important to "stop the moment" and make sure everybody understood that the deadline was going to change. I felt better about it when there was more than one person in the room when this happened. That made it harder for any kvetching about it. The truth is that I don't remember any kvetching from anybody, but it was a prominent feature of my own imagination. For some reason, I was born with a permanently in-session courtroom in my mind where I'd have to defend every action. I'm serious, it's really there. Maybe I should have gone to law school.

Steve Gerber knew deadlines were important but was incapable of meeting them. If I tried to act like the scripts came rolling effortlessly from my fingers, Steve made it sound like writing was the creative equivalent of giving birth. I'm not sure whether he was a procrastinator or just really meticulous (to be fair, his scripts were always more detailed and labored than mine), but he was always late. This was great for me, because if he hadn't fallen far behind, I wouldn't have been called in to help him at Sunbow.

The thing we all knew was that the show had to hit its airdate, so the work got done.

Buzz was like me, but without the cigarettes, and he was, quite possibly, faster, though we were both fast. For all of his extrinsic craziness, Buzz delivered a well-written product quickly and on time. For reasons that I still don't understand, it seems Steve and I were the only ones who fully appreciated Buzz. It might be because he made everybody else nervous. You never knew when he was going to try and slip something past (like the G.I. Joe B.A. scene) or whether something would get too weird.

Rick Merwin was the most mechanically perfect of us. His stuff was correct and on time and properly punctuated, and the grammar was impeccable—in fact, that was true of everybody but me, but I got away with it because I had swanky academic creds, so I fancy that people assumed I was making some whacked artistic choice. I knew somebody who lived next door to Rick Merwin, and they said that when they looked into his window, it appeared that he was working 24/7 in exactly the same position.

Everybody knew Frank Miller was a genius except Frank Miller, and I think he suspected it. He was an artist, and art is mysterious, so he didn't have quite the same deadline concerns as anybody else. Also, he was working on comics, and comics don't have a specific day and hour when they have to appear, and there weren't millions of dollars on the line for blown airdates.

The thing that amazed me about Frank was how hard he worked—and how hard he continues to work. He even did some covers for *Lone Wolf and Cub* that I'm not even sure he got paid for; I have this sense it was a favor. But anyway, I showed up at his place and I was ankle-deep in sketches. Big pieces of paper—I'd say two feet by three, but I might be wrong—with the same action covered from a number of different angles. I remember wondering if you could sequence them and have them play like a flip-book. And he had props: toy cars, guns, Polaroids. Meanwhile, Lynn would be across the way in her colorist area, which was always neat and orderly. She was a fascinating character, kind of a cross between Joni Mitchell and Michelle Phillips or Debbie Harry (in eighties terms), with a raspy voice and a big laugh. She was either wrapped up in some comics controversy or just a fun person to hang out with or both at the same time.

Paul Dini's working style involved having a lot of action figures around. He'd be writing a scene, and my sense was that he kind of staged the characters while he was writing. I don't know whether he actually did it, but he went to Emerson and had a lot more familiarity with actors and the stage than I did, so he seemed to stage things. He'd layer his wild ideas and visuals on top of it, but he seemed to be very interested in the character dynamics. He was also more experiential than the rest of us. He'd go on trips to Tasmania to find the Tasmanian Wolf, get chased off a dock by a Komodo dragon, that kind of thing. He didn't hunt, to the best of my knowledge, but he did search for mythical creatures in the real world.

Gordon Kent was the only one of that crowd that could make it as an artist, producer, voice director, or pretty much any other role in the animation business. The interesting thing about his work on *G.I. Joe* was that he did arguably the silliest script ("The Greenhouse Effect"), the grimmest script ("Cobra's Candidate"), and the most fantastical script ("The Gods Below") in the series. I never remember anything eccentric about Gordon's work style. In fact, I'm not sure I can ever remember actually seeing him at a keyboard. However, one look at his IMDb page proves that not only did he write, he wrote quite a bit!

Coopetition

ALL OF THE BEST creative environments involve something I call "coopetition." At one point or another, almost every combination of the people above helped each other on projects for no immediate gain of their own. In fact, given that we were all writers trying to sell our wares, we were in competition with each other on a certain level. But we didn't think of it that way. At least, not the people mentioned here. We'd jam together on ideas for no real explicit reason and we'd write or fix scenes and dialogue for each other for no apparent gain. We did it for the joy and thrill of it, and yeah, sometimes for the vulgar display of virtuosity—but the group here was a network, and everybody prospered as long as they remained part of one.

This phenomenon isn't limited to us. John Lennon and Paul McCartney tried to teach Mick Jagger and Keith Richards how to write songs while the Beatles and the Rolling Stones ferociously competed on their albums, but there were also numerous moments of collaboration, as if they knew their fates were bound together. The same would go for our film heroes during this era: Francis Coppola, George Lucas, Steven Spielberg, John Milius, Brian De Palma, and Martin Scorsese (to name a few) found themselves, to varying degrees, in coopetition with one another. Professional athletes are lying when they say they don't care about their personal stats—of course they do, as they're competing against the other team, history, and even against the other guys on their own teams who are trying to take their jobs. But with that last group, all the same, if they don't cooperate, they don't win.

It almost goes without saying that not all competition is good.

And, I suppose, that not all cooperation is good.

But the magic in a network is when you find a lot of coopetition.

TF: The Movie Recording Sessions
Fall 1985

REWRITES WENT ON UNTIL the recording sessions, which primarily took place at Wally Burr studios. A lot has been written about them, which is for the best, as the truth is that the recording sessions are a blur to me. It's probably chronicled to the minute on some fan site, but to me they were a confusing blur of famous people coming in and out of Wally Burr studios. And I wasn't present for some of the recordings. I think I was on the phone for Eric Idle's recordings and probably said nothing. Working with a real Monty Python member was a very big deal to me.

Killing off Optimus Prime was one thing, but replacing him was a whole different thing. You can't get a more archetypal hero than Optimus Prime. Ultra Magnus was the obvious choice, but in some ways, he was more of the same, just with not as much gravitas. He was doomed to fail, so he served as a transitional leader. The default was to go with a type of David and Goliath model, where an unlikely character selected by fate becomes the leader. Despite all of the immersion in Joseph Campbell, I don't remember anybody articulating it this way. We all just kind of knew it. But we wanted a model for it in the world.

I didn't have to look any further than my favorite quarterback, Jim McMahon of the Chicago Bears. He was young and brash and irreverent, and for a time threw the ball as well as anybody the game had ever seen. He led what is quite possibly the best team in NFL history to a Super Bowl rout of the New England Patriots. Anybody who's sick of seeing Tom Brady show up at the Super Bowl every year should watch a replay of that one. It might make you feel better.

The point is, we wanted to replace Optimus with the opposite of Optimus, and then watch him grow in the role throughout the movie and season three. Of course, other events would intercede, and Rodimus would remain in a kind of leadership limbo, but that was the plan. And, to his credit, Rodimus Prime (a.k.a. Hot Rod) has a legion of devoted fans.

Hot Rod was played by Judd Nelson, who was part of the Brat Pack and very cool at the time. I had no idea what I'd talk to him about in the prerecording lull. It took about twelve seconds to figure it out: the Miami Dolphins. Led by Dan Marino and Don Shula, they were my archnemesis team at the time. I had two teams then: the Raiders and the Bears, and the Dolphins/Raiders shootouts of the time were among the best games I've ever seen.

Bear with me, this is all going to get relevant to *Transformers* in a moment. But the sore subject was that the '85 Bears had a perfect season, *except* for one Monday Night Football game against the Miami Dolphins (who remain the only team with a perfect season—though asterisks apply). The Bears' defense that year, which was arguably the best in the history of football, suffered tipped passes that went for touchdowns and had a bizarrely bad night. It wasn't a lot better for the offense. So Judd Nelson's love of the Dolphins led to lively conversation. The kicker, though, is little did he know he was playing a character based in part on Chicago Bears quarterback Jim McMahon.

See, one of the mental tricks I play when working with large numbers of cast members is to peg them to something else—a set of people I know. I try to stay away from other fictions so that I don't imitate. There are so many Transformers I don't remember, but from what I recall, Kup was kind of like Mike Ditka, Springer was Walter Payton, Blurr was Willie Gault, Kevin Butler was Bumblebee, the Dinobots were cartoon versions of Danimal (Dan Hampton), Richard Dent, Dave Duerson, Otis Wilson. Howie Long was kind of Blitgzwing, and Gary Fencik, the only Bear to go to Yale, was Perceptor, because I kind of felt that was a free safety thing. And so on. It'd be a fun game to try and match the Bears up to the Transformers. I'm quite sure that Lester Hayes, Mike Haynes, and Jim Plunkett made it in there somewhere. Marcus Allen was kind of a Hot Rod guy, too.

Meanwhile, the Decepticons were various nemeses from other teams, like Lawrence Taylor, Clayton and Duper, Joe Theismann (and various Redskins), Mark Gastineau, and so on. I won't bore you with any more of this, except to say that the Quintessons were, of course, the referees.

Robert Stack was kind of a unique guy in the history of Hollywood. He wasn't some rags-to-riches story; rather, he was an heir, I believe, to Occidental Petroleum. And yet he was one of the humblest people I've ever worked with. He openly confessed to being a little nervous because he'd never done voiceover before. He was great as Ultra Magnus. Of course, he would go on to do *Unsolved Mysteries*, which called for a lot of ominous voiceover. I remember thinking that he sounded like a voice from beyond the grave.

I don't remember Leonard Nimoy recording, so I might not have been there. It's also possible that I was there, but in the back of the booth. I just have no memory of it. I did run into him a couple years before his death at the Sports Club LA. I was working out in a small circuit room and there was only one other person there. It was Leonard Nimoy. He saw that I recognized him and smiled. I smiled. I didn't say anything. This was West LA, and in West LA we're supposed to be way too cool to geek out over running into Mr. Spock.

However, Orson Welles was the big one in every sense of the term. As I said, I'd met him before, and he probably vaguely remembered me from the meeting with Gary Gygax, but I didn't bring it up. However, as I recall, it was a short staff day there. I think a lot of people were dodging that session or hanging back because there was a tape going around that featured him eviscerating some poor fool of an advertising executive. The tape was circulating among the sound guys. Wally had a copy of it, and he played it for us the day before Welles came in. Nobody wanted to be the poor fool advertising executive.

On the big day, Orson Welles showed up in what looked to me like a big old beater that had been specially retrofitted for his wheelchair. I'd heard that he'd had various financial ups and downs, but it felt a little bad. You expect Orson Welles to roll up in a thirties limo with klieg lights following it. That wasn't what it was like. For some reason I remember it being a rainy day, but that sounds unlikely in LA. Maybe it was overcast with June gloom, or maybe I'd just rewatched *Citizen Kane*. I don't know.

They rolled him in, then he used a walker to get to the stool before walking the last few steps. He had some French manager who said he had bad knees. He also weighed about four hundred pounds. Orson Welles was a big guy. I'm 6'5", and he was eye-to-eye with me. Usually celebrities are smaller than you expect them to be.

His opening line was, "I hear I play an entire planet." In any event, he looked the part. We then talked about his character a little bit. We didn't have to. He got it. We talked a little about Mercury Theater, because along with the pulps, I'd discovered old radio and this was *The Shadow*.

When we did his recording, he was all pro. He didn't trash the material. He asked how lines should be read. He was a little wheezy and quite obviously wasn't in the best of health, but he nailed it.

He died a week later.

The Shit Story

In 1980, there were four ratings for movies. G was General and was for kids. Specifically, little kids. PG was for older kids. R was for adults and meant the film might contain graphic violence or nudity, and X was for dirty films and/or extremely violent films. In 1984, in exactly the period I went to Lucasfilm, PG-13 was created for *Indiana Jones and the Temple of Doom* because of a violent heartrending scene.

That opened up some air around PG. With PG-13, there was no twilight zone between PG and R anymore, and by extension, G became a toddler rating. Tom Griffin and Joe Bacal knew that *Transformers* would die if it were released as a G movie, so they had to do something that ensured a PG. The solution was to throw in a single, solitary "shit," knowing that would move the film out of G without throwing it all the way to PG-13.

The question was who to give the line to.

The last thing Hasbro wanted to see was kids playing with one of their toys saying, "Oh, shit, what are we going to do now?" So they gave it to an Adult Spike who was not, himself, a toy.

Inhumanoids

ON FRIDAY NIGHT, NOVEMBER 1, 1985, for no discernible reason, my life changed. It's still something mysterious to me. I was sitting on my tapestry couch in the living room. I was headed to a Halloween Party somewhere, and I was pausing to have a smoke and decide whether I was going to do my effort-free Invisible Man costume with the trench coat and the ace bandage and sunglasses again, or whether I could whip something else up.

I pulled my Camel Filter out of the pack, like I did at least twenty times a day. Maybe I looked to see whether the Jane Russell-looking femme fatale was still hanging out on the Camel's leg, maybe I didn't—but I did check that a lot. I also looked closely to see if there was a 7-Eleven in the ancient Arabic minaret town on the back cover. (I used that town as a mental map for a fantasy town in Sagard.)

Anyway, I put the cig in my mouth, lit it up, and a psych bomb went off. I looked at the cigarette, got a wave of alien dread from it, felt revolted, and quit. It's probably not an accident that it was the Friday before my thirtieth birthday. I've never smoked since. I still chew nicotine gum and sometimes do patches, but no cigarettes. I'm not sure how to sell this as a therapy, but somehow it worked for me. Fifteen years of happy smoking, and then it was over. And I knew it was over. I've had nicotine issues my entire life, but cigarettes were over. I went through a cigar period fifteen or twenty years later, but cigarettes were done. There was no program, no conscious effort, and no looking back.

Not long after, I was sitting in my newly ashtray-free office at Sunbow with a box of nicotine gum and an outline for *Inhumanoids* on my screen. I decided I was going to get the miniseries that started *Inhumanoids* done in a week. I'm not sure why. I think it was partly to distract myself while I went through withdrawal and partly to see if I could pull it off.

Oddly enough, in my professional career I avoid that most of the time. I'm not a binge writer. I am kind of a boring drone. I get up every day before 5 a.m. and write until I either run out of ideas or have gotten rid of the dread I wake up with every morning. This is probably somehow linked to a recurring dream I have about being at the end of a quarter in college and suddenly remembering a class I signed up for and never attended. This didn't happen in the real world, but I still have dreams about it.

Inhumanoids was a unique project for me. It debuted on a strange show Sunbow had called *Super Sunday*, which was a half-hour show that contained three sub-shows. Each show had one act that worked like an old-time serial cliff-hanger. So the order was for thirteen episodes, but it wasn't that simple. The first thirteen of the seven-minute episodes were to be editable down to four separate twenty-two minute episodes as a tool to launch a thirteen-episode season.

Of course, the math doesn't work. We'd need ninety-one minutes, but this would only produce eighty-eight. And keep in mind that every episode had to end with a cliff-hanger, and every episode had to start with the resolution to the previous cliff-hanger.

Our solution was to make the series one long continuity. We wanted to end every episode with a super cliff-hanger, but we had to think of the acts as mobile blocks hinged by cliff-hangers and resolutions. And we realized that we needed promotable B-stories. B-stories weren't new—we had them all the way back to *Mister T* (every episode had a character learn a lesson)— but the trick here was that each of those stories would need to interweave so that as one plot thread was winding down, another was building up. Now, of course, this is pretty much the modern formula for "binge" series;

however, we were doing it in 1986 in a world where people really didn't get it. It was an alien format.

We had one thing going for us that was very subtle, though, in that this was the MTV era. In the MTV era, it was more about the song than the story, but many videos had some story. The stories were disjointed, with musicians who may or may not have acting skills playing out a fantasy that usually involved some weird love affair and dance number. Michael Jackson turned "Thriller" into a monster in more ways than one, but he had a budget—which most videos didn't. That changed as MTV prospered, because at the time the music business was doing quite well, but the point is that this led to a much more impressionistic kind of storytelling. With videos, the song and repetition of viewing caused viewers/listeners to assemble a story.

So instead of doing stories where every plot element was stated and restated, we just let it kind of flow. We decided that the "bug" of an extremely complex format was really a feature. *Inhumanoids* was horror, and monsters aren't supposed to be rational, so we didn't have to belabor the villain's goals or purpose—it became more about horrifying images. If we'd thought about it, we would have put heavy metal songs in there, but that was a lot.

We wanted this show to be different. Since I'd immersed myself in comics, I liked the idea of split screen, and you'll see it through the early episodes until we ran into production problems. We wanted very moody lighting, a kind of German expressionism brought to cartoons. We wanted something that was very scary and funny at the same time, because humor is the thing that makes horror palatable to parents.

We wanted a political overtone. It had to be about more than just rampaging monsters. In fact, most monster movies are about more than rampaging monsters. *Godzilla* was code for the risks of nuclear weapons. *Dracula* was about Victorian repression. *Frankenstein* was about the threat of unchecked science. *Inhumanoids* was about greed and corruption.

The political undertone was both a product of watching too many Alan Pakula films, a lifelong love of conspiracies and tinfoil hat stuff, and that feeling that kids would like it just the way I liked the Mayor Linseed references that I dimly perceived in the 1965 *Batman* show. Also, we knew parents watched these things, too. We wanted them to be watching and realize that the show was kind of smart.

And just as we were mirroring the oil crisis of the eighties in *Transformers* and growing terrorist worries in *G.I. Joe, Inhumanoids* had an environmental message of sorts. Only in our version, nature wasn't some passive victim—nature was honked off and striking back. There was no intention to make *Inhumanoids* a didactic preach piece, but the metaphor is there and there's no point in pretending that it isn't. Inhumanoids were unleashed because we invaded their territory and they got pissed off.

Also, the fact that the "Terror That Lies Within" is about monsters coming from the same places that our oil and minerals come from was irresistible to me, and it played well with the idea that the most terrifying stuff in the show was the greed and nastiness within humans. But don't for a moment think I sat there writing and editing episodes trying to tune the message. Mostly I just tried to figure out cooler and cooler things to do with our heroes and monsters under the earth. Later on, I realized what I was really writing about.

Just as Frank Miller was with *Dark Knight*, I was reacting to the media world we found ourselves in. With the advent of cable TV and smaller video recorders, the face of media was beginning to change. There were more hours to fill on TV, and the news was becoming more of a business than a public service, as it had been in the past. CNN wouldn't fully bloom until the Gulf War in 1991, but the stage was being set. The airwaves were overrun with magazine shows, daytime shock shows, and nighttime specials, hence the array of media figures who would be reporting various plot twists in *Inhumanoids*. Hector Ramirez, who may or may not bear an uncanny resemblance to Geraldo Rivera, has his own section in the book.

The fun thing about the Earth Corps was that they had a crap budget that was always in danger of being cut by the nefarious Blackthorne Shore and by Senator Masterson, who was running his own scam and wanted our heroes to fail. Fortunately, Blackthorne had a sister, Sandra Shore, who was a philanthropist (guilty over being partly responsible for unleashing D'Compose) and was able to bankroll the Earth Corps. In some ways, the financial aspect of *Inhumanoids* was a reaction to the recession at the time and to budget cuts. It was also a reaction to our other shows, in which it seemed that everybody had an unlimited budget. Sure, the Earth Corps tech was expensive, but it was fun to have a scrappy group that had to make things work and work against the system.

Another sign of the media environment at the time was Granahue, a rock equivalent of Phil Donahue replete with a very successful daytime show of his own. Donahue always seemed to me to be a symbol of the emasculated male. Granahue is made of granite, but he's always wimping out and putting forth wiener arguments for why they should take inaction. Not that they should fail to take action, but that they should actively do nothing. In other words, the Granites were strong and worthless.

The Redwoods functioned, as did all of the Inhumanoids, like environmental terrorists, but ultimately figured out that they had more in common with the "flesh slugs" than they did with the horrors from within. After all, they live on the surface of the Earth and don't benefit from the planet being covered with lava (or primal energy) by Metlar or being decomposed or living at the mercy of the Cthulhu-esque Tendril.

As with a lot of what I do, there's a lot of Lovecraft/Howard (I see them as one meta entity) in *Inhumanoids*. The curious thing is that while I've read all of Lovecraft, I'm not really a scholar of it by any means. But I love the feel of it. My Lovecraftiness is really more a sense of what I think Lovecraft should have been than what Lovecraft really was. It's the same thing with H. R. Giger, but different. Giger's stuff, when I actually look at it, seems pervy and weird to me, but I don't focus on that. I have some editor in my brain that auto-censors the grossorama stuff and just sees what I want it to be. I'm not sure if everybody works that way, but I'm often surprised to find out that my influences are awfully auto-impressionistic—which is my overblown way of saying, I see what I want to see and often miss the obvious.

But my biggest influence while writing *Inhumanoids* was chemical. Withdrawal from nicotine.

All of that having been said, the actual writing process while going through withdrawal was absolutely unique. It was like my head was filled with cotton, and no thought lasted for more than fifteen seconds. While writing, I worked in a document where I had the outline actually in the script document. This was a new, post-digital (though nobody said "digital" in the eighties; post–word processor would be more true to the period) way to write. You couldn't exactly do this before word processors. You had to retype everything every time—or you had to do some paste up, but I never did that myself.

So, right on the screen, I had where I'd just been and where I was going, and I'd plow through the outline and literally reformat to make script. This was very easy on the DECmate II computer, and I've never been able to exactly replicate it on any word processor since then. Microsoft Word is always outsmarting me. I've got work-arounds, but none of them work as well. I'd love to have a DECmate emulator. In any case, it allowed me to work well even though I had about a fifteen-second attention span or thought focus range due to the nicotine withdrawal.

I could do everything in the moment. One thought. Get it down. Go to the next one. Forget the last one and not be quite sure what's coming next. I'm not sure I'd recommend writing while going through withdrawal, but it somehow matched this material. *Inhumanoids* has a fascinating pacing for that reason. It feels "in the minute"; it feels like it jumps as far as a synapse can go. It's staccato in parts. Of course, some of that isn't due to me at all. It's in part due to the damaged production process we had.

I was constantly adrift in the moment. Sometimes I'd have to read back to see what I'd written less than a minute before, and I'd dig forward in the outline. (I had the outline done before I quit smoking.) It was a fascinating exercise. It gives the show a jagged urgency that wasn't in anything I'd done before because the process of writing was urgent. I had to get a thought down before it vanished. I had to keep moving forward.

I turned episode five in on a Friday five days after I started. Tom Griffin was in town, and he looked at me with his trademark slightly bemused expression. "You know, we're not trying to set the script speed writing contest record here," he said.

"You don't like it?"

"No, I think it's great. I just don't want you to kill yourself in the process."

"No chance of that. I'm actually prolonging my life in the process."

He kind of smiled and walked away.

Jay Bacal went along on the ride, too. "No question that this is the most bizarre show we've ever done or maybe anybody mainstream has ever done, but if our intention was to make something wild and terrifying and funny, we're accomplishing it."

What he was really saying, whether he knew it or not, was that we were into a whole new territory with *Inhumanoids*. It almost wasn't a kids' show anymore. Later, after it had aired, Mike Weirich, a friend from high school whom I played UNCLE/THRUSH with and read comic books with, happened to catch the show. He had no idea I'd written it. "So I saw this thing called Inhuman or something…I can't believe they're showing it to kids."

"Oh, you're talking about *Inhumanoids*. That's my show."

"What kind of kids are you writing for?" he asked, with legitimate indignity in his voice.

I remember thinking, "Kids like we used to be," but I probably wasn't fast enough to say it.

My dinged state and the odd format weren't the only reason the show was weird. We also had serious production issues. While the show was still a Marvel/Sunbow production with Toei in Japan, we were using a different company overseas. The Sunbow/Marvel relationship was going through a rough patch, and the different production house was one of the intended fixes. It didn't work out that way. In truth, I don't know what the problems were, because certainly Sunbow and Marvel had had a lot of success together, but something was wrong. Changing animation houses in Asia was not something I cared about until I saw the results. We did the script, voice, and storyboards in Los Angeles and sent it all off and forgot about it until it came back. We'd look at the assembly, call for fixes, and send it back. It would usually come back fixed.

Inhumanoids was different.

When the stuff came back, there was significant stuff missing and there was no time or will to fix it. We had airdates to hit and we somehow had to come up with seven-minute shows out of six minutes' worth of material. We had to get creative. *Inhumanoids* was the first time since making my own films in school that I'd have to "make it in post." This wasn't "fix it in post," mind you—it was "make it in post."

Oddly enough, though relations between Marvel and Sunbow were strained at the top, I never worked more closely with the producers and editors than I did on *Inhumanoids'* post. Stephanie Graziano (I can't remember whether she was married to Jim at that point) was great. We just kind of smiled and shrugged and went into fix-it mode. It was the one and only time in animation when I sat for hours at a moviola with the editors, trying to fill holes in unsent animation, trying to figure out what we could cut to make the scene work and still tell the story. Where we could insert a voiceover line to tell something that we didn't have the animation to show. It was like being back in film school—in a good way. It might have been a crisis, but it didn't mean it wasn't fun and challenging. No part of me worried about making the airdate; I was just interested in cobbling together the best show we could. We stole animations from other shows, we reused shots but would flip them so it wasn't as obvious. We broke the action axis in the process, but it was *Inhumanoids*—viewers expected weird and disorienting.

But for every trick we had, we still came up short on the episodes. We had a couple last tricks up our sleeve. We had extended recaps (in which we told bits of the story that may not have made it on the screen before) and coming attractions for the next episode (cobbled together with past footage). But we were still short. We had to do something. Fortunately, I'd always wanted to do "baseball cards" with the shows. The idea with a baseball card was that we'd focus on one character and do fifteen or thirty seconds just about them using old footage. The baseball cards were a featurette that mirrored the back-of-the-box copy on the toys.

To be honest, I was proud of the result, and I thought the episodes were better than they would have been if we hadn't had the crisis. That having been said, missing scenes are missing scenes. However, the whole experience taught me a lot about storytelling and making the best of a non-optimal situation.

It did well enough. I seem to recall somebody telling me $70,000,000. In an ordinary world, that would be a hit; however, for Sunbow, with three different phenomena going at the same time, and for other reasons we'll go into later, the show and toy line were considered failures. The toy line was canceled, episodes we wrote for the next season were never produced, and aside from a small but fanatical cult following, the show vanished with little trace.

Months later, we were sitting in the Sunbow conference room, commiserating about the failure of the Inhumanoids toy line. It might have been the last time that Joe Bacal, Jay Bacal, Tom Griffin, and I were all in the Westwood office together. I asked Joe what he thought went wrong. He picked up the figure of a character named Tendril (a foot-tall Lovecraftian-looking thing) and started walking the action figure across the table. It was a clumsy mess. He skidded it. It hobbled around and was zero fun. "Sometimes you can't get past the reality of the product."

But *Inhumanoids* didn't start off as a bad idea. The idea with the giant monsters was that they were simultaneously a giant action figure and a playset. Omega Supreme would be another example of that. Well, the concept of *Inhumanoids* was to make the action figure and the playset the same thing. This wasn't really executed except with D'Compose's rib cage, which opened up to be a jail for Earth Corps members. And the Inhumanoids toy line was lame, if we're honest about it. I mean, did anybody want a stubby telescoping redwood tree as a toy? (Yes, I'm aware of the adult gag lines here, but you get my point.)

And there was another thing about *Inhumanoids*. Until the proposed third season, there weren't any human bad guys (Dr. Manglar was a first). And the good guys looked weird. They were sold in their Earth Corps suits. The problem was that when you took off the helmet, they looked like pinheads.

And they were age-confused. You look at the Granites, and they look like children's toys, and our show wasn't really a children's show. *Inhumanoids* was simultaneously bizarre and, to the extent that a limited animation show can be scary, it was scary. So you had kid toys with an adult show. I'm proud of that show, warts and all. And it had production warts and story warts. Try writing a show that is thirteen stand-alone episodes at seven minutes each and which edit to four half-hour three-act episodes and can be reedited together to form a movie. It's challenging. It forces economy and discipline.

There were a lot of good ideas there, but sometimes good ideas don't gel into a great project. Much later, Bob Prupis would say, "Yeah, if things were a little different, we could have taken a real run at *Inhumanoids*."

Nowadays, I think any toy company would be happy with a $70,000,000 product line. But we're in a different world now. Though before we leave *Inhumanoids*, there's one more ironic thing. *Inhumanoids* was probably the darkest, most violent, most disturbing animated show of the era. We had skeletons that "decomposed" people, things that ripped out of the ground and snatched people, epic destruction, and cackling monsters with worms for arms. And there was no complaint from Thomas Radeki or Action for Children's Television or from any other watchdog group. We also had a guy who lived in a lava pit with horns and maybe a pitchfork called Metlar, who had an amusing relationship with the Statue of Liberty, but no religious groups complained. Instead, the controversy that reigned in that period was a hullabaloo (I like using that word) over a butt tattoo on a *My Little Pony* character that, to some, looked like a secret satanic symbol.

Go figure.

The Strange Case of Hector Ramirez

IT MIGHT SEEM A little bit odd that the Joe Team and Cobra would have been either unaware of or not interfacing with the Autobots and Decepticons, given that they operated in the same *G.I. Joe* universe. It also seems odd that neither group encountered the *Inhumanoids*. Who wouldn't have wanted to see a "decomposed" Zartan or what would happen if an Inhumanoid had touched a Transformer. (Would they have rusted? Would they have returned to a monstrified protoform?) And Jem and the Holograms never seemed to have come across any of the Joes, though a double bill with them and Cold Slither might have really been something to see. None of it happened, though it would be fun if it had.

However, there was one character that crossed between *Jem*, *Transformers*, *G.I. Joe*, and *Inhumanoids*. It was a pesky reporter named Hector Ramirez. How did Hector, and only Hector, have the power to do this?

Did Hector have some clearance granted by one of the various presidents or politicians in the Sunbow shows? Did he have an ability to invisibly slip through the various alternate universes of *Jem*, *Transformers*, *G.I. Joe*, and *Inhumanoids*? Or was he an animated human Easter egg who moved through the shows with a will of his own? By the time he shows up on *Jem*, he is interviewing Flint Westwood. I'm not making this up. It's both a riff on Clint Eastwood and on myself.

Meanwhile, he bombards my character in *G.I. Joe* with questions, and we find out he's a dupe of the Baroness. He showed up on *Transformers* as a reporter in "Prime Target," cowritten by Buzz Dixon and myself. He also showed up in a season four script that I don't remember having anything to do with but which is credited to me and Meg McLaughlin. I credit Buzz Dixon with the creation of Hector Ramirez.

Hector Ramirez was Sunbow's parody of Geraldo Rivera, though I don't remember it ever being discussed. He fit into Sunbow shows because he was the closest thing to a Sunbow character who existed in the real world, and we always needed investigative journalists in our stories.

Anybody who was alive in the eighties remembers *Geraldo!*, which at the time was regarded as "trash TV." Nowadays, it would be mainstream premium fare. (Okay, I'm being cynical, but it *was* the precursor to reality TV, which would be more or less invented by the 1988 Writers Guild of America strike.) There was no topic too outrageous or inflammatory for Geraldo. At one point there was a brawl between white supremacists, anti-racist skinheads, black activists, and Jewish activists live on the show. Geraldo got his nose busted in front of millions of Americans.

He soon got fired by ABC for protesting the fact that they wouldn't air a report about the relationship between Marilyn Monroe and John F. Kennedy. (Ted Kennedy was a partial inspiration for Senator Masterson on *Inhumanoids*.) Undaunted, he found out about a secret vault buried beneath a Chicago hotel in which Al Capone had allegedly stashed his loot. In a scene straight out of *Inhumanoids*, he brought a medical examiner along in case they found bodies, and an IRS agent in case they found money.

Again, I'm not making this up.

In my version, they open the vault and—*sslliikkkk*—a tendril rips out and grabs all three of them and drags them deep under the earth. They are then taken to Metlar's molten Shangri-La, Infernac, where the head Inhumanoid introduces Geraldo to his new trophy girlfriend, the former Statue of Liberty—Metlar filled statues with "primal energy" and brought them to life—and made him do a friendly story about the Inhumanoids.

Of course, that didn't happen on either the Geraldo special or in an *Inhumanoids* episode, but it should have. In the real world, he opened the vault and there were a couple of old bottles in there. He claimed they were moonshine and then went across the street to blast down some tequila.

On the *Inhumanoids* show, he was decomposed and turned into something horrific, but the truth is we had nothing but affection for Geraldo. If you want a quick before-and-after that serves almost as a metaphor for the difference between the eighties and the teens, watch some YouTube of eighties Geraldo in the vault and then watch him on Fox News. It seems like he got recomposed and reinvented and found a way to thrive long after the eighties.

Far beyond Geraldo's career, the idea that a character wandered between worlds was novel in those days, and this kind of stuff paved the way. Later on, we'd do a sort of crossover with Marissa Faireborne. It was never explicitly stated, but we thought of her as Flint and Lady Jaye's daughter. As far as a formal crossover, it would have been interesting to do, but I don't remember it ever being suggested.

Steve Gerber's Bulletin Board

IT'S ONE THING TO glimpse the future and quite another to know what you're looking at. In 1985, everybody had a different kind of computer. Some had

IBM PCs and were working on programs called Word II Star or Word Perfect or Microsoft Word. We had things like Scriptor, which would turn your text into screenplay format after the fact (or something like that). Spellcheck was an exotic and time-consuming new invention, and dial-up modem speeds were 256k and then the dazzlingly fast 512k. The net effect of this was that you could load an entire episode in about ten minutes. Maybe it was faster than that in something called ASCII. What came out was something that looked more or less like a script on whatever your resident program was, and you could edit from that. It was a glovotch of a process, but when the only other option was to retype the whole script, it was turbo as far as we were concerned.

Somewhere in late 1985, Steve Gerber set up the "Sunbow Bulletin Board." At least I think that's what it was called. It was originally for Sunbow writers and story editors to upload their scripts, but in short order it was populated by half of the animation and comic book industries. It was well-intentioned, worked most of the time, and served as a vision into the future. Steve's bulletin board would give us all a glimpse of Facebook and Twitter a couple of decades before social media took over the world. If we'd known what we were looking at, any one of us could have been Mark Zuckerberg—but we didn't, and we aren't.

A byproduct of this was that he also had a "mail" area on the program that functioned like a chat room. It seemed to me that it functioned more like a series of emails, but maybe I'm wrong. But it worked well enough that people could post messages very quickly in threads kind of like a Facebook topic. Soon this became the center of animation conversation. And all of the bad behavior that we'd now recognize as social media appeared in microcosm.

We got into stupid flame wars. Titanic animosities grew out of nowhere. I was arguing with people I didn't even know. J. Michael Straczynski, whom I knew as Joe Straczynski at the time, and I argued about God knows what and thought each other were smoking rectums until we actually met. Turned out he's a really good guy.

I remember somebody was hitting on Linda on there and ended up messaging something like, "Dump Flint, he's a loser." It probably wasn't something the guy would have said if I were around, or if Linda was, for that matter. I'd had my first whiff of the vicious, false anonymity of the Internet. And these people were known to me, but protected by pixels. I don't even think people would have behaved that way on a phone call. And what nobody knew then is that everything you write is a public document; unless there was a hard drive crash, it existed forever. All of this was happening in 1985.

And then something even weirder happened. I got together with Steve Gerber one night in some dark bar. He started telling me about his new girlfriend. As the conversation developed, it slowly dawned on me that Steve had never actually "met" his new girlfriend. They had fallen in love in a chat room. At the time, this seemed utterly bizarre and more than a little unhealthy. It never occurred to me that one day I'd have hundreds of friends who existed mostly virtually and whom I'd never actually met.

I remember thinking I had to take a harder look at this "cyberpunk" stuff that Mike Dobson at TSR had been telling me about and which seemed kind of gross. I knew I was seeing a version of the future, I just didn't know whether I wanted to live in that future. But, yeah. The eighties might have been the last analog decade, but already you could see the coming age sneaking a glimpse at us from the future, and it was unsettling.

The Sunbow chat room became something so pernicious that Candy Monteiro, everybody's agent, started railing about it one day, saying we all ought to just get off of it. Three decades later, I'm still wondering if that was good advice we didn't heed. The interesting thing was that at some point the bulletin board went down and nobody clamored very hard to get it back. The analog world still seemed to hold infinite possibilities.

And maybe it opened a window for me to other worlds. Maybe this wasn't true of other Sunbow people, but I pretty much only knew the people whom I happened to encounter directly in my path. With the exception of Steve's BBS and occasional parties or chance encounters, I had no idea who was doing anything farther than one degree of separation from me. It was like I was running a race and there was nobody in front of me. Being out in front feels strangely alone. Everything else was ambient noise of unknown origin. Speaking strictly, I didn't watch competing shows. My cover story was that it was because we didn't want to be influenced by them, and there might have been some truth to that—you can't plagiarize things you haven't seen—but the reality was that I'm just not that academic. Every artist has their own well they draw from, a muse they follow, some winky they're after and their own way of finding it—or reason for not finding it.

I knew almost nothing about *Voltron, Mask, Jayce and the Wheeled Warriors*, and various other shows. I had this vague mental image of what they were, and that was that. Same goes for *Robotech*. That just felt more hardcore, and I lumped it in with the mech games I'd seen at Gen Con and then kept running. I could make an argument that I should have worked completely differently and paid attention to everything everybody else was doing, but I didn't. I treated it like a race. Run your race and don't pay attention to the competition.

One of the odd phenomena of having multiple projects going at the same time is that you almost forget about them when they are actually being produced. The flurry of the summer and fall before, in which I wrote three of the four Sagard books, had turned into a slow-motion process of doing minor rewrites, approving art, seeing galleys, etcetera.

A couple of boxes of the Sagard books showed up in the stable office, and Gary and I did a signing at a book fair, where they had a giant standup of Sagard that was almost as tall as I am and which I wish I had kept. Not sure what I would have done with it, but it would be cool to have it.

My actual first contact with the Sagard books in the wild was a very quiet affair. I found copies at a bookstore in Carmel. Not Thunderbird, where I spent so much time, but a smaller one in Carmel Plaza. There it was, on the shelf with everything else. It was just another book. It was a letdown. There was no endcap or display. There were three copies of *The Ice Dragon* and *The Green Hydra* sitting in the shelf spine out. They seemed so lost and forgotten. I showed them to my mother and then turned them face out. It was kind of a lonely and pathetic feeling.

Sagard was a quiet release. In fact, the whole thing was quiet. The sales weren't actually bad, but so much had changed since the summer before that there wouldn't have been any more than the first four in any case. By the time the Sagard books came out, Lorraine and Gary were at war and relations between Gary and I were strained, and my career in novels was moving forward with Dave Marconi on *Agent 13*.

For me, the Sagard books were incredibly important. They taught me to write like a pulp writer, spinning prose nearly as quickly as I could think. And that's not a bad way to write. Larry Greene, a rhetoric professor of mine at Berkeley, had told me papers that were written the night before they were due were often just as good as papers that people labored over. And he was right. When you're writing fast, your writing tracks your thinking.

Having a book with your name on it is a great feeling, different than having a show with your name on it. It's tangible. It's right there. They've aged a little bit on the shelf, but they're still there, and they're mine and Gary's (and Ernie's and Luke's).

I was juggling *Inhumanoids*, *Transformers*, and another show—possibly the most obscure thing I've ever worked on—called *Bigfoot and the Muscle Machines*. That one was so obscure that I don't even remember when I wrote it, other than it also premiered on *Super Sunday* along with *Inhumanoids*, *Robotix*, and *Jem*. *Transformers: The Movie* was still rolling through production, and we were flying high.

And, if all of this wasn't enough, Dave Marconi and I were barreling along on *Agent 13*.

The Birth of Video-Game Narrative

Destroyer of Worlds

I WOULDN'T WRITE OR design any video games until the period after this book, but given where the next phase of my career went, I can't not land a glancing blow on the issue. It's the elephant or moose or pick your animal in the room.

Even with the earliest video games, I'd superimpose narrative onto a bunch of raster screen asteroids and a triangular ship with a couple different kinds of UFOs firing white plasma torpedoes at me. I couldn't have imagined in the early eighties that I'd spend decades working on different narratives on games and giving meaning to math, but given a few cues, some garish art, and a handful of sound effects, I couldn't help but try to answer the question that all gamers eventually ask:

"Why am I doing this?"

Sometimes I'd think, "I'm the last hope for the solar system—or galaxy or cosmos or whatever—and if I survive, I win." Every level had three acts. "The Call to Adventure" was the deployment of ships. "The Ordinary World" was introduced by a low bass heartbeat and giant asteroids rolling out. "The Road of Trials" began as you started shooting and the giant asteroids turned into smaller and faster asteroids that would whiz across the screen, forcing you to avoid either hitting them or being hit by them. That was death. You got three deaths unless you earned extra ships. The second act was introduced by large, highly inaccurate UFOs that flew out and shot at you. Just often enough, they killed you. Then the third act began, when the small ships came out all fast and deadly. You had to clear the screen fast. Too many asteroids and small ships, and you were dead. Then came the Confrontation. At this point, there was a moral choice to be made. Did you "lurk," or did you fight organically? Did you destroy the last asteroid and start a new level, or did you have a series of shootouts?

Though, looking back, I'd put a very different narrative on *Asteroids*. I was a destroyer of worlds. The innocents I wiped out were sending out their best defenders, and I ruthlessly mowed them down before heading off to destroy bigger and bigger worlds.

But that's just my version of it.

Pros could play for hours, but it always ended somehow. It would be fascinating to know, and this is unknowable, whether there has been a minute on Earth since that time when nobody was shooting asteroids.

The greater thing was the immortality. If you got into the top ten, you got to put your initials on the wall. They would stay there until better players pushed you off or somebody unplugged the machine. *Asteroids* is primitive, but I defy anybody to name a simpler, better-designed game.

It ate a lot of quarters.

As *Asteroids* morphed into *Galaxians*, *Galaga*, *Starcastle*, *Pac-Man*, and a thousand other things, video games came into the home. I remember Gary Gygax showing me a prerelease version of the *Dungeons & Dragons* Intellivision game. It would seem hopelessly primitive now, but at the time this was a huge step up from text adventures and crude exploration games. Who knew it would spawn *World of Warcraft*, arguably the most successful entertainment product in history?

And the magic infected our music. Synthesizers had been out for a while, sure. In fact, the first time I'd noticed them was Wendy Carlos's soundtrack for *A Clockwork Orange*, and then I'd listen to an endless amount of Emerson, Lake & Palmer, and Yes in the seventies, but those synths were really just a different riff on classical instruments. They went mainstream in the eighties, though, and suddenly everything seemed to bounce with the weird beats and rhythms of something from an arcade. In fact, I look at eighties music as a partial product of arcade games. It was all of the same flesh.

Our cartoon shows rolled out in the MTV era. Video games set the pace and music videos changed mood. A combination of increasingly mobile cameras, telegenic stars ("Video Killed the Radio Star"), high energy, low budgets, and a whole new wave of filmmakers came out of the frenetic, dream-like world of MTV.

Videos played in the ambient background of our world. They were everywhere—in gyms, in restaurants, in bars, in stores. The music industry was killing it with arena rock, hair bands, and an endless array of new stars as the classic rockers slid into middle age and disco was swallowed whole by a new style.

There were other new things happening in that period. Cable television and syndication came rolling in. That meant an endless number of channels and a desperate need for programming. A lot of it wasn't good. When Bruce Springsteen wrote "57 Channels and Nothin' On," nobody had any problem understanding what he was talking about.

Quantity wasn't quality.

The vast emptiness of endless cable TV channels created a form of media consumption called "video surfing." The remote was more an interactive device than a convenience tool. Your night of entertainment wasn't about making an appointment to watch a TV show; it was about whatever assembled itself semi-randomly as you flicked through channels.

Old movies, infomercials, foreign shows, music videos, and news snippets all added up to a somewhat tedious but entertaining experience. In Transformers terms, it turned us all into Junkions. But every once in a while, you'd discover something new and unexpected. It could be anything from some anime film running for no apparent reason to a particularly compelling guy on cable access. Things that had absolutely no relation to each other juxtaposed in such a way as to imply connections that in no way really existed. Culture became fragmentary. And somehow our brains were trying to assemble a narrative. Looking back, it was all prep for the Internet, but nobody was talking about an Internet at the time.

Also, televisions got BIG in the eighties. Big-screen TVs had been around for a while, but these were a whole new animal. Once again, bigness didn't mean quality, but cable meant no more static, rolling screens, or interference. The words "home theater" pretty much summed it up and spelled trouble for the actual theaters popping up in malls everywhere.

TF: The Movie
Production/Post-Production

DIFFERENT FILMMAKERS VARY IN their opinions on which segment of rewriting is more important. Some like to start with a pristine script and doggedly shoot it; others start with a loose script and encourage improvisation; others shoot endless alts and puzzle it together in post. There's no right way of doing it. If there were, everybody would be doing it that way.

The rewriting in production of an animated project mostly happens during storyboard and voice recording. Usually, storyboarding comes before recording, but there are no laws about this. Sometimes the film kind of grows up organically together with a lot of retakes. Sometimes an actor delivers such a transformative performance that the entire film changes (think Robin Williams in *Aladdin*).

The movie you have in your head when you're writing is very different than the one that appears in a storyboard processed through somebody else's vision. That has to be reconciled. You realize things when you see the script visualized. In the case of *Transformers*, sometimes the size of the characters is utterly different than what you saw in your head. Sometimes characters have dropped out of the story, and you have to decide whether to put them back in or dial them further back. Sometimes the visuals convey things you didn't expect and the dialogue isn't necessary. In a standard episode, I tended to over-explain, knowing I could take the dialogue out. A movie is such a massive effort that there's little chance anything will slip by. And, of course, sometimes additional dialogue is needed to explain the visuals. The point is that story editing is in some ways very much like game design: the filmmakers make a series of meaningful choices.

Animated movies usually start with an animatic, which is sometimes called a leica reel. The directors and producers will put in scratch track dialogue—which is them reading the lines more for timing than dramatic purposes. And then as production grows, newer and newer elements are laid on top of the assembly reel. First, there are animation tests, then real voices, then fully animated scenes, then rough music tracks, then songs (which differ from the dramatic music tracks), then sound effects, then processed voice tracks, until finally every scene is animated and scored and sound effected and the dialogue is all in.

In live action, most directors get a "master" and then go in for coverage shots and close-ups so that when they are editing, they'll have a number of ways to put together the puzzle of the film. It doesn't work that way in animation. Very little extra footage is shot. It's expensive and wasteful, so picture editing is minimal.

The animatic is the first time the filmmakers get a chance to see how the film will play. Is it too fast? Too slow? Can you follow the story visually? As animation by its very nature is highly planned and the goal is not to waste animated footage, there is rarely much choice as to what scenes to use in post-production. Animation doesn't shoot coverage like live action. A probably apocryphal story about Jeffrey Katzenberg watching *The Little Mermaid* illustrates this. Eventually he asked, "Do you have another angle on this?" In animation, there are no other angles.[11]

There is an opportunity to add sequences and scenes if they're necessary, so the process isn't as rigid as it might seem. It is a different process. And for the record, of course, Jeffrey Katzenberg was a very fast learner and went on to have a string of hits rarely seen in Hollywood.

In order to explain what post-production on *Transformers: The Movie* felt like to me, it's necessary to talk about how animation production works—or how it worked in the eighties.

As production goes on, you write the "music cues" to somehow compare or contrast to the emotion of the scene. Sometimes whole songs are inserted ("The Touch," "Dare to Be Stupid") and they define the scene and even the movie itself. Sometimes you call music "stings" to highlight the mood. For instance, an ordinary scene of the Autobots rolling down the road feels very different when a menacing music cue goes over it. You're waiting for the attack. Sometimes the right music cue makes dialogue unnecessary. Point is, usually you want to go with the images, but sometimes you want to work against the images.

Then you really go into post. As I say this, note that there are about a hundred asterisks to what I'm about to say, and the "friction" of production ensures that not everything happens when and how it is supposed to, but at some point, the picture has to be "locked" and the whole thing viewed in its entirety.

You have a "rough cut" of the whole film, but now there are a whole new set of issues. Is the story clear? Does it flow? Somebody along the way

---

11   Storyboards, which are part of production, contain extra shots and scenes, but excess is usually cut out in storyboard so that it isn't animated. Thirty years after the movie, somebody found a copy of the "final" storyboard and asked me to write dialogue and scene descriptions for the unused scenes—it was a fight with Devastator at the Autobot Fortress. Not only was this flattering, but it might be the beginning of a new genre of animating left-out scenes long after the movie has been released. In the eighties, finished was final. In the second decade of the second millennium, nothing is ever final.

told me that there's only one question pros ask, and that is, "Does it work?" When you're in post-production, it is all about solving problems. In fact, every phase is about solving problems. From the first day, *Transformers: The Movie* was about introducing a whole new line of toys while "discontinuing" the old toys.

At some point, you have everything: picture, music, SFX, and dialogue. Now you have to decide how to mix them. Do you bury the dialogue under the sound effects? Do you bury the sound effects under the music? What is most important? What tells the story best?

It's a fascinating process.

The thing that struck me about the soundtrack, watching it for the twentieth anniversary DVD edition, was how wonderfully eighties the soundtrack was. The Stan Bush and Vince DiCola songs, especially, took me back decades to Arena Rock, "you can do it" aspirational power ballads, and what I consider to be the last purely fun decade. The sheer guts of putting Al Yankovic's "Dare to Be Stupid" in there and the optimized *Transformers* theme define a moment in time better than any other soundtrack I can think of (I understand that many will disagree).

1. "The Touch" (Performed by Stan Bush) (Produced by Richie Wise)
2. "Instruments of Destruction" (Performed by N.R.G.) (Produced by Ernie Burns)
3. "Death of Optimus Prime" (Performed by Vince DiCola) (Produced by Vince DiCola and Ed Fruge)
4. "Dare" (Performed by Stan Bush) (Produced by Vince DiCola and Richie Wise)
5. "Nothin's Gonna Stand in Our Way" (Performed by Spectre General) (Produced by Randy Bishop with Spencer Proffer for Pasha)
6. "The Transformers (Theme)" (Performed by Lion) (Produced by Richie Wise)
7. "Escape" (Performed by Vince DiCola) (Produced by Vince DiCola and Ed Fruge)
8. "Hunger" (Performed by Spectre General) (Produced by Spencer Proffer for Pasha)

9. "Autobot/Decepticon Battle" (Performed by Vince DiCola) (Produced by Vince DiCola and Ed Fruge)

10. "Dare to Be Stupid" (Performed by "Weird Al" Yankovic) (Produced by Rick Derringer)

Of course, during production, we'd get cassettes of tracks they were interested in. "The Touch" was almost used in a Sylvester Stallone movie called, ironically, *Cobra*, but it wasn't, so Sunbow snapped it up. We loved it. We didn't know why, but we knew it would work.

The movie version of the *Transformers* theme playing side by side with the TV show theme is a great exercise in musicology of that era.

Spring 1986

ONE DAY I MET A girl coming up the stairs with short-cut, fiery red hair. I think she was coming to have lunch with Marty Pasko's girlfriend, Becky, but I might have that wrong. Her name was Linda Woolverton. Everybody said she was a great animation writer. Whatever she was, she was certainly interesting. I kept trying to figure out ways to actually meet her.

Our first "date" started at an *Inhumanoids* editing session. Linda, for her part, might have been an animation writer, but that didn't mean she wanted to hang around with a bunch of geeks. It just wasn't her thing. When I'd met Linda, she had a red buzz cut, but now her hair was growing out. She reminded me of Ripley from *Aliens*. When her hair grew out, she became more Diana Rigg as Emma Peel, with intense blue eyes. She was especially Emma Peel in her red convertible sports car. She had whippet energy and never seemed to get tired.

Linda would tell you she had a damaged childhood, and she's even written a book about it called *Running Before the Wind*. And maybe she was damaged, but she never played damaged. There was nothing self-destructive about her. The other thing was, and this mattered, that she was mega-talented. Nobody disagreed on that point. We might not have known that she would end up the highest-grossing woman writer in the history of the WGA—we couldn't have—but while all of us had our own set of magic skills, everybody sort of knew that she was probably the best writer. Or, at a minimum, none of us were better, let me put it that way.

And she had another hidden advantage: she walked into geek world with her own sophistication. She'd worked at CBS and knew exactly how the networks worked. She'd also been an actor in college and part of the theater group.

Linda always chided me about not writing from the heart. And she had a point. It's never really been my intention to touch people's emotions, and when I've actually found myself in a position where I had to, it's always felt weird—like I then had to go somewhere way over the top just to even out. She claimed that her secret was heart, but she was about a lot more than that. She had a Stephen King quote from *It* printed on her wall, and she had a habit of blindsiding you with plot surprises. You should have seen them coming, but you didn't. Go ahead and watch *Beauty and the Beast, The Lion King,* or *Maleficent* and see for yourself.

Watching her write was an entertainment experience all its own. She'd be working away, laughing at stuff, sometimes tearing and sort of unable to explain what she was laughing about, which was okay. It hit the page. She's one of those writers who hits the page. If it doesn't hit the page, it doesn't matter how good you are, just like it doesn't really matter how good you look in practice.

And this is the lesson for writers and would-be writers. Where do you write from?

Not that I can answer the question. I'm still not sure where I write from. Sometimes from my brain, sometimes from my biceps, now and then from my gut, but rarely from my heart. It's just not the organ that interests me.

Chris Latta (Collins)

Summer 1986

THE ALARM SOUNDS. PEOPLE are running. It's my chance to escape. Wait. I'm not in prison. The bell is my phone. I run my hand across a stack of paperbacks, trying not to knock over a coffee cup or a Coke can on whatever table I had next to my bed, reaching for the phone. The digital alarm clock from the seventies that has little leaves that flip down on a cylinder says it's 3:00 a.m. I pick up the phone. Starscream is on the line. He's in the North Hollywood clink and needs me to bail him out. Or maybe it's Cobra Commander in his other guise as Chris Latta. He's done something bad and has to be bailed out. Same drill as last time, except a different place. Last time it was the regular Hollywood station. Same price. $1,250.

Rolling through my mind was, "Why is he calling me? In what universe am I the adult you call when you're in trouble?" Maybe it was because he knew I needed him at a recording session, but more likely it was because he pegged me as a guy who a) was stable enough to have a working checking account and/or credit card, and b) I'd come get him and not make an issue out of it. In short, maybe I was kind of a dupe. And perhaps this is significant or even proves that point, but he was the third person that summer I bailed out of jail. It was a big summer for that.

I hit the floor and pull on whatever is nearest in the closet. It'll hurt too much if I turn on the light, so I won't know for a while what I'm wearing. I throw water on my face, brush teeth, spray deodorant, put on my ubiquitous sports coat, microwave yesterday's coffee, and get my checkbook. The checkbook is mission essential. The pokey takes checks. Who's going to write a bad check to the LAPD? I get into the Mustang convertible feeling like a cheap detective, check the Thomas Brothers map (car GPS only existed in James Bond movies), and soon I'm rolling into the night.

So what happened next?

It was 3:00 a.m. in North Hollywood or Van Nuys and the jail looked exactly like it did on all of the TV shows of the period, and the police weren't really forthcoming about what he was in for, which was fine. It didn't matter to me. It was the same $1,250. Chris eventually turned up rumpled with a big smile on his face. He had a removable front tooth. Sometimes it would be in, sometimes it wouldn't. We went to breakfast. One of the times, we just hung out until the recording session, which probably started at ten or eleven. I just remember killing a lot of hours in a diner near Wally's. It might have been the Coral Tree on Burbank Blvd. Or it might have been somewhere on Hollywood Way. Whatever it was, it was open all night. I don't remember what we talked about, but Chris wasn't a hard guy to spend a few hours with once you got past the heightened sense of paranoia and rage.

He would have me believe the problem was jaywalking. "In New York, nobody pays any attention to jaywalking. What the f#*& kind of city is this? Jaywalking, indeed."

Maybe it *was* jaywalking. I'll never know.

My price for the bail service was that he had to do the extended version of his "heroin enthusiast" routine. He had this great riff. I hope to hell it's found its way to YouTube or somewhere. The memorable lines to me were, "I am not a junkie, I am a heroin enthusiast. People say we don't work, but you try carrying two TVs down a fire escape and tell me that isn't work…" And so on.

Chris would invite Doug and I down to the Belly Room at the Comedy Store or wherever he was doing stand-up. I'd go one time in three and make sure I clapped when he was introduced, because his gag was that he made somebody in the audience who hadn't clapped clap alone. He had that scary edge that some stand-ups have, where part of the fun of watching them was the fear that you'd get called out. Didn't happen to me. I stayed near the back, in the shadows.

Chris brought a whole energy with him. Seeing Chris and Frank Welker, who was to voice acting what Jimi Hendrix was to guitar, was worth the price of admission. Absolutely opposite characters. Frank is the consummate pro and can do anything. Chris was a chaotic force of nature who could only do Chris. Okay, he also played Sparkplug Witwicky, Wheeljack, Gung-Ho, and a host of other characters, but to me he'll always be D'Compose, Cobra Commander, or Starscream.

The other voice actors all had their stories about him, too. He was frantic and he sweated a lot. Some think it was drugs. For somebody who went to Berkeley and worked in Hollywood, I was pretty naïve about that stuff. Still am. So they have their stories, and I won't step on them, but ask Michael Bell about him sometime, or Peter Cullen, Neil Ross, or Gregg Berger. They're voice actors, and they tell the stories better than I do.

If I had to pick somebody who gave the unique flavor to Sunbow shows, it would be Chris Latta (his name is also Chris Collins, I just always knew him as Chris Latta). I saw Chris several times after the Sunbow days on various voice things, but the time I'll never forget was the time he showed up at my house unannounced with several thousand dollars to pay me back for various bail bonds. I hadn't billed Sunbow for the money and just figured it was some kind of a contribution. In those days, I had plenty of money and not a lot of expenses, so it was easy to just ignore.

Apparently, he was going through AA, and one of his steps was to atone and pay his bills. Linda Woolverton was at my place that afternoon. Chris came through the door, and he was different. Clean shaven. I don't think he was wearing black leather. One micrometer under his skin, you could see the manic, but he was different. He was in a program, turning his life around. Chris walked us through how he'd never been around sober behavior in his life. His family were drunks. His uncle was a drunk. Everybody they knew was a drunk. Everybody he worked with was on something. (Not the Sunbow voice actors, but at the comedy clubs.)

When he left, Linda was zooed. "That's the most intense person I've ever met in my life."

The last time I worked with Chris, it was doing voiceover for a trailer for Republic Pictures on a project we were doing to revoice and reedit their serials into a series. It didn't go anywhere, but it was a cool idea that Buzz Dixon and I came up with. It was one of those ideas that had one huge fan at late night TV, and he was fired before we could present it.

Almost a decade after I met Chris, Carole Weitzman called to tell me he was dead. Neither she, nor anybody else, had an explanation or a solid story as to how or why he'd died. There was a lot of speculation, but in the end, it doesn't matter. Raymond Chandler was right: "What did it matter where you lay once you were dead? In a dirty sump or in a marble tower on the top of a high hill? You were dead, you were sleeping the big sleep, you were not bothered by things like that."

Thief in the Night, Blow-Up Over Carbombya, and Other Controversies
Spring/Summer 1986

BACK TO TRANSFORMERS.

Along came an episode called "Thief in the Night." The episode was written by Paul Davids. I don't remember who came up with the name "Carbombya." It sounds like a Buzz name, but it might have been one of mine. In any case, Casey Kasem didn't think the references to Abdul Fakkadi and Carbombya were funny.

Casey Kasem voiced Mark in *Battle of the Planets* and several *Transformers* characters: Bluestreak, Cliffjumper, Teletraan I, and Dr. Arkeville. He left *Transformers* during the third season due to what he perceived as offensive caricatures of Arabs and Arab countries. In a 1990 article, he explained:

"A few years ago, I was doing one of the voices in the TV cartoon series *Transformers*. One week, the script featured an evil character named Abdul, King of Carbombya. He was like all the other cartoon Arabs. I asked the director, 'Are there any good Arabs in this script for balance?' We looked. There was one other—but he was no different than Abdul. So I told the show's director that, in good conscience, I couldn't be a part of that show."

I don't think Paul Davids or anybody else was intentionally trying to offend Arab Americans. Abdul Fakkadi was a very thinly disguised reference to Muammar Kaddafi.[12] We didn't know, nor honestly care, that Abdul was an Arab name and not a Libyan name.

In the real world, the US had a very hostile relationship with Mr. Kaddafi, who was deemed responsible for various terrorist attacks including a disco in Germany, TWA Flight 847, and the Line of Death controversy, which "A Thief in the Night" was sort of a reference to. As for the name Carbombya, car bombs were a daily occurrence in the mid-eighties, and we have to remember that this was during the ongoing energy crisis and while America was still smarting over the Iran Hostage Crisis.

I don't remember the recording session or any particular problem at the time. What I do remember is that Casey Kasem complained about it to Sunbow (Tom Griffin and Joe Bacal). I vaguely remember seeing a letter, which complained that the name Abdul was offensive. Joe and Tom didn't scold anybody and didn't seem to care.

Apparently Casey Kasem left the show in 1986, but by that point, I was only sporadically going to the sessions because I was focused on *Inhumanoids, Visionaries,* and *Muscle Machines.* There's all the potential in the world to analyze this in terms of Arab-American relations. You've heard the story, come to your own conclusions. But remember the context.

The only anecdote I remember about Casey Kasem was sitting with him in Wally Burr's green room, just the two of us. I was trying to make conversation, and my only real reference to him was a top-forty countdown show he'd done forever ago called American Top 40. For those who don't remember the show, Kasem told stories and interesting anecdotes about all of the bands on that week's top forty before playing the songs. American Top 40 had gone on as long as I could remember, and though I don't ever remember turning it on, it was always playing at car washes, shopping centers, burger joints, etc. It was a great piece of Americana from my high school world, and it felt good.

So I went ahead and asked him something about rock and roll, to which he gruffly replied, "I don't like rock and roll" before going back to whatever he was reading. It was one of those moments, like when you realize as a kid

---

12   There are about a million ways to spell Kaddafi, so I picked the one that most obviously transposes to Fakkadi.

that you probably care more about the outcome of a mid-season baseball game than the players do.

When a fan pointed out that I'd worked with him again on the video game *Scooby-Doo Unmasked*, I thought it was possible. Amazon says that along with Adam West, the Scooby-Doo cast appeared on the game. Wikipedia, however, says that Scott Innes played Shaggy. So I guess I never did work with Casey Kasem again.

GEN CON Revelation
1986

I WAS STANDING IN a small line, waiting to get up to a dealer's table at Gen Con. I don't remember which one. There were two guys in front of me talking about a space battle. Maybe it was from Star Frontiers. The way they talked about it, it was like they were there. It was as real and present as if they were talking about some football game they'd actually played in.

The memories were that real and crisp.

And they weren't talking about die rolls or anything in a rules-based system—they were talking about a desperate battle where they were swash-buckling ship invaders while trying to shoot enemies who were attacking from outside.

The point is, it was a shared experience and it existed only in their imaginations, and later it probably *was* as real as if it had happened. I believe that to this day. What you remember from an experience is as important, and probably as real, as the experience itself.

And, while we're at it, let's not forget childhood imprinting.

Now, return to that scene in Sunbow with Frank and Steve. There we were, dead center of the eighties. Frank and Steve had come from a medium that had gone on pretty much the same way since it started sometime around World War II, when some guy figured out that you could fold and staple newsprint a different way and have a whole new medium.

Frank didn't know it, but he was busy transforming a stagnant medium as well as a stagnant character. Batman hadn't had an upgrade since the Adam West show in the sixties. That having been said, it would be almost impossible to overstate the importance of that show and the strange surreal shockwave it sent out. I was just a kid—young enough not to get the humor, but old enough to know that there was humor in it that I didn't get. I tried to take it seriously, until that broke, but if you go back to the night when Frank Gorshin appeared as the Riddler and Jill St. John was meeting a horrible fate and Commissioner Gordon was calling Batman—it was a moment that would torque the television world around.

The world didn't know what hit it. Some people thought it was the "camp," some people thought it was psychedelia, but whatever it was, it served as a kind of precursor to what would happen later with *Star Wars* on an epic sale, in that everything became a reaction to it. *The Man from U.N.C.L.E.*, which began as a reaction to James Bond, became camp for a couple sorry seasons. Everybody was going camp. Movies like *Yellow Submarine* and Peter Max drawings would go mainstream. A guy named Stanley Ralph Ross, who was a writer on both *Batman* and *The Monkees* (and the first person I met when I arrived in Hollywood), would later be a voice actor and writer for us at Sunbow on *G.I. Joe* and *Inhumanoids*. And make no mistake, the DNA for what we did in the eighties is found in sixties TV.

Remember the Jack Kirby joke? About how the golden age of comics is twelve? Never underestimate the power of childhood imprinting. It is very hard to get past the thrills and intrigues and fascinations of childhood in your adult work. It pays to have an engaged, vibrant childhood. It doesn't have to be a chaotic one with endless influences. Frank came from a small town in Vermont. Steve grew up in St. Louis, though everything about him screamed New York. But all of us reached back to things that impacted us when we were kids. Remember Frank and *The 300 Spartans*. Same thing with me and Davy Crockett dying at the Alamo. Same with the puzzle of "Why are adults laughing at *Batman*?" Steve Gerber and I never strayed far in our conversations from *The Prisoner* with Patrick McGoohan, and that could have only existed in a world of James Bond and Batman and the Beatles. It's no accident that "All You Need is Love" plays in the final episode.

And, of course, I was twelve the summer it came out.

Still, it's a great show no matter when you watch it.

And the following section is another "Belly of the Beast" journey into all of the imprinting that was almost invisible to me, save for one obvious thing that would subconsciously serve me to this day. The belly of the imprinting beast had a high point in summer or fall of 1986 (neither Paul Davids nor I can remember the date), when we visited The Ackermansion.

Paul Davids set it up at some *Transformers* recording session, and we took a field trip to this shrine of geekdom back in the days when "geek" was a bad word. I don't remember whether I was looking forward to it or if it was something I wanted to do, but I'm quite sure I had mixed emotions. Nevertheless, I knew it was important. If James Bond, *Batman, The Green Hornet*, and *The Prisoner* were my influences, these were the influences of the people who had created all of those things. It was like entering a necropolis of dreams from before my time.

Neither Forrest J. Ackerman nor geekdom were completely new to me, but this trip was a revelation. I'd first heard of Forrest J. Ackerman years earlier, when my father was researching a second volume of *The Collected Works of Buck Rogers*. Apparently Ray Bradbury, whom Dad had gotten to know when he wrote the introduction for the first edition of *The Collected Works of Buck Rogers*, had recommended that he contact "Forry," because Forry knew everything. As I was doing nothing with my life in my lost years out of college, I was helping Dad sift through the stuff for his book and came upon an envelope with two things in it. One was a copy of *Amazing Forrys* magazine, and the other was a letter saying that Forry did not give out information for free and that he was charging a hundred dollars an hour (or something, I don't remember the number) for consultation.

This puzzled me. I'd never heard of somebody charging money for telling old stories. I'd just never seen it before.[13] And I'd never seen a magazine that somebody had self-published to promote themselves. It

---

13   Yes. I am aware of the irony here.

kind of stunned me. I knew that there was once a magazine called *Amazing Stories*, but I had no idea who Forrest J. Ackerman was.

I commented on this to Ray Bradbury later on, to which he replied, "I think that's my fault. I just felt that Forry was giving too much away for free and that he ought to get paid for his work. He just kind of got carried away."

And it was true. I wasn't used to nerds in the sense that they are socially awkward, and it was really just the way he phrased it that I found off-putting. That was my problem, not Forrest J. Ackerman's problem. I just figured that anybody with an Ackermansion didn't need money. I had a lot to learn about how the world really works.

So here I am, five years later, and what had looked weird to me in 1980 doesn't look weird to me in 1985 while knee-deep in geek world, when I'm producing *Transformers* and *G.I. Joe* and TSR is owned by my family. TSR now owns *Amazing Stories,* and Steven Spielberg is making a TV show out of it. I am fully aware of money, and I'm fully aware of Forrest J. Ackerman's position at the leading edge of what we would now call "fandom." This guy was way out ahead of everybody, and the "garbage" in his Ackermansion was pure gold.

My recollection is that the Ackermansion, which was only sort of a mansion, was just rooms and rooms and rooms of old pulps, movie props, books, comics, and framed art that Forrest J. Ackerman had collected over a lifetime. My biggest impression was that one stray match or an LA wildfire could wipe it all out. I had fantasies about underground salt mines with climate control while I was there. I remember keeping an eye out for fire escapes. (It never burned down, by the way.) At a deeper level, the Ackermansion was a museum of stuff that was considered mostly crap and refuse when it was made. A Louvre of disposable pop culture.

Forry[14] was aware of me, vaguely, for the shows I was doing, but there's no reason they would mean much to him, because his mind was back in the Golden Age, and that's a good place for his mind to be.

And, yeah, at that point, I'd had years of dealing with every form of nerd and geek imaginable and had probably become one myself without noticing it. The whole fact that I was looking at *Star Trek* props and Maria

---

14   I use that name because that's how I was introduced to him. However, I only met him a couple of times, and I don't want to imply a closeness that didn't exist.

from *Metropolis* was not lost on me. And having grown up in a house full of antiques, I knew exactly how valuable this stuff would become.

Amazing what a few years can do.

I remember wondering what would happen to all of that stuff when he died. I remember thinking, and still think, that somebody should turn this into a real museum, because these old pulps and props and comics and posters really are the American treasures. This is our Louvre. Our Library of Alexandria. These comics, I'd argue, were what stimulated America's first Wonder of the World—the space program—in exactly the same way that Dante triggered the Renaissance.

Okay, maybe that's a bit overblown. But you take my point.

I, of course, did nothing about this instinct. I hear the stuff was all auctioned off after his death. It's my hope that it is sitting in some climate-controlled silo under the desert somewhere, waiting for the day that a proper museum is built. But that is probably pure fantasy.

The point is that Forry Ackerman and Ray Bradbury and a few others were my link to that bold and exciting time before mass geekdom, when people actually thought about thrilling new futures and anything was not only possible but probable. It was a world of Esperanto and starry-eyed modernism when modernism made a lot of sense, a world where some of the most brilliant and visionary authors the world would ever produce released their work in much maligned pulp magazines. We're talking Asimov, Heinlein, and on and on and on. Pure genius disguised as worthless pulp with gaudy covers (which were also some of the best and least recognized art America has ever produced).

I'm reminded of Charles Champlin's column, which predicted that *Annie Hall* would beat out *Star Wars* for the Academy Award under the reasoning that "America hates what it does best." Hopefully somebody will do a streaming series about the wonder of those old pre-geek times. Also, see Paul Davids's *The Sci-Fi Boys*, shot when Ray Bradbury, Forrest J. Ackerman, and Ray Harryhausen were still with us. It will open a whole world for you.

I knew it just wasn't in my range to become a superfan. I just don't have the attention span. I wasn't like my friend Gregg LaPore, who in high school would endlessly read sci-fi novels and listen to reel-to-reel audio recordings of *Star Trek* episodes while drinking lukewarm ice tea that came from a glass jar and smoking his pipe. A part of me thought it would be cool to be like that, but there are things that you are and things that you aren't. That having been said, it was Gregg who got me started with writing. He was working on a novel, and so I decided I'd try my hand at it.

But for science fiction and fantasy, yeah, I'd read the big stuff: *The Lord of the Rings*, *Dune*, *Starship Troopers*, everything by Bradbury, and some obscure stuff that fell down the chimney, but there was nothing encyclopedic about me. Nothing voracious. It was high school, and I was busier badly playing bass guitar and making Super-8 films.

And this gets to something that's strangely personal, but it's relevant, and that's that in Geek world—especially for Forrest J. Ackerman's generation—I'm royalty via my grandfather and Buck Rogers. This is a very weird position to be in. It comes with this sense of illegitimacy. Whatever my grandfather did, I didn't do it. I've met various people who are real royalty. It happens in Hollywood now and again. The guy in the strange suit at a dinner party is really a Count or something. And my reaction is eighty percent "So what?" and twenty percent "Hmmm, this is kind of interesting." Royalty, which is dependent, by definition, on bloodline, brings with it a sense of illegitimacy.

And the other irony in all of this is that at exactly that moment, I was out there doing pretty much what my grandfather was doing, but more than fifty years later. You think about this and it goes ouroboros fast. So I didn't think too much about it, but like everything that's intrinsic to yourself, it's something to factor in when the world starts treating you weirdly. You're a lot of different things to different people. But what does royalty do, other than create a lot of awkward conversations?

It's like a backstage pass. And like real backstage passes, sometimes it works, and sometimes it doesn't, and you find yourself in exciting places and in places you which you don't really belong. By the time I found myself in the Ackermansion, I was deep into what alternate reality games call a "rabbit hole," in reference to *Alice in Wonderland*. You go into a rabbit hole and you're in a whole new world. If you're even reading this, you're in a rabbit hole and may not know it. You've already met the White Rabbit and fallen into some hole or maybe multiple holes, at a minimum.

The first question is how important it is to you to be able to see the light from the outside world. It's like the underground catacombs in Paris. People have elaborate maps, and there are markings all over the walls in cryptic languages. You're in there, and you hope to hell your guide knows what to do. The concept of being lost in a necropolis is horrifying. You get too lost and it's about running out of food and wandering endlessly and trying to remember the rule about always following the right-hand wall.

Or is it the left-hand wall?

Some people take up residence in rabbit holes. They're some of the happiest and weirdest people I know.

Once I was in Fiji, and our cruise boat (a small scow—don't think floating Iowa) had a side trip to explore some caves. We didn't have scuba equipment. This was a network of caves right next to the shore. You swam under a low rock wall and moved from cave to cave. The guides had flashlights. The farther in we went, the less we could see the comforting blue light of the real ocean. Finally, by cavern three or four, we couldn't see it at all. That's when the thrill and paranoia started. What if the flashlight breaks? What if they play a trick on us? What if this is a black hole of lost tourists? In the rational light of day, that's all kind of silly, but in a dark underwater cave in Fiji, these are very rational thoughts.

I remember seeing one of the guides slapping the water in a strange way and wondering what he was doing. Was he placating some real or mythical sea creature with bulbous eyes, sharp teeth, and tentacles that was looking up at our feet, treading the water?

The fan rabbit hole is something like that. How deep do you go in? How much do you care about the light outside? At what point are you cut off from the skiff that's going to take you back to the real world?

And at the same time, the cave was cozy and comfortable. Maybe you could live there. Learn to catch shrimp or something.

That's how I think of the fan rabbit hole. I look at some people that show up at the cons with extreme haircuts and piercings and face tattoos, and I wonder what they're doing at 2:30 on a Tuesday afternoon. I think the same about people I see at concerts and in clubs. What does this look like in daylight? The important thing is that they're committed. They've created their own world, and they usually have friends that live in these worlds too. They're all the way in the rabbit hole and probably don't know or care about the way out. Maybe you never need to come out. A part of me fears their fate and a part of me envies them.

The Ackermansion was, almost literally, a rabbit hole—if rabbits built bookshelves, I mean. But it was a warren. We walked through room after room of movie props, comics, books, posters, and magazines. I remember being shocked to see all of the *Secret Agent X* original pulp print series collected on a top shelf with Operator #5 and The Spider. I wanted to ask to look at it but didn't. I was afraid I'd crack or bend something.

Forry Ackerman's place was rabbit hole grand junction. All of the subcultures seemed to meet in that one place. He was not only a collector, but also a creator and a scholar of popular culture—like some hoarder who then discovered that the newspapers really all did contain secret treasure maps and that the bottles he collected contained genies. It was pure gold.

Transformers: The Movie Premiere
August 8, 1986

TRANSFORMERS: THE MOVIE PREMIERED on August 8, 1986. It is one of the few dates in this book that I can pin down. That was a Friday. I have to guess then that our premier was either Wednesday or Thursday of that week. The big premier was probably in New York, but I remember one in LA. I believe it was at what is now the Landmark Regent Theatre, but it might have been at the Village. I might be confusing it with the *My Little Pony* premiere. As I said, memory is strange.

Some people call it a classic now, but it sure didn't feel like a classic at the time. At the premier, there was a guy sitting behind me cursing. The film would be going on and I'd hear "$#@$!!" every few minutes. I faked like I was looking for something or maybe like I was talking to my date, who was probably Linda, and got a look at the guy.

I didn't know him. I was thinking, "It's not great, but it's not *that* bad." I winced every time he cursed. Fortunately, it didn't seem to be in sync with the dialogue, so I figured he wasn't cursing the script. After the movie, I stood up and was trying to get out of my row without making eye contact.

Of course, the guy started speaking to me.

Turns out he was perfectly friendly. "Hey, Flint…I did the Dolby on the B-track (or something like that). Did you hear how messed up it was? Way out of phase! Screwed up the whole mix!"

Of course, I didn't notice the Dolby B (or whatever it was). It sounded fine to me. But I learned something there: everybody who works on a movie only sees their part of it. If the whole movie was, to me, from the script out, for him, it was the sound mix. And maybe that's the way it is supposed to be.

There is little objectivity in the universe.

I remember seeing a full-page ad in the *Los Angeles Times* and Jay calling to say that he'd seen it with a bunch of different audiences and particularly enjoyed the ones who were shouting at the screen at all the key moments, like, "Don't trust him! Look out!" as Megatron was going for his gun to kill Optimus.

And then it kind of passed.

I vaguely heard that Hasbro had been disappointed with the box office, but I was way too green to know where this would go. In reality, I was probably hunkered down doing what would be my final work on *Transformers* for a couple decades, and that was springboarding the season. At that point, we'd started thinking of the entire season as one long story. After *Inhumanoids*, everything was what I now call "arced episodic." Episodes might not cliff-hanger into each other, but there was a general sense of growth and continuity in the story. We had to be careful with this, and every episode had to be viewed as stand-alone, because in 1986 there was no assurance that some guy in a TV station in Wichita was going to air the episodes in the right order. So we couldn't change too much, but we did think in terms of sequence.

"Five Faces of Darkness" was both a kind of sequel to the movie and a five-part kickoff for season three. I'd probably written it in the late spring or early summer, but there was still plenty to be done. I was technically still a coproducer and story editor, and I'm sure I went to recordings and the like, but at that point there were a lot of different projects in every phase from pre-development to post, and life was a blur. I realize as I write this that so much overlapped because the development and production cycles were so long.

Not long after the movie came out, crisis struck. Crisis focuses things. The story was that some kid had locked himself in a bathroom and wouldn't come out for a week after he saw the movie. I think the kid in this urban legend lived in Michigan. And here's the bizarre thing: I believed that story. It wasn't until decades later, as a parent, that I realized how absurd this was. No parent is going to let their kid lock themselves in a bathroom for a night, much less a week. But I wasn't a parent at the time, so I bought the story hook, line, and sinker. Alarm bells went off. We had to fix this problem. We had to bring Optimus Prime back and bring him back new and shiny. Nobody wanted to tell Hasbro that we already had an episode in the pipes where Optimus came back as a zombie and was killed again. Eventually we glued "Dark Awakening" and "Return of Optimus Prime" together and everybody was happy. Or at least less unhappy.

After the crisis, things were never really the same. If I had to pick a moment that felt like the beginning of the end, it was the movie bombing and the bad reaction to the death of Optimus Prime. But there was a lot of other stuff going on, too, and I only knew some of it. I suspect the rest. At some corporate level, somebody had seen somebody stumble and was trying to take advantage of it. That's the way the world works. Ambitious people never want to let a crisis go to waste. I'm quite sure nobody really believed the kid in the bathroom story, but I'm equally sure that they saw an in. It's rarely the crisis that kills you—it's the chain reaction that the crisis sets off.

At any rate, rumors of kids locked in Michigan bathrooms aside, *Transformers: The Movie* underwhelmed at the box office. There isn't another way of putting it. It would become something of a cult classic, but that mostly means the general audience doesn't love it, though it has fanatical followers. I think that's a fair statement. In 2015, we packed the house at the Egyptian Theater in Hollywood with a screening of the movie. In 2016, I was at a TFCon in Toronto and there were probably three hundred people in the main room for a screening of *Transformers: The Movie*, and my impression was that they knew the movie better than I did. Of course, they didn't have memories of all of the versions of the movie that never actually got made. And there's a difference between the way the fans perceive the work and the way the writer perceives the work.

Why did it bomb? First off, the idea of TV shows becoming movies was relatively new. In the eighties, television was a decidedly lower medium than film. And in the realm of television, animation was the bottom rung. But more than that, people didn't want to pay for something they could get for free. Also, while Fandom (with a capital F) was beginning, it wasn't there yet. There was no Internet to turbo the movie, and marketing hadn't really figured out how to hype it. Also, in reality it was a "fan" movie. It was not accessible in the normal sense. We weren't doing what Michael Bay would do thirty years later and provide an introduction to *Transformers* in the form of what is now known as a reboot. We were doing a movie in a continuity, and if you were not well versed in *Transformers* lore, it is a very hard movie to understand. It was a movie done for a cult. And if that was the target, it hit its audience like a bullet. Hence, I'd argue that as a long-term brand-building movie, it was brilliant. However, as a short-term moneymaker, we probably shouldn't have made it. Sometimes the enemy is expectation.

From my office at Sunbow, I just saw it as a speed bump. My mind went back to the giant *G.I. Joe* aircraft carrier we used as a coffee table. The way it was explained to me, they didn't make the carrier to make a profit on it, they made it as a show of commitment to the property. At the time I kind of wondered why *G.I. Joe* needed a show of commitment; I figured that was some calculus way above my head, but inside I had the creepy feeling that maybe the sales numbers had slowed. But I didn't give it a lot of thought. Nor should I have. My job was to make the next episode the best episode I could make it.

So, at some level, we knew it wasn't good news that the movie had bombed, but I just saw it as a setback. Move on. Your team had a turnover. It happens. You have turnovers. Get back on the field. Stop the other team. Get the ball back. Get your own turnover. Score.

Looking back, the writing was on the wall. At the very least, we weren't going to be doing any more movies. Later, we'd learn that there was a serious cutback in shows ordered. There were vague rumblings about problems at corporate, but we were sheltered from this. What we weren't sheltered from were the repercussions of the death of Optimus Prime.

But before we get there, let's pull way back to the eighties context of *Transformers: The Movie*. In 1985, animated movies, outside of a few Disney releases, were a dead medium usually reserved for foreign art house releases, the occasional indie, and an occasional toy movie. And even with Disney, there had only been a slight bump with *Oliver and Company*. I remember Jay Bacal talking about how big the numbers were given that there was no discernible groundswell. But Disney was Disney, and they had cache in the "family" arena.

The Little Mermaid would come out in 1989 and really begin the roll of Disney animation as a dominant force in the movie industry, but that was still three years in the future. It doesn't seem like anybody in Hollywood saw what demographics called "the baby boom echo" (the children of the Baby Boomers) coming. It was about to hit feature animation like a hurricane, but not yet. In some ways, the success of toy lines in this period was a precursor. In those days, few mommies would take their sons to see a chaotic movie with giant robots blasting each other, even if they did turn a blind eye to their kids watching it on television. Violence in children's TV was still a very real issue, too. Being worn down by your kid in the TV room is one thing; heading out to a theater to see a movie you don't want to see and paying money is quite another.

So, though nobody explicitly said this, Hasbro could have had three motives for making a *Transformers* movie: 1) it might make money, 2) it shows commitment and belief in the toy line, and 3) more practically, it is a huge commercial for the 1986 toy line. It would serve as a showcase for a whole new line of characters at every price point.

And the key word here is "new." Remember, at its heart, Sunbow was an ad agency, and "new" is one of the two magic words in advertising ("free" is the other one). Hence, you have the introduction of Rodimus Prime, Kup, Ultra Magnus, Arcee (the first female transformer), Galvatron, the Sweeps, Unicron, Blurr, Wheelie, and a few others. On top of all of that, we had an incredible marquee: Orson Welles, Judd Nelson, Eric Idle, Leonard Nimoy.

And that's not to mention people who meant a lot to Mom and Dad: Robert Stack, Lionel Stander, and so on. You start adding all of this up, you've got a legitimate bet.

And something would really happen. Something shocking. As a matter of fact, a lot of shocking things. But there was a big one: Optimus Prime would die. So would Megatron (to be reborn), and so would Starscream. You talk about guts. In retrospect, we were going all in. At some point in the beginning of the process, we probably were cognizant of this, but somewhere around draft ten, we were over the shock.

I've talked elsewhere about writing the scene, but my larger sense of it is that if we hadn't killed Optimus Prime, *Transformers* would not be remembered now. I'd make the same argument for Sherlock Holmes's death on the Reichenbach Falls, J.R.'s death on *Dallas,* or James Bond's apparent death at the end of *From Russia, With Love.* (Everybody has forgotten about this, but at the end of the book, Bond collapses, having been kicked with Rosa Klebb's poisoned shoe knife. Allegedly, Ian Fleming intended to kill off James Bond until Raymond Chandler talked him out of it. It was an intentional cliff-hanger.)

The more I see *Transformers: The Movie,* the more I realize how brilliant Nelson Shin is. Nelson not only worked on the Pink Panther films (check out the opening titles), he also animated the lightsaber blades in the original *Star Wars.* Nelson is a genius with lighting and storytelling. In fact, he's one of those guys who's so brilliant that you don't even notice it until you really look at it. Take a look at the lighting in Prime's death scene. Who else in the history of film would have thought of showing a character was dead by having them turn to black and white? It was amazingly powerful. Most every other director would have had some power light go off and have somebody say, "He's dead." Nelson visualized what it was for life to leave a robotic entity in what might be the most scarring death scene of a generation. Tasteful. Almost mystical and brilliant. The same goes for the laser scenes and the surreal battle inside of Unicron. You stand back and look at it out of context, and it looks like an animation art exhibit.

I didn't know him well when we were doing the movie. He was in Korea most of the time, and I was in America, but he was always polite and gentle. At one point, he submitted his own version of the movie script, and it met the same fate as the version Jay and I did (*The Secret of Cybertron*). I vaguely remember seeing a fax that said, "Nothing?" Meaning, "You are using nothing in my script?"

My guess is that lots of Nelson's script made it into the movie, but that's not the point. The point is that it's simply not healthy for scripts to suddenly appear from nowhere. It is disruptive and chaotic. Tom Griffin and Joe Bacal were the producers, and they needed to control the process. In the end, all three of the "first scripts" for the movie were important, but none of them, in and of themselves, were seminal. And bear in mind, every draft had input from Tom, Joe, and Jay to begin with, and if somebody had to claim paternity of the film, it would be some combination of them. If you want to control a movie, TV show, or film, you have to control the script. Control the script, and you control the show.

Last time I actually saw Nelson was when we did the voiceover track for the twenty-fifth anniversary edition of *Transformers: The Movie*. He looked unchanged and looked at me and said, "You're still young…" thus earning a place in my heart forever. Sue Blu was there too. Sue is great. She's an actress and voice director, and always fun and interesting to talk with. I couldn't imagine any other voice for Arcee, the Wonder Woman of the TF universe and the only female Transformer character in the film.

Ixnay with the Lab Coat
C-SPAN Midterm Election Coverage
Fall 1986

November

THIS NEXT SECTION GETS to my point about how chaotic life is. At what was probably the same moment when the death of Optimus Prime crisis was being handled by the creative team, I flew back to Washington, DC, to appear on C-SPAN as a "researcher" from Aristotle Industries and hang out with some old friends. This story is set against real-life political events: the 1986 midterm election, which took place in the middle of Ronald Reagan's second term. I can't even remember what the issues were or who I was rooting for, if anybody, or what was going on. Huge events were coming—most of them good—but this seemed to me like a quiet period.

To put this in context, remember back to *Lounge Lizard*, the failed project I did with John and Dean Phillips in the spring of 1983. At this point in time, John and Dean Phillips were licking their wounds from John's second congressional run, which platformed off of his fifteen minutes of fame as "the A-Bomb Kid." I make a guest appearance in his book *Mushroom*, which detailed how he designed an atom bomb while flunking out of Princeton (he'd transferred from Berkeley in his junior year) and later ran for congress twice as a Democrat in Connecticut. After *Lounge Lizard*, they were starting up their own political software company, Aristotle Industries, based on software that Dean had written for John's campaign.

The software, Campaign Manager, took off from extremely humble beginnings. Three years later, by the election of 1986, they had a number of products, owned a magazine, and convinced Brian Lamb of C-SPAN to let them do the election night coverage. John called and asked if I wanted to come out and be an "election analyst" or whatever he was calling it, and frankly, not getting in on this ridiculous ride just wasn't an option.

I don't think any of us had any idea what we were doing, but combined, we had enough knowledge. This was the eighties, and the election team consisted of me, John, Dean, Patty, Wendy, and a couple other Aristotle Industries staffers. Patty and Wendy had been models, so they were naturals. I knew what I had to know about a camera and broadcast, Dean had the tech side covered, and John was the captain of this particular pirate ship.

We were issued Aristotle Industries lab coats and reported the results, looking very scientific. It was a midterm election. I can't remember which side won, but it didn't matter much to me.

The real story here is that Aristotle Industries is still going strong—a perfect blend of Dean's tech genius and John's flair for adventure. As I write this, they are booming with secure software for candidates in the wake of Wikileaks and Russian hack threats. They also manage campaigns in dubious countries, own either part or all of PredictIt, and still sell software to both parties at every level of government. I'd have to say that John and Dean (John and Patty later married) have been doing the same thing at the same company longer than anybody I know. That being said, Aristotle Industries is a great, endlessly morphing operation and to this day hasn't gotten boring.

Buck Rogers

MY BUCK ROGERS STORY takes a certain amount of personal setup and going back in time. Unlike any other project I've ever been involved with, Buck Rogers was neither a personal creation nor something I did for a company. I was born with Buck Rogers. To his credit, Buck Rogers opened some doors for me, but without blowing the analogy of a pay toilet out of proportion, nothing in life is free. Doors don't open for free. There's always a cost. But we'll get there.

Buck Rogers is nearly forgotten now, but in the 1980s, it had been a TV show on NBC for three seasons. It starred Gil Gerard and Erin Gray (I've since come to know both of them, and they're great folks), but it was time for what would today be called a reboot.

But that's not the real story here.

Buck Rogers is literally in my DNA. My grandfather was the "originator" of Buck Rogers, syndicated it and owned the rights. That's why you see John F. Dille Company on every panel. Guess what the "F" stands for? Then it would say National News Service or National Newspaper Syndicate. I have zero interest in getting into some debate over who created what. I wasn't there. I wouldn't be born for twenty-five years. I can tell you what I think happened and leave it at that. A couple paragraphs and we're out.

Phillip Francis Nowlan wrote a story called "Armageddon 2419" for *Amazing Stories* magazine. The cover of that issue has a guy in a jet pack on it. The "amazing" thing is that it had nothing to do with Buck Rogers—it was an illustration for another story. "Armageddon 2419" was a Rip Van Winkle story about a guy named Anthony Rogers who fell asleep in 2019 and woke up five hundred years later. It was set on Earth and involved various techno-tribal organizations rising up against their Han overlords in America. It had ray guns and backpacks, but what's most significant is what wasn't there. Buck Rogers has been known as a space hero, but Anthony Rogers never leaves Earth. There are no space ships, no bubble helmets, no Warlords of Mars, Venusians, or anything else space-related.

Somewhere in the transition from short story to comic strip, Anthony Rogers became Buck Rogers. There are various theories on where the name "Buck" came from. Some say he was named for my grandfather's dog.

After sophomore year of college, my summer job was to read through nearly fifty years of Buck Rogers and synopsize it. I sat in a dark, musty basement at the bottom of the Gotham City–esque building—20 North Wacker, Civic Opera Building, home of National Newspaper Syndicate— with a single light bulb hanging down. I'm not sure why I didn't haul the boxes up to the office, but it was kind of cool being deep underground and reading that stuff. Bingeing comic strips is kind of a hypnotic experience.

I developed a theory about what was my grandfather's. It is utterly scientifically indefensible, but the ways in which brains work are partially genetic—I think. There were certain ideas, inventions that seemed like something I'd think of. Just unique fingerprinty things. I guessed those were my grandfather's. By all accounts, my grandfather (JFD) was hands-on. Nowlan would die in 1939 of cirrhosis of the liver. My grandfather had hired Phillip Francis Nowlan to write it, but Nowlan missed deadlines and couldn't quite wrap his head around it.

While he syndicated numerous other comic strips and columns, Buck Rogers was his toy. He had very specific ideas about what he wanted it to be. If you read it, it's shockingly modern given that it comes from January 7, 1929. Women were emphasized (though there was to be no social message), and everything was supposed to be scientifically possible or probable.

This wasn't fantasy, it was science fiction. While this seems obvious to us, remember, this was 1929. It went on to be a hit.

There are a couple of amusing family stories from the period. One was that JFD had the second-highest income in Chicago in 1936. He loved cars and had a sixteen-cylinder Black Cadillac. One day, as he was fishing his car out of the parking garage, the attendant said, "Mr. Dille, take a look at this." He led JFD over to a car that was identical to his own. My grandfather probably said something like, "Yeah, that's my car," but however you would have said that in 1936.

Then the attendant showed him the back windows. The glass was two inches thick, bulletproof. The car belonged to the real richest guy in Chicago: Al Capone. After that, JFD kept the car in Evanston. You don't want to look like the guy who ordered the St. Valentine's Day Massacre, particularly if you don't have bulletproof glass.

The other celebrity story was that William Randolph Hearst (who also owned a Newspaper Syndicate) invited him out to San Simeon (a.k.a. Hearst Castle, a.k.a. Xanadu of Orson Welles' *Citizen Kane* fame). He went. Eventually, Hearst got to the point.

"I want to buy Buck Rogers."

My grandfather responded, "Anything else? That's my pet project."

"You realize I'm going to have to compete with you."

"At least you tried to buy it before you stole it."

Hearst hired Alex Raymond, and soon thereafter *Flash Gordon* was born. And, in fairness, *Flash Gordon* was different. It was science fantasy. Flash showed up on Robin Hood planets and was not bound by the known laws of physics.

JFD died in 1957, a couple months before I turned two years old. I have one, quite possibly manufactured, memory of him sitting in our living room. The only thing that makes me believe it was a real memory is I remember him in an "up" shot from the floor. He seemed like a grumpy old guy, but it was a big deal that he'd come over to the house. And in fairness, all old people seem kind of grumpy when you're two.

My first conscious memory of Buck Rogers was sitting on the floor in the den. I was probably around five years old, and the den was the room that had our only TV. It was Saturday morning, and I was probably playing with toy soldiers on the floor. WGN in Chicago ran old movies and serials opposite the network's Saturday morning fare.

Anyway, an old black-and-white serial came on. Spaceships zipped awkwardly across the screen with sparks trailing out of them, loud music played, and all of a sudden the room came alive with relatives telling me that this was *Buck Rogers* and that my grandfather had created it. The show looked old and goofy and fake to me, even at that age. I wasn't that interested. Maybe I suspected *Buck Rogers* would be a frenemy for the next several decades.

Buck Rogers was present in my house and at my dad's office at the Lyric Opera Building. There were big wooden rocket ships that I couldn't play with and old metal rocket guns that I also couldn't play with. I still have them, framed, and I don't play with them. There was a Buck Rogers solar system map, a standup in the Murphy Anderson style. With this kind of stuff imprinted in my brain at that age, it's not a big surprise that I had an intuitive knowledge of transmedia and franchises decades later.

Buck Rogers certainly didn't play a huge role in my early childhood; it was just kind of there. But it was responsible for a life-changing moment in 1966. We went to New York on a business/pleasure trip. We stayed at the New York Hilton. A couple years earlier, we'd been there and the place was surrounded by teenage girls, as the Beatles were allegedly staying there.

In summer 1966, the family traveled to New York City. ABC was interested in doing Buck Rogers as a TV show. My mother and sister went shopping, so Dad took me along on the meeting. I was eleven. A guy named Mr. Siegel was our executive. Two decades later I would know exactly what a network executive was, but then I could only guess. He had some elaborate theory that if Twiggy and Yellow Submarine went, Buck Rogers would go. I've puzzled over the logic of that ever since, but it kind of makes sense. You look at Twiggy on the cover of David Bowie's *Diamond Dogs* album and she looks like Wilma Deering, and the Yellow Submarine kind of looks like a Buck Rogers ship, but it doesn't matter what I think. The world was in the surreal, psychedelic Batman phase, and the network was very close to Madison Avenue circa Don Draper. In fact, Tom Griffin and Joe

Bacal were probably young ad executives in that period, but we wouldn't meet for a couple decades. Anyway, the sixties Twiggy/Yellow Submarine Batman show never happened, but what did happen was that when they wanted to park me somewhere so they could have real meetings, they sent me in to watch two of the new shows for that season: *The Green Hornet* and *The Time Tunnel*.

It had never occurred to me that you could watch a TV show on a big screen like a movie. It was the coolest thing that ever happened to me. They ran the pilots for both shows. A kid in a screening room watching the kickoff shows for the best night ever on television. If there are ten experiences that set my life in a direction, that was one of them. I wanted to get back into that room, though I had no idea how.

The other notable thing about that trip was that they were selling the James Bond paperbacks in the store in the lobby. I bought them one at a time. Still have them. I'm not sure I read them then—I was pretty dyslexic, and it would have been a fight—but I'd seen *Goldfinger* and *Thunderball,* so I'd been hooked on Bond from about age eight.

My next memory of Buck Rogers is coming back from Boy Scout camp and seeing years of comic strips and promotional materials and toys laid out on an enormous oriental rug in our living room. Dad was assembling the book that would eventually be called *The Collected Works of Buck Rogers in the 25th Century,* behind which he did a national book tour and appeared on *What's My Line?* and *The Johnny Carson Show.* There's some debate on the Internet whether he appeared on "ROBERT C. DILLE 01-14-1970" or "ROBERT C. DILLE 01-21-1970," but if I had to guess I'd say it was the latter, because it seems he was bumped one time. In any case, Alan King was the host. I remember watching it and having a sensation for the first time that I still have every time I see somebody I know on a major television show. It felt fake, like somebody had made a fake version of the show. I think that same thing when I see myself on videos.

The book did well, apparently, because it was reprinted numerous times in numerous formats. Dad signed one for me, but I can't find it. I'm hoping it's sitting in the same "Lost Ark" storage box that has the *The Secret of Cybertron* and *The Scepter of Seven Souls.* I'd also love to see the show. It may or may not exist. A friend of mine who is a Johnny Carson aficionado says that a lot of the episodes where he wasn't host just don't exist anymore.

Ray Bradbury wrote the book's introduction. He was a hardcore fan. In fact, if there was a moment I realized that "fans" existed, it was when I read his intro. Until then, I never knew that adults still thought about things that excited them when they were kids. I think I just figured that when people got done being kids, they forgot all about their childhoods and moved on. Of course, I'd heard of "nostalgia," but fandom didn't exist back then the way it does now.

My dad and Ray Bradbury became good friends. I was a huge fan. I'm not sure any book has influenced me more than *The Illustrated Man*. I wouldn't meet him then, but years later, while Dad and I were driving from LA to Chicago in a convertible Mustang, we had drinks and dinner with him and his wife, and I began to realize that while I couldn't aspire to being Ray Bradbury, it was possible to be a writer. I was a junior in college at the time, and Ray was extremely encouraging early in my career.

One object that did have a profound impact on me was a Warren Paper Company ad that featured comic panels of Buck Rogers alongside the real-world inventions inspired by the comic strip. It presented me with an idea that I've been processing ever since: the relationship between science fiction and real invention. Fascinating thing to think about. I'm quite sure that the iPhone wouldn't exist in its current form without the tricorder, and I believe that smart watches were implanted in the human consciousness by Dick Tracy.

Dad did several "special feature" reprints and tinkered with doing a sequel. I remember coming home from college once and he was creating his own alphabet that could be electronically scanned. I remember thinking for the first time that despite having a great life and inheriting the Newspaper Syndicate, Dad probably would have been just as happy or happier if he'd been an inventor or an architect or a historian or something. After he sold the syndicate, there was talk that he'd want to be a professor. He didn't live long enough to realize those dreams. It's easy to overanalyze these things, but I can't escape the notion that I'm living a version of the alternate life he would have liked to live. That's not to say he didn't seem to love his life. He did. It was just too short. It's weird to think, as I write this, that I've lived longer than he did.

Finals week of my senior year of college coincided with the release and explosion of *Star Wars*. Not long after, Universal Studios optioned Buck Rogers. The proposed show coincided perfectly with my graduation from college and the "what am I doing to do with the rest of my life" phase. When the show was announced, I had this fantasy that I could go down to LA and work on the show as a gopher and write episodes and jumpstart my life.

We made the deal. A production team was announced. It was headed by Andy Fenady with David Gerrold (who's on my Facebook page to this day). I went down somewhere in late summer or autumn of 1978 and had lunch with David Gerrold. Except for Gerrold, I couldn't get anybody on the show to look at my ideas. Gerrold, who wrote "Trouble with Tribbles" for *Star Trek* and a great book about franchises called *The World of Star Trek*, along with a number of other novels and TV shows, is still writing away. Great guy. But his team was scrapped, and Glenn Larson and his team had no interest whatsoever in having the grandson of the creator and son of the licensor anywhere near the set. For whatever reason, I couldn't understand why.

At the time, they were in what looked like converted trailers just off the Universal lot on Lankershim. It wasn't far from the Egg Company where I'd have an office later at Lucasfilm (or from the adobe where the peace treaty that made California a state was signed). I think this was David Gerrold's first story editing job. He gave me a copy of the bible and a pilot outline for a script called "Rustom's Raiders." Fenady seemed to have a western bent to him. At lunch at the Universal Commissary, David Gerrold gave me his interpretation of *Star Wars*, which was, "It's *Wizard of Oz* with hardware." Now I'm quite sure that Gerrold had far more complex thoughts about *Star Wars* than that, but remember, he was talking to some noob son of the licensor. And by that, I don't mean that he was in any way patronizing or condescending, but he was considering his audience and was probably giving me more credit than I deserved at the time.

So I went home and wrote up some premises. One was called "Atgame's End," and though I don't remember the exact story, I'm guessing it was a riff on "The Most Dangerous Game" but set on another planet. Except my real way into that story probably didn't come from "The Most Dangerous Game," but from an *Avengers* episode where Steed and Peel receive mysterious invitations to a party on some island, after which murder ensued. He sent back notes. I reacted to them. Sent them back. Then nothing.

The show was on hiatus. The current staff was gone. The show was in limbo. Calendar pages flip, seasons change, and *Buck Rogers* came back with Leslie Stevens and Glen Larson producing it. At the time, they were also doing *Battlestar Galactica*.

Dad and I went down and had lunch with Leslie Stevens. He spent much of the lunch talking about *Battlestar Galactica* and how Apollo and company are really the ancient astronauts. He talked about the helmets being vaguely reminiscent of Ancient Egyptian effigies (think King Tut's headdress). I thought of it as a space *Aeneid*. Sounded more interesting than Buck Rogers.

I got a tour of the set and met Erin Gray and Gil Gerard for the first time. Forget the fact that "Wilma Deering" was weapons-grade beautiful, Erin is now a great businessperson. Gil is a hoot. Exactly what you want him to be. I got to know him and Erin in 2008 or 2009, when we were shooting a streaming Buck Rogers retro homage in upstate New York. He's the only person I've ever seen slam his fist on a table to make a point and make the cup jump off the saucer without spilling anything. This usually only happens in cartoons.

My only other involvement in *Buck Rogers in the 25th Century* was when I snuck onto the lot (you could do that in those days) and slipped some premises to Glen Larson's extremely attractive assistant. She called a couple weeks later and said he liked them.

Nothing happened. The closest I came to working on Buck Rogers was working on *Battle Beyond the Stars* for Roger Corman. But this long-winded story is all prequel for the first time I actually got to work on Buck Rogers with TSR. And that falls well into the mid-eighties. Conventional wisdom would dictate that the whole Buck Rogers experience at TSR was a disaster, but conventional wisdom should sometimes be challenged.

Somewhere in 1986, we started developing Buck Rogers at TSR for a bunch of complicated reasons that are a subject all their own. My concept was that it was kind of *G.I. Joe* meets *Transformers,* and I even had a take for Hasbro like this. Nobody bit, however, and maybe that should have been a warning. But as it was about games, the important thing wasn't the characters as much as the world. And I loved the world. Our solar system five hundred years from now. Colonized, using real planets in our solar system. Robotic and genetically engineered creatures. Pure strain humans. Spaceships. Interplanetary intrigue. No speed-of-light travel. Everything had to be plausible. That was the first rule of Buck Rogers. Not actual, but scientifically defensible. It would all grow up to be Buck Rogers XXVC, which spawned board games, role-playing games, computer games, novels, comics, and more.

The TSR I walked into for Buck Rogers was completely different than the TSR I'd known in Los Angeles. Gary was gone, and unlike before, I didn't have the cushion of DDEC. It was a company on shaky financial ground, and there was a kind of corporate culture I'd never experienced before. There was a lot of history, not all of it good, and there wasn't the money or forcing production function of Sunbow, Ruby-Spears, or Lucasfilm. The company was built around Dungeons & Dragons, and aside from some trips to Top Secret, Star Frontiers, Gamma World, Boot Hill, and some other things, it was mostly a company designed to do medieval sword and sorcery. It seemed like nobody wanted to do Buck Rogers, and they sure as hell didn't want to do it with some guy from LA who wrote cartoons.

The first meeting we had with the team was one of the toughest meetings I've ever been in on any project. At one point I said, "Look, if you don't want to do this project, I don't want to force you." People left the room. They actually did. I was simultaneously amazed and relieved. I thought it would lessen some of the tension. It didn't. That project never got easy. Long afterward, Warren Spector and I, who'd gone several rounds over a rule in the board game, agreed it was one of the better projects we'd done in that period.

I'm quite sure that no small part of the difficulty was me. I was young and had never worked in board game culture, and what I was to TSR back in the Gary days didn't lend me much credibility now. In other words, as usual, I was a noob again.

At that point, the TSR Buck Rogers team felt like anything but a team, and that felt strange to me. Unlike all of the other teams I'd played on, where the creatives thought of themselves as freelancers who'd temporarily found themselves at a corporation (and always had their outside projects—in fact, outside projects were encouraged), the TSR folks were actual long-term employees of a real company.

It was a period of a lot of soul-searching. Was I just a bad leader? Wasn't I the exact same guy at the exact same time who was running the Sunbow shows? Context matters. And that gets to the frenemy part of Buck Rogers. With every other project I work on, I'm there as Flint Dille—writer or game designer or whatever title. I'm there because people want me there. With Buck Rogers, I'm there because I was born with it. It's as if all of the other dues I've paid don't count. It is a weird feeling.

Ironically, there is no project I've ever worked longer and harder on than Buck Rogers over the years and harvested less. I don't remember ever directly making money on Buck Rogers (indirectly, maybe) except when Joey Thompson and I received a commission for the Sega *Planet of Zoom* game in 1982, but somehow the dues are never considered paid. And this goes far beyond TSR. To this day, people who know me and know me well routinely either pitch me new takes on Buck Rogers or look at me incredulously, wondering why there isn't a movie or a TV show coming out.

Dumbass Brother with a Trust Fund

IF I GIVE UP THE point that no small part of my issues with the TSR team was my fault, sometimes there are other things that play a factor. I didn't know it at the time, but the standard perception of me was that I was *"Lorraine's dumbass brother who had never held a job and was born with a $7,000,000 trust fund given to him on the day of his birth."* You can still find traces of this rumor on the Internet more than thirty years later.

Rumors are fascinating things. We can debate whether I'm a dumbass, but the "never had a job in his life" bit was clearly manufactured, and pretty much everybody I dealt with directly at TSR was aware of my past projects and jobs. Still, the fascinating thing about rumors is that people can know they're not true but still believe them. Pete Townshend said in an interview, and I'm paraphrasing, "There are all sorts of stories about the Who, and I was there and know they're not true, but I still believe them."

People believe what they want to believe sometimes. And the particularly fascinating thing about the almost gothic detail of the $7,000,000 trust fund *given to him on the day of his birth,* as if somebody handed me an envelope in the nursery, is that it's so specific. Somebody had to consciously make this up.

If such a thing exists, I remain unaware of it to this day. And if I were such a lazy dumbass, why was I working so hard on the Buck Rogers game?

Which is the other interesting thing about rumors: they often don't make sense.

I'm sure somebody will do—or has done—a PhD thesis on the psychological underpinnings of rumors that allow us to believe things that don't make sense, and there is a practical lesson here. I don't think I was ever properly introduced, and I probably did a very bad job of introducing myself. There was never that moment in the meeting where I said, "I am Flint Dille," along with some kind of biographical information. I'm sure I thought that stuff was partially a waste of time and wholly embarrassing.

I now see the importance of it.

Nowadays, we have IMDb and Wikipedia and the entire Internet, but that doesn't solve the problem. It assumes that people do their research. Don't assume that. My unsolicited advice is to learn how to introduce yourself and listen very carefully when other people are introducing themselves: how they do it, what they emphasize, what they leave in the rearview mirror, what is important to them, *and* what they're not saying.

While we're on the topic, I'll throw this in. Jim Boyle, the legendary USC screenwriting professor, said something fascinating that echoes around in my head to this day: "Listen for the clunkers." The "clunkers" are the things that aren't said, the sudden promotions or jobs that came out of thin air. What are they leaving out? Maybe it's that their uncle hired them or they were in a relationship with somebody in the production. The clunkers are the things that are unsaid, the holes in the story, the things that don't add up. They're the things that are glossed over. And if nothing else, listening for the clunkers is a great game to get you to pay attention when people are introducing themselves.

For instance, my biggest clunker was always Buck Rogers. Always. While Buck is a true frenemy, the fact that my family owned an intellectual property that still had some cache in the early eighties meant people assumed that Buck Rogers was the reason I continued to get work.

And there's some truth to it. I met Joe Ruby and started my career because of a Buck Rogers meeting. He never made a serious offer for it, probably because the networks didn't want to do it (I'm sure he tested the waters). But it was what got me into the room. Even when "The Hundred-Year-Old Mystery" went big, there was talk that NBC wanted to revive Buck Rogers for Saturday morning and that's why my script had been singled out. Gary Gygax never once expressed the slightest interest in it, but people would explain my meeting him that same way.

There's a grain of truth to it, in that Joey Thompson, the agent who introduced us, also represented Buck Rogers. Later on, when talking about *Easy Riders, Raging Bulls*, I asked John Milius if all that stuff about the beach house is true. He said, "It's like all the best lies. They start with a grain of truth."

The Buck Rogers explanation died hard after I got the *Droids* job at Lucasfilm. A friend of mine, who will go nameless here, asked: "Do you think George Lucas is interested in Buck Rogers?"

"No. I think he's already got a space property."

In fact, if there's a rant in this book, this is it. I am surrounded by creative people. I am a member of their community. In all other cases I'm an equal, but somehow, when it comes to Buck Rogers, I'm suddenly a guy who fell off the turnip truck from Bundor Falls, Iowa, and just happened to find a rare painting in my attic. Some tell me earnestly that I should take it to an appraiser, others try to "take if off my hands" for free and get mad when I don't go for it. And imagine how many "takes" I've heard on Buck Rogers over the years.

"What if Buck Rogers is a seven-year-old and ends up in the future…"

"What if Buck Rogers doesn't exist and everybody is looking for him. He's a legend. A ghost…"

"Imagine if the whole thing is like *The Wizard of Oz*, and he never goes to the twenty-fifth century…"

"In the reboot, we should call him 'Dollar Rogers' (Get it? Buck, Dollar?). He's a con man who sells fake trips to the future."

Okay, I'm making some of those up, but nothing surprises me. It's simple: Buck Rogers is a guy from the twentieth century who goes into suspended animation and wakes up in the twenty-fifth century to become a sci-fi space hero. Take every word of that and change it and you can generate a reboot take. In fact, somebody could make an app for it. What if Buck becomes "Stud Rogers" and it's an adult film? (Or perhaps there's a better name he could use?)

"What if Buck Rogers is Steve Rogers' (Captain America) brother and you sell it to Marvel?" Oddly enough, that makes a strange kind of sense, but I'm not a fan of everything turning into a family story. That doesn't mean it doesn't work—*Star Wars* is a hidden family story—but when you get to Ernst Stavro Blofeld being Bond's "brother," you're arcing through the air looking down at a Great White.

It's the twenty-first century. He should come from now. I've probably heard a few hundred variations on who he is. For the next legion of people coming up with takes, let me give you the banana peel that all of the takes slip on. And I'm using "banana peel" as a technical development term—it is the vulnerable point that nearly every franchise has. Solve the banana peel, and you've solved the franchise. When people approach Buck Rogers, they rarely think past the origin story. People look at me with shocking earnestness and say things like:

"Who was Buck on Earth in the twentieth century?"

"What has he left behind?"

"Does he have survivor's guilt?"

And I'll grant you that these are all valid questions, but it is so damn easy to slip on the banana peel of Buck's past. The problem is that 99.9% of the story happens in the future. People go vague fast when we try and figure out the world he's actually going to be living in. And the problem with looking back is that it always leads to the graveyard. It always leads to a scene where he finds an ancient tombstone of his a) wife b) parents c) children d) pet husky. That plays for a minute (done very well in the seventies show, in my opinion), but it stops there until somebody comes up with the breakthrough idea that they always come up with:

"What if he isn't the only person from the twentieth century?"

And the smart ones—and a lot of the people who've pitched me these stories are very smart and creative and experienced—ask *the* question: "Why does the twenty-fifth century need Buck Rogers?"

That's the question.

I've heard hundreds of answers for it, and I've probably made up another five hundred of my own. The most developed of mine is in *Arrival*, a novella of mine that launched the XXVC book series: "Buck is a hero from now and his return in the future is kind of like the Return of the King." I even used that one once. It kind of works. "Buck has secret knowledge from the twentieth century which tips the balance of power in the twenty-fifth century."

But back to the Buck Rogers Reboot Generator. Specifically the "is a guy" part.

"I've got it! Buck Rogers is a woman, and Wilma Deering is her lover."

Don't laugh. I've heard that.

Then you get to the world of modern feature films and television series. Is it procedural, or is it a continuous story? Nowadays, almost every-thing is a continuous story one way or the other, but the question is, does the audience have expectations? The audience expects that it will be a normal day in Gotham City, and then pick your villain. The Joker commits a crime, so we go to Commissioner Gordon and then to stately Wayne Manor, and we're off and running. Somebody shows up at 221B Baker Street with a problem—maybe after a grabber. James Bond makes a daring escape at the end of a mission we haven't seen, the villain does something bad, and Bond shows up at M's office—often after some banter and innuendo with Moneypenny. This is the interesting question you get to with Buck Rogers. Once you've got him in the twenty-fifth century, where does the story start? Is he a pilot with the Earth Defense Force? Is he a Han Solo-esque rogue?

In Joseph Campbell terms, what is "the world as it is"?

If you want a franchise, you have to build your world first. It isn't about coming up with the great first script. Of course you do need the great first script, but it's more than that.

Do you have to tell an origin story?

"Let's skip all of that 'from the twentieth century' crap and just go to Buck Rogers as a space hero…" Believe it or not, that was my idea after hearing too many takes on who he was in the past. Nobody is going to do it, but it's a great thought experiment.

Oh, yeah. And how do we get him off Earth? And how do we educate him real fast on life in the future? You don't want him walking around like an idiot for hours.

In short, it's a tricky property. So is *Transformers*. That was why I was much more charitable about the Michael Bay films than many. It's hard.

Fall 1986/Winter 1987

I DON'T REMEMBER WHAT I did on New Year's Eve in 1986. The days of Edy Williams standing over lights probably felt like a distant memory, but if I took a moment to review the previous year and project on the next one, I knew that a lot had changed in 1986 and that more change was in the air for 1987. But few things ever end in a day. Not something as big and complex as this era, which took almost a year to end. The *G.I. Joe* movie seemed to have an unknown fate, as did *My Little Pony*. We still had plenty of things to do and we were still getting paid, but the machine was shutting down. There was a lot going on off-screen, and even if I didn't know what it was, I could still feel it.

The relationship with Marvel had deteriorated. We made a deal with TMS to do *Visionaries*.

Meanwhile, the D&D mansion stood empty most of the time. Gary, Luke, and Ernie were gone. A skeleton staff was still there, but I didn't go up very often. It was depressing. Golden ages are like flowers: they grow, they bloom, they die.

Curiously, I don't remember being that upset about it. Even in the best of times, you sometimes get a sense that you have to move on. Or maybe not "move on"—I hate that overused phrase—but evolve into something else. The world is a dynamic and chaotic place. Things rise and fall. I'd seen TSR when the wave appeared to be cresting, I saw it fall, and I saw it rise again. Ruby-Spears went from promising new studio to dominant 1983 studio to struggling—all in a period of three years. Lucasfilm, at the exact moment I was there, appeared indomitable. Then they released a bad movie, mothballed their biggest franchise, and came out with *Howard the Duck*. They would survive in the form of Industrial Light & Magic (their visual effects and animation studio) and rise again, but that year it looked bad. And now the same thing was happening with Sunbow.

I've never actually surfed in my life, but surfing is probably the best analogy for how I viewed my career from then on. You can't control the waves, but you can ride them. And if you wipe out, you have to find your board and wait for another wave. If you don't wipe out, you're probably not trying to do that much. Everything is a wave; new waves come along all the time, and sometimes, unlike in the real world, you can make your own waves. *Agent 13* was its own mini-wave that rose again thirty years later.

So the advice is this: Always have three things going. Two of them are actual paying jobs, and one of them is a project you are incubating. Of course, in order to do this, you have to be constantly out there, networking, submitting, pitching, woodshedding, kibbitzing, and, yes, going on fool's errands. You find a lot of fool's gold before you get real gold.

And not all waves are epic. Some waves are small. Some are duds. And every once in a while there are three epics in a row.

Every time you do a project, you learn from it, the résumé gets deeper, and just when you wonder if you're relevant, something old suddenly becomes fashionable again. That's happened multiple times to me. And that blast powers the next blast.

So here are the pieces of advice:

- Boom towns bust.
- Bust towns can boom again.
- Everything changes.
- Old is new and new is old.
- Even in the richest mines, the dirt-to-diamond rate is high.
- Always be in motion.
- You spend a lot of time paddling against the waves to find the right one to ride.
- Always be making your own weather.
- Don't swim or surf alone. Have friends, allies, and networks. Encourage them. Help them.
- Collaborate, even when there is nothing in it for you.
- Sometimes you have to trim your network.
- And, yeah, there are sharks and Portuguese man o' war out there. Steer clear of shark-infested water. People say sharks are solitary, but that's not true.
- Sometimes you have to find another beach.

Activity breeds activity. Success breeds success. All the clichés are true. But there's luck, too, and luck comes and goes. I've been extremely lucky in times when not being lucky would have been fatal to me.

And luck isn't always luck. One of the reasons I switched from chess to Avalon Hill games and SPI games is that I liked the randomness of die rolling. It more closely mirrored real life. And the rolls aren't really random. They have what's known as a combat results table. The results aren't binary. It's not good/bad; the range goes from really bad to great, with a lot of shades. So when you make a move, you have meaningful choices to make. What happens if I win? What happens if I lose?

This one's not about cardboard pieces, but resources in terms of time, effort, money, and relationships that you stand to gain and lose. Combat Results Tables come in all forms, and I'm imagining a one-die game here, but the principle holds.

Combat Results Table

1	2	3	4	5	6
REALLY BAD	BAD	SLIGHTLY BAD	SLIGHTLY GOOD	GOOD	GREAT

The point here is that sometimes you really do have a run of bad luck, like landing on Park place with another player's hotels on it and then rolling snake eyes. That happens, but in real life, every month, day, hour is a different die roll, and the results are cumulative. Real life isn't all in on a die roll, but more like Risk: every die roll is short-term excitement, but ultimately the odds even out.

In other words, you can have a bad run, but if you keep at it, luck turns. And the Combat Results Table is also about relative odds. If you want to win at a military sim, you know not to attack infinitely more powerful forces when you can't afford to get a bad roll. When you're rolling wildly, you're not playing a smart game. The normal cycle is that you gather your forces, attack, heal, rearm, and prepare for the next assault.

That metaphor holds true to real life. I've never met anybody whose career was one long steady flow of successes with no setbacks and no dead times. Smart people use those dead times to arm up for the next assault. Sometimes you have to retreat. Sometimes you have to defend. But you can't conquer anything if you never attack. I'll get out of this before the metaphor breaks, but you get the idea.

And, let me say this one time, explicitly: on healthy days, I think of life as a very long game (yes, it can end at any moment) in which no single turn is critical and, in the end, luck evens out, for good or for bad. Effort, over time, is the thing that flips the odds in your favor, and, to borrow another thought from games, you level up.

In the winter of 1987, another door opened: Michael Chase Walker, the executive at CBS behind *Pee-Wee's Playhouse* (a paradigm-bending show), called me up one day and asked if I had bandwidth to do a really wildly different project. I figured it was James Bond, because I knew that Michael knew Cubby Broccoli and was a Bond fanatic.

I said, "Let's talk."

We talked, and it wasn't Bond. Instead, it was something called *Garbage Pail Kids*.

In the early eighties, there was a phenomenon called Cabbage Patch Kids, which were essentially dolls, though they were called "soft fabric sculptures." The shtick was that each doll was unique and kind of damaged, as they were handmade. When they became a phenomenon, there was a shortage of them at Christmas retail, so, of course, there were numerous stories of fracases breaking out at stores. A few years later, a parody called Garbage Pail Kids emerged. In 1985, they came out as trading cards from the Topps Company, and they're credited to Art Spiegelman, Mark Newgarden, and John Pound.

And this is more than a little interesting at a number of levels. Topps, long known for doing Wacky Packs, sort of came out of the tradition of *Mad Magazine* and parody humor from the sixties and seventies. There was also a whiff of "naughty" to it—or really "anti–political correctness"—but it wasn't coming from where you'd expect it to come from.

Art Spiegelman is a very interesting guy. He edited *Raw*, an underground comic, and did stuff for *The New Yorker*. He's most notable, however, for *Maus,* a graphic novel about the Holocaust, which in addition to finding itself on roughly every list of essential graphic novels also won him a Pulitzer Prize. And frankly, on the face of it, you don't expect Garbage Pail Kids to come from a Pulitzer Prize–winner.

When Michael Chase Walker first mentioned Garbage Pail Kids, it felt all wrong. I'm not really a comedy writer, and it seemed like a passing fad. However, I thought about it, and a big enough idea did eventually come into my head. What if we did it as an anthology show but for Saturday morning? *Mad Magazine* was as powerful an influence in my mind as there was. It had everything: movie parodies, *Spy vs. Spy*, the Fold-In, the little drawings on the pages, Sergio Aragonés, and (my favorite) *Dave Berg Looks at...* as well as the odd assorted things like "Rewriting Your Way to a PhD" (which changed my life) and enough funny political stuff to make me think I understood something about the world.

What if we could do all sorts of topics glued together with the Garbage Pail Kids? After all, there was no real story to GPK, it was just a parody on the ultra-successful Cabbage Patch Kids. A send-up that poked fun at the smug self-righteousness that many people saw in Cabbage Patch.

Of course, I had to get approval from Tom Griffin and Joe Bacal to do outside work that could be perceived as competitive. They didn't care if I was designing games or novels, but this was television animation. Around that time, Joe Bacal happened to come out to LA, and I asked him if it was okay if I did a development for the show, since it was fairly evident that things would be slowing down at Sunbow in 1987. He went along with it. They were great guys, and it was at that moment when I'd go from being an employee to an ally. And there's a life lesson in that. I owed a lot to them, and I decided I was going to put everything I had into my last project for them: *Visionaries*.

Visionaries

Winter/Spring/Summer 1987

BACK THE STORY UP almost a year. The first thing I saw of *Visionaries* was when Bob Prupis and Kirk Bozigian of Hasbro came into town and showed us the art and prototypes of the Visionaries. The whole gag was that the action figures had a hologram built into them and the characters could channel their spirit animals. The animals were mostly cool. The good guys had lions, eagles, bears, dolphins—think the NFL, pretty much—and the bad guys had nasty animals like lizards, gorillas, sharks, and a few that were a little inexplicable, such as phylots, mollusks, and armadillos. I never knew or thought to ask how we arrived at snail (mollusk), because snails don't seem to be the stuff of action toys. But production had already begun, so there was no point in pushing the issue.

If the toy is a snail, well, I have to make a snail cool—end of story.

I remember *Visionaries* through holographically colored glasses. It was the last Sunbow show, and some believe it was the best show we ever did. It didn't start that way. It started horribly. There were a lot of cooks in a very crowded kitchen. The property had been created by the Gentili brothers, and so I spent a lot of time with Anthony Gentili. It was simultaneously being developed as a comic book by Marvel, and as I recall, the meetings between Sunbow and Marvel went immediately bad. We showed up with a development plan for the *Visionaries* show and Marvel showed up with a development for the *Visionaries* comic, which they felt should lead the charge. And while I can't remember a single issue in the meetings, I remember that they were contentious, almost hostile, and I didn't get why. Marvel was represented by Brian Augustyn and Tom Defalco, both good, smart guys— but in this scenario, we were adversaries.

Larry Hama might have been in the mix somewhere. The irony was that despite the fact that our names appeared on dozens of shows together, I never met him until a Comic-Con panel sometime in the last decade. I have no idea whether I named a character Falkhama, but it is interesting to note that there is just such a character in the show.

I was utterly unprepared for this kind of conflict. It wasn't all that different from the TSR fights over Buck Rogers, except they hadn't really started at that point. In the past, the Marvel comics based on Hasbro products had been more or less invisible to me. A lot of fans ask about differences in the continuities between the *Transformers* and *G.I. Joe* comics and our TV shows, but the truth is that we paid near zero attention to the Marvel comics, and I didn't get the feeling that they were watching our shows. Life was just too busy for that.

So to answer the most common fan question: To the best of my knowledge, nobody ever tried to sync them up after the first episode. It was hard enough getting shows done without syncing with another creative team. Besides, they were two different mediums. I just got character drawings and back-of-the-card bios (sometimes), and we pretty much ran off on our own. Our characterizations beyond name and look pretty much depended on what we felt would best serve the series. Same thing with *Transformers,* except that after a while, Hasbro was turning out the toys faster than the comics could absorb them, so we'd receive raw designs with maybe a vague concept of what the characters would be, and we'd go from there. There was no comic for *Muscle Machines* that I know of, so we didn't worry about that, and from what I saw of *Jem* (I was in maybe a couple early creative discussions, but that was mostly Christy Marx), that was developed in-house.

On the other hand, the *Inhumanoids* comic was pretty much a transcription of my scripts, so I was surprised when suddenly the comics guys were in the *Visionaries* mix. I didn't hate it, I just didn't know what they were doing there, and it also meant there were two competing visions of the show. This was just a dress rehearsal for something that would happen very often later in my career, but this was a new experience for me at the time.

The whole gag with any take on *Visionaries* (Full name: *Visionaries: Knights of the Magical Light*) was that the characters, futuristic Knights of the Round Table with barely concealed roots in Arthurian legend, held staffs that had totem animals on them. For the totem animals, I defaulted to what I'd learned in anthropology class a decade earlier and John Boorman's film *The Emerald Forest*. The idea was that each of the knights could turn into their totem character when they got into trouble. I'd later draw from that same well with a game called *Dead to Rights,* except Shadow wasn't a spirit animal—he just functioned like one.

I didn't know any other way to approach the material than to look at the reality of the product. There were five good guys, five bad guys, a couple vehicles in there, and there were plans to release an Iron Mountain playset like the one they had at Toy Fair, which the good guys and bad guys battled over in the series pilot.

When it came to developing *Visionaries,* we had models that looked pretty high-tech, but the show was about magic and animal totems, so we decided to set it in a civilization that was once extremely developed but the tech had been destroyed when three suns aligned. The cultural context was this: It was 1987, the era of the Harmonic Convergence when a whole New Age movement believed that the world would change when the planets in our solar system aligned on August 16–17, 1987. There were global meditation events, and maybe it worked, maybe it didn't work (the Soviet Union did go out of business not long after), but Harmonic Convergence was in the air—the same way that the word "quintessence" was in the air and we created Quintessons. (Actually, it was the name of a store down the street from our office in Westwood.) Anyway, context matters.

Looking back, my guess is that the fight was about something else. On its face, it was about the pilot and the series and character and plot development. In reality, it might have been some proxy fight between Marvel and Sunbow. I knew the relationship was deteriorating. There were rumors of sinister plotting in corporate throne rooms over whether Marvel would just take the show over or whether Sunbow would control it. That thought probably didn't cross my mind at the time. Honestly. I took it as a sincere creative battle. Looking back at it with a whole lot of experience, this battle wasn't really about the creative side of things at all.

In any case, at some point, Tom Griffin pointed out that millions of people watch the TV show while thousands of people read the comics, so the TV show development had to take the lead. As brutal as his argument was, it also happened to be true. It went as one would expect. The first comic played out just like the TV show, and the other four went off in another direction. This didn't exactly improve relationships between Sunbow or myself and Marvel, but it was what it was.

And the kicker was that Marvel didn't do the animation on the show. It was done by another company that was making a name for itself in LA called Tokyo Movie Shinsha, or TMS. And they were great.

The Marvel/Sunbow relationship was all but over.

If the pilot was a pitched battle over every line and action, the rest of the series was done in a period of benign neglect. As I look at the writer credits, I wrote about half of the episodes, and the rest were written by Doug, Buzz, and Rick Merwin. We were all playing out our contracts. I was both co-producer and story editor, and as we knew it was the end, I put everything I had into making it the best goofy King Arthur kind of show I could. Of all the shows, this one came the closest to realizing what we were intending to do.

And before we move on, a word about pilots. They are their own animal. If you don't believe me, just try this exercise. Go back and watch the pilot of a show you know and like. It will probably seem weird, and this isn't even just true of modern shows. I watched some early episodes of *The Andy Griffith Show,* and the Andy Taylor and Barney Fife in the first episodes are not the characters we came to know and love over the decades.

The elements were there, but they just hadn't jelled. Andy was a little bit nasty, and they hadn't figured out yet that this wasn't a show about "hicks." In a pilot—even an animated pilot—the actors have to get to know their characters and how they interact with one another. Accents get dropped or buffed, relationships deepen, and so on. Sometimes writers skip the pilot and write some later episodes first. *What is the show really going to be about?* The idea is to avoid dealing with all of the intros until the team knows who and what they're intro-ing.

So, if you're going to watch *Visionaries*, get past the pilot. The rest of it is some of the smoothest, most natural stuff we ever did, and this was in no small part to do with Tokyo Movie Shinsha and the producers, Kaoru Nishiyama, Sachiko Tsuneda, and Zahra Dowlatabadi, who were the people I actually interacted with. And before we drive past this, here's a bounce-back for you. The head of TMS was Yutaka Fujioka, whom I'd already had a relationship with when he was making *Little Nemo* and trying to make *Buck Rogers* five years earlier. It's a small world.

I had worked a lot with TMS and went to the recordings, which featured an all-star cast, including Chris Latta, Peter Cullen, Neil Ross, and Malachi Throne, who was on *It Takes a Thief,* which was one of my favorite shows as a kid.

After it was all over, a movie called *The Princess Bride* by Rob Reiner with Mandy Patinkin, Andre the Giant, and Robin Wright in it came out, and Jay called me up and said to go see it and "you'll know what the fourteenth episode of *Visionaries* would have been." And he was right. It had the same mix of seriousness, comedy, self-parody, and improbable characters that we had.

The Sunbow LA Office Shuts Down

Spring 1987

Los Toilay wasn't really the name of the Mexican Restaurant; it was just the name we gave it. It was really called The Acapulco, and it was around the corner from Sunbow in Westwood. We didn't call it Los Toilay because the food was bad—it wasn't. We called it Los Toilay because it was the place Tom always seemed to take people when there was bad news to deliver or a hatchet was coming down. Tom was anything but a hatchet man, so firings were very rare—but they did happen.

The handwriting was on the wall at Sunbow for anybody willing to read it. There were rumors that somebody very high up at Hasbro was very ill. There were rumors of palace coups. Our shows were winding down. When the day finally came that Tom came into town and took us all to Los Toilay to tell us the office was shutting down, it wasn't much of a surprise. It was sad, but it wasn't a surprise. The toy show era would morph into *Power Rangers* and spike and then wheeze on for a few more years, but the heyday had passed.

They didn't lock the door that day. The end of Sunbow LA stretched out for weeks, or maybe even months. People sort of phased out when their projects were over. Hildy stuck around the longest to turn out the lights.

I was heading into the Garbage Pail, but there were still several more *Visionaries* scripts to be written, so things didn't change very much for me. I vaguely remember packing up my box from the office and carting everything out to my car. To this day, I regret not walking off with the General Flagg aircraft carrier, but it wasn't really mine. I still have boxes from that period in deep storage. One day I'll dredge them out.

Into the Garbage Pail

So as I headed over to CBS's Television City to begin work on *Garbage Pail Kids*, leaving the comfortable Sunbow home. Did I know that I was heading up the writer's equivalent of the Nung River in *Apocalypse Now*?

I don't think so, but I knew I was going to need help. Linda Woolverton, and ignore the fact that she was my girlfriend, was everybody's first choice for this adventure. Linda was the flipside of me. She once told me there were two kinds of shows, "squishies" and "toasters." Squishies were the soft shows—*Smurfs, My Little Pony,* and so on. Toasters were the tech shows. *Transformers* was the ultimate toaster. Linda also had another secret weapon. She'd worked at CBS and could speak the secret language of network. I didn't speak network, but I've always loved the way executives talk about projects. I might think I've come up with a brand-new, wholly original idea, and an executive will say, "I get it...this is a door movie."

"A door movie?"

"Yeah, the main character walks through a door and enters a whole new world."

This can cover anything from *The Chronicles of Narnia* or *The Wizard of Oz* to *The Bonfire of the Vanities* or *Guardians of the Galaxy,* but to executives, they all fall into the box of "a door movie."

Anyway, after Linda, there was another prominent animation writer and actual veteran of *Rowan & Martin's Laugh-In* named Rowby Goren. Rowby was also a vet animation writer, having worked on everything from *Masters of the Universe* to *Fat Albert* to *Berenstain Bears.* Rowby is as wild in person as the work he does.

Then we turned to Gordon Kent, who had traveled my animation journey every step of the way from Ruby-Spears, through Sunbow, and who I've already noted had written arguably the darkest, silliest, and most fantastic episodes of the *G.I. Joe* series, respectively "Cobra's Candidate," "The Greenhouse Effect," and "The Gods Below." The secret to Gordon was that he could do everything and was the perfect Swiss Army knife for the project.

Michael Chase Walker was a star after bringing *Pee-Wee's Playhouse* to CBS and single-handedly redefining Saturday morning. *Garbage Pail Kids,* with its edged parody, novel formatting, and artsy crassness, was supposed to do the same thing for animation. CBS was going to be the edgy hit-making network. And they were going to do something different. *Garbage Pail* was going to be an in-house production.

What could go wrong?

I thought I was heading from one big time to another, and even in retrospect, I can see why I felt good about it: Linda, Rowby, and Gordon were a dream team. Michael Chase Walker was a winner on a roll. I'd talked to Judy Price on the phone for hours before meeting her, and she seemed like a smart, interesting woman. I thought I was heading out to conquer a different world. I'm not sure I had any big network ambitions—I rarely have articulable ambitions—but this felt like a good step out of a dying world and into the mainstream.

Little did I know that Saturday morning TV was dying too.

Other than Judy on the CBS team, there was Carrie Broom, an attractive and articulate executive, and a guy who seemed oddly familiar to me named Ralph Sanchez, who was a creative development executive. Ralph was simpatico in a way I didn't expect. He was, and is, a huge gamer. Hardcore. Since that time, we've worked on all sorts of projects. Most recently, he went to work for Blizzard. But back then, he was a seasoned industry guy. He was about my age, and that should have told me where I remembered him from.

We didn't figure that out until having coffee in 2016. It turns out we were both in our first screenwriting class together with Jim Boyle, the legendary instructor who taught screenwriting like it was Camp Pendleton. That had been seven years before *Garbage Pail*. We should have remembered, but we didn't. But it was the same class. We both remembered Ed Morgan, an ex-Nixon guy who went to Lompoc for backdating Nixon's VP papers and wrote the best script in the class (according to Boyle).

Boyle hated my script. "I really resisted *Swords and Daggers*," he'd said, "but of all of [the scripts], it's the most likely to sell." So I had the dubious distinction of being the most commercial.

So as I went over to the CBS campus at Fairfax and Third in the spring of 1987, I was feeling good about the world. And even in retrospect, I can't blame myself. I'd been on a nice long roll since my debacle at Lucasfilm.

As with most properties I worked on in that period, GPK drew aggression from various pressure and protest groups. This was to be expected. Everything was protested. Some of it was sincere, and some of it was cynical. There was a lot of earned media (a.k.a. free publicity) in protesting stuff. Any group that could pay for a letterhead and fax something could generate a quick, easy story for an increasingly voracious media. And obviously they were doing everything they could to provoke controversy. When you have a character named Adam Bomb with a nuclear blast detonating from his head, you push some buttons. When you have Leaky Lindsay with gallons of snot coming out of her nose, you push gross-out buttons. Bony Tony is always unzipping his face, revealing a cracked skull. I'm sure somebody thought it was about teen suicide. Swell Mel, a guy in a dress, would probably raise more hackles today for making fun of gender identity, but in some ways the eighties were less rigid. Somebody would probably say that Drippy Dan makes fun of child murder, as he's a kid who's drinking a bottle and apparently leaking out of bullet holes. Patty Putty's face is distorted and could be interpreted as a deformed child.

I'm sure that if the show had aired *and* it was criticized, there would have been a lot of hand-wringing over the characters. The thing that reviewers and people who haven't spent time in a lot of collaborative creative environments err in assuming is that there is a lot more meaning to things than there is. I still have my sheet of uncut cards, and I vaguely remember the selection process. It wasn't scientific. A lot of it was practical. For instance, we knew they'd need a vehicle, so we used Rustin' Justin. We wanted boys and girls for the larger group adventure segments—one section of the show, for instance, was a troupe of Garbage Pail Kids doing movie parodies. Other characters who were more limited, like Garbage Mouth Gilbert (a garbage truck with a face in the back), would just be used for incidental parts in guest cameos.

In the early, halcyon days when anything was possible, we had endless numbers of characters and endless numbers of segments, and we had music video sections with custom Garbage Pail songs and fake Garbage Pail advertisements and so on. The sky was the limit. I wrote the bible, and it was quickly approved. Of course, as I would soon learn, in network in-house productions, "approved" is only approved until it is unapproved.

Nobody I've talked to remembers when things started going bad, but it was pretty early on. I do remember getting a call from one producer who seemed to be kind of cagey with script notes. It turned out there were some story inconsistencies, and he seemed angry about it. This was the kind of thing that I was used to, but without the anger. Scripts go through multiple steps and drafts, and we miss things. This happens in two-hundred-million-dollar movies, too. It wasn't much to fix a couple sentences, but when stuff like that happens, you know you're seeing the tip of some iceberg. Sometimes you get weird notes, and sometimes notes come from weird places, and it isn't really about the notes. It is usually about something else. In most cases, it's a political game being played somewhere above your head or at least out of your sight. The notes aren't the disease—they're just the symptom.

Judy started having more problems with the bible and the scripts. At this point, there were a lot flowing in. Looking at the writers list on IMDb, most all of the writers were very familiar people. By my count, nearly everybody on the list except Donna Kuyper and John Pound were people I worked with at Sunbow (also Rowby and Linda).

Flint Dille...(developer) (13 episodes, 1988) Gordon Kent...(12 episodes, 1988)Rowby Goren...(10 episodes, 1988) Paul Davids... (2 episodes, 1988) Buzz Dixon...(2 episodes, 1988) Michael Charles Hill...(2 episodes, 1988) Linda Woolverton...(2 episodes, 1988) Doug Booth...(1 episode, 1988) Paul Dini...(1 episode, 1988) Donna Kuyper...(1 episode, 1988) Richard Merwin...(1 episode, 1988) Marv Wolfman...(1 episode, 1988) John Pound...(trading cards) (uncredited) (unknown episodes)

I guess my feeling was that I wanted to keep the band together. These were people familiar to me whom I trusted. As I recall, the scripts were good enough, but I wasn't used to the network way of doing things. It seems like there was constant loss of forward progress and constant rethinking of everything.

Michael Chase Walker left CBS very early on. I can't remember the reason, but with him gone, the edgy, friendly buffer between Judy and I disappeared.

So as we sailed into summer, life was in the garbage pail, and it seemed like a new adventure was just beginning, but just as with the end of a TV series, there were all sorts of subplots to tie up.

1987 COMIC-CON
G.I. JOE Movie Launch Dinner

As of this writing, I've been to Comic-Con thirty-four of the last thirty-six years, and I'm heading down there again. For me, Comic-Con is a kind of measuring stick. What am I doing now? I've been there in good years, and I've been there in bad years, though few were as memorable as 1987.

We were at a swank restaurant in the Horton Plaza near the US Grant. It seems like everybody was there. Well, almost everybody in the Sunbow West Coast family. It was the last hurrah, and we'd never assemble that way again.

It was a very long table. Linda and I were sitting somewhere near the middle. Buzz and Sook-Ok were there, as were Gordon and Donna. We premiered the *G.I. Joe* movie earlier that day. I remember riding over on a bus with Frank, which is more than I remember of the movie—but I was there.

Anyway, it was early evening, magic hour, and Jay was the only New York Sunbow person there. Kaoru Nishiyama, a producer on *Visionaries*, which I was still finishing at the time, stopped by the table, as she was eating nearby. Zahra Dowlatabadi, who was also with TMS on the project and whom I'd get to know better much later on, was there too. Steve Gerber was down at the end of the table. Doug and Yolanda were somewhere near the end.

It was an eighties night. I probably did something obnoxious like order White Zinfandel because it reminded me of Kool-Aid and the room just got shinier. The era might technically have been over, but it didn't feel that way at the moment. The world was in full swing. It was exciting and fun.

But the real star of the night was Christy Marx's husband, Peter Ledger. He was down at the end of the table. I was vaguely aware of a cart being rolled out to him and him sampling a number of wines. It seemed like something expensive was going on, but I wasn't paying attention.

It's a cliché, but Peter Ledger was a larger-than-life guy. The reason the cliché works is that years later, when I was writing his eulogy, I described him as being a gigantic guy, and Christy corrected me. Peter was 5'9", though I was totally convinced he was 6'7".

He was a loud, charismatic Australian guy. If you were casting Professor Challenger, he wouldn't have been a bad place to start. By trade he was an artist, but on this night, he was a wine connoisseur and raconteur. Man, he had a lot of stories. I'm not sure which ones he was telling that night, but I was probably hearing them like an ambient soundtrack.

As the check came and I was pulling out my wallet, I realized that things were getting awkward at the far end of the table. It seemed Peter was under the impression that Sunbow was paying. And this check was going to be big—like down-payment-on-a-car big. One look at Jay's face told me he hadn't intended on footing this one. I'm not sure anybody else would have noticed the look, but I knew him quite well.

Eventually Jay just decided that Sunbow would eat it and that he'd explain it to Joe and Tom later on. I knew them well enough to know their reaction would live somewhere between amused and annoyed.

Whatever their reactions ended up being, they sure as hell didn't hold the dinner against Christy. She'd end up being their story editor on *Conan* a year later. Strangely, despite the fact that I was working with TSR and Gary, that Christy was working on *Sisterhood of Steel,* and that Steve Gerber was doing *Void Indigo,* I don't ever remember talking about medieval sword and sorcery with either of them in that period. On top of that, Jerry Conway was working on *G.I. Joe,* as was, I think, Roy Thomas. I don't remember ever once talking about *Conan.* Sometimes things have a way of just being in the air. You could be working with somebody all day every day, but we were all doing multiple things and very rarely explicitly talked about them. Writers are different. Some people talk about their projects, others keep quiet.

In any case, if I had to pick a moment when the Sunbow era really ended, it was when we all stood up from that table and wandered off into the San Diego night.

With the Garbage Pail era, my life moved to the Fairfax district. Linda lived there. CBS's Television City was there, along with the farmer's market—though the Grove hadn't been built yet. The Garbage Pail team would go out for lunch and have a couple glasses of wine, usually at Muse. Some people got happier. Some got edgier. It was a weird, anxious team, and there was some component of anger in there, too. I'm not sure what it was or where it came from, but some teams are like that.

Sidney Iwanter, who was an executive at various different places along the way, eventually tried explaining to me what he'd already explained to Judy Price, the producer on *Garbage Pail Kids* and the head of children's TV for CBS. Basically, he said I'd come out of syndication and was used to swashbuckling. I'm not sure exactly what that meant, but I mostly translated it to mean that I wasn't all that housebroken in terms of dealing with networks. I wasn't sure how to process that. I just kind of rolled with it, like I was saying "whatever" long before anybody said whatever. I wasn't an alien to network TV—I'd been at Ruby-Spears for three seasons—but apparently that didn't matter. They thought of me as syndication.

When the going gets rough in comedy, and when you don't have enough clear ideas and the environment isn't conducive to experimentation, there's always one obvious option: parody. Parody is a weak hand to play, but if it's the best hand you have, you play it. We did a *Garbage Pail* version of James Bond, and probably a version of Indiana Jones, and right on down the franchise line. We planned to do fake commercials and had some other bits that were conceptually fun. This was my first pure comedy. I'm not really a comedy guy. At least not that kind.

But that wasn't really my problem with the show. My goal was to get the thing running well. I'd trust Linda, Rowby, Gordon, and the rest of the team to bring in the other kinds of comedy. After all, this was a variety show, which by its very nature relies on a lot of different kinds of comedy. I figured one way or the other, we could make it work.

But some shows just don't want to work. I'd been involved in things that didn't work before, and I'd done things that didn't work before, but I'm not sure I'd been in this kind of an uncomfortable environment before. I'm quite sure I was part of the problem, but I'm also quite sure that I was only a small part of it. This one was a big problematic puzzle. It wasn't like *Droids*, in which I was in a benign environment but just couldn't seem to please; this felt like a non-benign environment in which nobody really *wanted* me to please.

At the time, luckily, I had a lot of other things to turn my mind to. There were still episodes of *Visionaries* to do, which served as an umbilical cord for me to a comfortable world. Also, Buck Rogers was taking shape as we were working on the prototype for the Buck Rogers: Battle for the 25th Century strategy board game. The premise was simple: imagine Risk if the continents (planets) move and you have to time your attacks, plus different kinds of spaceships and drop troops. Multitalented game genius Jeff Grubb was working on the overall bible.

Visionaries and Beyond

WRITING THE LAST EPISODES of *Visionaries* was bittersweet. As working on *Garbage Pail Kids* got worse and worse, things with *Visionaries* continued to get more and more compelling. If I had to define my peak of writing for animation, it was probably the end of that show. One of the producers told me she'd developed a crush on me after reading "Trail of Three Wizards." And while I'm not exactly sure I believe that, the show did pull something out of me that I hadn't ever realized I had.

After the *Visionaries* pilot, it seems like there was almost no adult supervision from Marvel or Hasbro or any other stakeholder. It was just us creatives and a great animation team at TMS. I wrote seven episodes, and Doug and Buzz wrote three a piece. I was coproducer, story editor, and head writer. Jim Duffy came over from Marvel and produced it, and I remember him as maybe the easiest of the Marvel producers to work with.

There's something liberating about ends. You only have to care as much as you want to care. In some ways, your attitude toward the end says everything that needs to be said about the whole experience. It's the net at the bottom of the balance statement. It's kind of like being a soldier and knowing this is going to be your last charge, so the only real decision is how you die.

Everybody involved with *Visionaries* wanted to go out on a high. We kind of knew the product line was doomed and thus the show was doomed. It didn't matter. Doom is liberating too. We just did our best, and I think you could make a good argument that on an episode-by-episode basis, *Visionaries* was the best show we did in that era.

It's Not Going to Work

Summer/Early Autumn of 1987

"THAT'S NOT GOING TO work with Judy, Flint."

I have no idea what I was trying to do that got Ralph Sanchez to say that. I might have been trying to move the schedule or expedite an approval or who knows what. It doesn't much matter. By the time you're having conversations like that, it's time to start making other plans. It's over. Done. Gornished. Call the coroner. Or perhaps that's a bit too grim. Maybe it was more like fourth-and-ten from midfield, with no time on the clock when you're down seven.

Sometimes the Hail Mary works. Though, this time, it wouldn't.

Ralph, who was a sympathetic messenger at this point, was saying, "It's over." There was no fat lady singing yet, but she was walking to the stage, clearing her throat, and she was going to start unless something dramatic changed.

Nobody wants to be fired. Nobody wants to fail.

Not all games are winnable, of course, but you still have to play them until they're over. Just often enough, they turn around when you least expect it, so you go on the death march, you walk bravely to the guillotine, you make the last call to the governor for a stay, because sometimes there are no other options.

I was doing everything I could, and it just wasn't working. Maybe it was my fault. Maybe it was their fault. Maybe it was a failed concept for a show. At that point, I knew that unless something drastically changed, this was going to end badly.

One positive came in the form of personal growth. I didn't react like I did with the epic fail at Lucasfilm. There wasn't panic. There wasn't scrambling. There wasn't the dark fear. That's the great thing about losing and coming back. You're a survivor. You're not a noob anymore. I'd argue that the best lesson both sports and games teach is that losing is part of it, and it's even a good thing if you can learn from it and get better.

Losing was a problem to be managed, not an existential threat. And to the question of how you manage impending loss, all of the clichés work:

Hope for the best, prepare for the worst.

Keep calm and carry on.

Do the next right thing.

Throughout all of this, I'd stayed in contact with Michael Chase Walker. I didn't know what his falling-out with Judy Price was over, but it didn't have anything to do with me. I did have the good sense not to mention to her that Michael had invited me and Linda to a launch party for some comedienne whose name I don't remember at the Santa Monica Airport. (In animation world, you didn't get invited to a lot of "Hollywood" events, so you pretty much took whatever was offered.) Little did I know that this was the "Call to Adventure" that would lead to the end of an era and spark a whole new adventure.

The Magic Flight

The Bald Guy and the Woman in the Leather Jacket

It was the night of the Michael Chase Walker party. I was dressed and ready to head out and pick up Linda. I got to my car, and Bill Winter's stupid station wagon was blocking me in and Bill was nowhere to be found. I can't remember why Bill was there or why he was blocking me in, as it wasn't like him. He was anything but inconsiderate, but all the same, there was his stupid station wagon blocking me in, and his keys were nowhere in sight.

Looking back, Bill's car seems more like a literary device than a real physical object that was blocking me in, but it really was there. I don't remember why I didn't call Linda and ask her to pick me up, but I decided I had to move the car. It became a mission. I went inside and grabbed Roger or Bill Guttman or whoever was couch-surfing at the time and asked for their help in moving this turd out of the way. Fortunately, he'd left it unlocked. Still, the mission wasn't trivial. Moving it meant backing the station wagon into the street on a hill, stopping the car, moving mine out, and rolling Bill's back in.

I don't remember being irritated as much as determined, though I'm sure the thought of having him towed crossed my mind. And for some reason, I was bent on going to the party, even though ninety-nine percent of the time I would have just blown it off. I wasn't much for going to events where I didn't know anybody, but still, the car had to move.

We put the clunky old hand-me-down station wagon into neutral, rolled it, got my car out, rolled it back, and I was off. The party was its own threshold, and the station wagon was its guardian. I'd been on the outskirts of the bigger entertainment industry, but I hadn't been to something exactly like this before. To this day I'm not quite sure what or who the party was for, but it was big. Some network or studio had rented out a hangar at Santa Monica Airport, hired caterers and valets and a band and decorators, and turned the hangar into a high-end comedy club for a night. I'd love to find out that it was somebody who went huge and that I was there in the beginning, but I remember nothing about her or the performance.

I don't remember showing up at an event before and having to check whether I was on "the list," but there were bouncers and a list this time. I don't know if they gave us drink tickets or nametags or whatever, but once we got past this set of threshold guardians, we went in search of the only people we knew—Michael Chase Walker and his wife, Jane. Eventually we spotted them holding court. In a different world, Michael would have been

Jack Warner, and my image of him that night is pretty much what I would have imagined a Hollywood mogul looking like. Jane was a costumer and had an incredible sense of style. I'd never seen gloves without fingers before, but they looked really cool. Michael is, and was, a James Bond fanatic, and at that moment I felt like I'd shown up in the James Bond room of the casino.

He introduced us to a few people. The first was a bald studio executive, and the second was Lisa Henson. I didn't know at that moment that she was Jim Henson's daughter, but she seemed like royalty. She was wearing a black leather jacket but somehow seemed a lot more Ivy League than biker, and we started talking. Linda wandered off with the bald executive, and I kind of monitored it out of the corner of my eye. It didn't seem menacing, and he was a perfectly mannered fellow, but you never know.

Meanwhile, Lisa and I—almost instantly, and God knows how—got onto the topic of her thesis at Harvard, which was on Achilles' shield in *The Iliad*. How something that coincidental happens I do not know, but I'm quite sure I was the only person in that loud, smoky hangar who knew that the shield that Achilles used in his fateful battle with Hector wasn't just a D&D shield with scary stuff on it, but a microcosm of the ancient Greek world from the cosmos to the mundane. At least, that's my interpretation. There are a hundred other valid ones, but they weren't represented in that particular room, and if somebody were to ask me to defend getting a worthless degree in ancient history and classical rhetoric, I would point to that moment.

Near the end of the conversation, which probably went on through the comedy show, she asked, "So what do you do?"

"I'm an animation writer and game designer," I told her, only suddenly realizing how uncool "game designer" sounded in that world. Luckily, she didn't seem to think it was uncool.

Lisa said, "We've got an animation project. Are you available?"

I figured that since I was about to be fired from *Garbage Pail Kids*, the answer was yes. In fact, by that point I'd figured out that one of the rules of being a freelancer is that the answer is *always* yes.

Lisa continued, "We're doing kid versions of the *Looney Tunes* characters."

A thought balloon opened up in my mind, and there was nothing in it. I followed with a real winner of a line. "I have to be honest. I'm not really a comedy writer."

"Yes, you are." She said it just like that. Like she instinctively knew something about me that I didn't know.

We must have exchanged phone numbers, because I got a call the next day setting up a meeting. Or maybe we did it that night. I can't remember. Somehow, a meeting was set up.

My overall impression of the meeting with Lisa was that it was something out of the *Odyssey*. It was like Telemachus meeting Athena disguised as Tiresias. In Campbell terms, it was "Woman as Goddess" signaling that childhood is over. Telemachus had to get off his butt and find his father, Odysseus, or his mother would be forced into a real bad marriage and he would be killed. I didn't face those stakes, but I did have to evolve into something else. The world I'd thrived in was dying. It was time to find a new world.

Linda's conversation with the bald executive was also ending, and we took off. When we got into the car, I asked, "So what was that all about?"

"That was Charlie Fink from Disney Animation. They want me to develop the baby versions of the Disney characters!"

"That's funny. Lisa wants me to do kid versions of the Warner characters…"

"We have the same project for different studios," Linda said.

"Well, we don't have any project, and other than Bugs and Daffy, I'm not even sure who the Warner characters are or who the Disney characters are."

The incredible thing is that for somebody who had been in the animation business, I knew as little as one could possibly know about classic animation.

"Roadrunner and Wile E. Coyote, Pepé Le Pew…" Images returned from childhood—the cartoon before the movie, the cartoons projected on the wall during naptime at summer camp, things running in the background on TVs. I'd seen a hundred of them, maybe five hundred, but never really watched them. They were just ambient background.

"Foghorn Leghorn," she said.

"Who's that?"

"You don't know Foghorn Leghorn?"

Foghorn would become my favorite Warner character.

The next few days of my life became one big bone up on Warner characters, with Gordon Kent as my professor. He had all of *Looney Tunes* on VHS and walked me through them. I could tell he was a little annoyed that I was having the meeting when he was the expert, but he never really said it or showed it, though he was right to feel that way. In a just universe, he would have been a more obvious choice.

If only he knew more about Achilles' shield, I suppose.

The one thing Lisa hadn't told me was that Warner Brothers' partner on the project was Steven Spielberg's company, Amblin. The phrase OMG didn't exist in those days, but it would have applied nicely. I couldn't believe I was going to be pitching at Steven Spielberg's company. I hadn't pitched anything anywhere since *Agent 13*, but at least I knew the drill.

I needed an idea. How do you make the Looney Tunes into a movie? What could the plot possibly be? There was no central neighborhood. They never appeared all in the same cartoon. They were clustered. Bugs, Daffy, and Porky would show up together. Tweety and Sylvester showed up together. Roadrunner and Coyote never had guest stars. Pepé Le Pew smelled, so nobody wanted to be in a cartoon with him. Foghorn had some dawg he tormented, but the dawg, unlike Foghorn, wasn't a real extrovert.

How do we bond all of these characters together?

The answer for me came from game design—specifically, my first game design lesson from Gary Gygax. *What's the dungeon? What's the resource base? What unifies them?*

In short, the question was: How do we create an ecology for *Looney Tunes?*

And it turned out the answer was obvious to any game designer: the ACME Company.

I'd already figured out that the Warner characters were about the seven deadly sins: pride, envy, wrath, sloth, avarice, gluttony, and lust. Bugs is pride, Daffy is envy (wants to be Bugs), Yosemite Sam is wrath, Foghorn Leghorn is sloth, they're all about avarice, Taz is gluttony, Pepé Le Pew is lust. Yeah, I realize all of this is up for debate.

All we had to do was create an ACME Company with resource bases in all of those areas. Today, this would be called world building (or retrofit world building), but in 1987, this was revolutionary thinking.

I just needed the hook of an idea.

Amblin was located on the lot at Universal. And if you want a thumbnail of the difference between George Lucas and Steven Spielberg, it is the location of their offices. George Lucas was a long drive deep into Marin County, past a local gas station called Miwok, named after a local tribe, and the Darth Vader rock to a compound. Okay, I don't think the rock is called Darth Vader rock, but that's what it looked like to me.

Steven Spielberg's was—and still is—a feature of the Universal Tour.

Anyway, I remember being on the 101 between Coldwater and Laurel Canyon when it hit me first as an image. What happens if Coyote actually catches Roadrunner? To me, they are the two quintessential Warner characters—this is highly debatable, of course, as most would go for Bugs and Daffy—and they're definitely the two most connected to the ACME Company. Coyote was constantly buying crap products from them that didn't work, in what I suspect was a reflection of the postwar days of "time-saving" gadgets and cars with defects and dishwashers that flooded your house and vacuum cleaners that jammed. This era was reflected in the eighties with frozen computers and hinky cable and a variety of Rube Goldberg products.

It felt relevant.

But the image was this. Coyote catches Roadrunner. Chows him down. Ecstatic.

Then something is wrong.

Confused look turns into crisis as we see a round shape coming up from his stomach to his throat. Choking, he spits it out cartoon style and realizes it is a gear with "ACME Corporation" stamped on the side.

He's puzzled.

Then he gets it.

The Roadrunner was a piece of crap from the ACME Company that was designed to get him to buy more pieces of crap from the ACME Company. And though Roadrunner doesn't talk (except in an obscure, failed series in which he's a mad genius), he might have a line. Or maybe you show it in text. Or maybe you show it as a set of cannons bombarding the ACME Company, but it all adds up to one signature Warner Brothers line: "This means war!"

Fear and nerves have blacked out the memory of my arriving at Universal, getting through the gate, being directed to Amblin parking, walking into Amblin and to the reception area.

Cathy Stewart, fresh, smiling, and charming, probably came and fetched me and led me up to Debbie Newmyer's office. Lisa was already there and just as stately, wise, and engaging as she was at the hangar. Debbie was as un-Hollywood as you could be and be at the epicenter of Hollywood. She was Steven Spielberg's director of development, Lucy Fisher's (VP at Warner Brothers) cousin, and producer Bobby Newmyer's wife. Yet the actual woman seemed like somebody who would be a really good mother, an image enhanced by the fact that she was pregnant at the time. And in a director of development, mother is a good thing, because all projects are children in more ways than one.

The BIG SURPRISE in the meeting was the arrival of Steven's story editor, Bettina Viviano. I didn't know her, but she knew me, or at least about me. She was a friend of Dave Marconi's.

Because of course she was.

Bettina got the right last name, too. She was, and still is, one of the most vivid people I've ever known. Imagine Madonna suddenly popping into the office with a crazy loud laugh, a bubbly aura, and a dangerous brilliance about her. And from the first moment, I knew Bettina was wild. There's not another word. Wild.

It turns out Marconi had given her *Agent 13*, and she loved it. So much so that she'd been thinking of us to write the next Indiana Jones movie. Of course, the actual fourth Indy film wouldn't come out for decades, but what a great thought. This was one of those moments in which everything went right. That moment when every die roll is a six, that moment when you drive through nine green lights in a row on Wilshire, or that moment when every shot rolls around the hoop endlessly and then falls through the net.

It was that moment.

They loved the idea of the gear in Coyote's mouth, which only about fifteen minutes old. But because it was so fresh, I pitched it really well.

From there, I may be conflating a couple meetings, but things happened fast. Very fast.

Something bad had to happen. I knew it. I'd get loudly fired from Garbage Pail. Somehow, I had to buy myself some time. Then the bomb dropped.

"So you worked at Lucasfilm..."

I was about to say that it didn't work out when she cut me off.

"I called them up. They loved you."

I thought, "They did? What? They fired me." Of course, I said none of those things.

I again remembered Paul Dini telling me, months after I was gone, that George had asked him, "What happened to that guy with the good ideas?" But I figured Paul was just trying to make me feel better. Maybe it was true. Maybe Debby Neumyer made it up.

After that, I just wanted to get out as quickly as I could. It was the perfect meeting, and that doesn't happen very often. In fact, I can't quite remember one that could have gone so poorly going that perfectly since...ever.

The funny thing was, later that day I stopped off to see Gordon Kent, and he said I actually hit on something that the network liked for *Garbage Pail Kids*. Suddenly, it looked like maybe I wouldn't get fired after all.

Still, I didn't care.

By late afternoon, as I was stumbling home, equilibrium had returned. In the real world, I figured it would be a long process before I'd actually get hired on *Tiny Tunes* and I should just return to life as normal.

When I got up to my office, my answering machine was blinking. I flicked it on. It played through my message, which was partly tired joke and partly premade excuse, in which I greeted people and then said, "If I don't call you back, it's because my a-an-answering machine was acting up." I slowed down and messed with my voice so it sounded like the machine was slowing to a stop. I thought it was big funny at the time. I still think it's a little funny. That joke cannot exist in the digital era.

It took me a beat to figure out who the first message was. It really did sound like my machine was malfunctioning. It was Judy Price, my boss on *Garbage Pail Kids*. The message was hard to listen to in more ways than one; Judy might have had an extra Chardonnay at lunch. "Flint...is this machine working? It's Judy Price at CBS." When somebody you've talked to almost every day for three months gives you their full name and affiliation, you don't really have to listen to the rest of the message. You're being fired. I'd learned that three years earlier with Miki Herman. The only interesting part left is how they're going to put it. "Listen. We've been thinking. It's not working out. We're going to go another way with *Garbage Pail Kids*. Give Carrie a call when you get this."

Or some such. I don't have the message, I'm reconstructing it from memory, but it was something like that.

I was fired.

I don't know whether I was sad or relieved or some combo thereof. I just had to hope word didn't get back to Amblin. I'd have to tell people about it, and that would be a little embarrassing, but nobody would really care.

I didn't have a lot of time to think about it before the machine beeped again.

"Hi, Flint, this is Steve Spielberg. I heard about your pitch, and we want to hire you for *Tiny Tunes*."

Somebody later told me that his comment was that it had taken him and Bob Zemekis a long time to figure out the ACME Company for *Who Framed Roger Rabbit?*, which was just beginning production. I had been fired by Judy Price and hired by Steven Spielberg on back-to-back messages.

I have no idea what I did next. Maybe I called my agent. Maybe I called my mother. Maybe I called Gordon or Michael Chase Walker. Maybe I called Linda. Maybe I sat down and stared at the wall wishing I hadn't quit smoking.

Who knows?

Who cares?

It didn't, and doesn't, matter.

My era of TV animation had ended and my era of movie writing had begun all in about the space of thirty seconds. An era that had begun with

Joe Ruby giving a noob a shot had ended with Steven Spielberg giving a noob a shot.

The thing I didn't know was that I would go on being a noob on almost every project for about thirty years, with a few brief moments of feeling like an experienced pro. I'd feel like a noob doing board games, then doing computer games, then directing, then working for the Intelligence Community, then for Google and Niantic and DARPA. Everybody has their own fate: mine is to be a professional noob. There are worse things to be. If you're a noob, you can't be a blown bag.

And that's where this narrative ends. But endings are never tidy. There are always threads hanging off, and there's always the question of what happened next.

Now to tie the loose ends together…

Aftermath

Master of Two Worlds

So, MY LIFE REALLY did change with two phone calls. Real life isn't as clean as fiction most of the time. Even after Judy gave me the flush, I had a couple of *Garbage Pail Kids* scripts left on my deal, and curiously, I wanted them to be great. I figured nobody would use them or care, but somehow, that felt like the best parting shot.

At that point, at TSR, we were doing early playtesting for the game that would be released as *Buck Rogers XXVC: Battle for the 25th Century* and doing the Buck Rogers bible. As I mentioned before, that development was one of the roughest experiences I ever had in the game business. It never got easy. Warren Spector and I had brutal debates, but eventually it won Mass Market Science Fiction Game of the Year at Gen Con and at DICE. More than a decade later, when Warren had gone on to stardom in the video game world, we agreed that it was probably the best thing we did at TSR.

It's hard to place exactly when the magic flight from the DDEC mansion happened, because it isn't really connected to anything else in time. The mansion had lain empty ever since the end of the Lorraine/Gary lawsuit. Maybe John Beebe was there with his wife Ingrid for a while. Maybe Matthew the caretaker and his wife Christina still tended to things, but Luke, Ernie, Gary, Gail, Donna, Penny, Peggy, and the various other guests were gone. I do remember cleaning the stuff out of my office alone, bringing my train set home—a tremendously sad moment. The sadness wasn't so much over the finality of things but foreknowledge of the ensuing loneliness.

One day, twenty years later, I was picking my son up from a playdate, and his friend happened to live almost directly across the street from the mansion. I drove my car up to the gate, which had a Do Not Enter sign on it, and looked like an establishing shot for a horror movie. Back in the day, Joe Ruby said it was the kind of place where the Mansons would have committed a mass murder. I remember thinking he had a point.

I looked over the gate, and there was nothing there. The house was gone, the stable was gone, Matthew and Christina's house was gone. I did some checking, and it turned out that some bozedorf had purchased it, torn it down, and forgotten to even leave up a chimney, and because of the strange zoning laws, that meant it couldn't be considered a remodel.

The place will never be permitted again because it is on unstable land.

There are about fifty life lessons from the DDEC experience, and maybe I'll write them all down someday, but here's the one that struck me. Except for the Sagard books with Simon & Schuster, I never got paid a dollar for any of the DDEC stuff. However, I did learn to design games and had experiences I'm writing about thirty-five years later. Truth is, I should have paid to have that experience. But the life lesson is that there's a twilight zone, somewhere after college, where it's not clear whether you should be paying to do something or paid to do it, and if you're not starving, always go for the experience over the money. That education has powered me for decades to come.

I would never really do syndicated animation again. I went to one meeting for a later revival of G.I. Joe and I passed. It wasn't because I was writing movies and felt it was behind me, I just realized that you can never go home again.

I couldn't imagine doing G.I. Joe or Transformers without Joe and Tom and Jay, though years later I'd do a couple of Transformers games and a trilogy of graphic novels with Chris Metzen and Livio Ramondelli, the latter of whom illustrated the cover of this book.

I did a couple Saturday morning things, but they were one-offs and limited engagements: *Spider-Man, Captain America and the Avengers* (with Stan Lee), and *Attack of the Killer Tomatoes*. I did the bible and pilot for a show called *The Pirates of Dark Water* and toured Toy Fair with Steven Spielberg years later. The funny thing was that I heard the soundtrack playing with lyrics and only vaguely recognized the lyrics I'd written.

I'd help Joe Ruby sell *Piggsburg Pigs!*, but I knew that wherever I was going, it wasn't back to TV animation.

There was no moment at which I decided, I'm not doing this. It was more that the path just didn't lead that way.

Over the years, I've worked with a lot of the people from that period and stayed in touch with a surprising number. I had dinner with Tom Griffin and Joe Bacal (who passed as I was writing this book) last spring, had lunch with Joe Ruby not long ago, and, on the day I'm writing this, I also emailed Joe to say that Buzz told me some guy at *New York Magazine* wanted to interview him for the fiftieth anniversary of *Scooby-Doo*.

Some people have passed on: Steve Gerber, Gordon Kent, Gordon Bressack, Peter Ledger, Len Wein, and Roger Slifer, to name a few.

I go over to Paul Dini's every year for Halloween and see him regularly and have worked with his wife, Misty, on Ingress. Cleaning out a storage locker this summer, I came upon a cynical story development we did back in the day called "Captain Trademark and his Amazing Presold Warriors." It was a send-up of the toy shows written while we were working on toy shows. We talked about dusting it off for Midnight Swim or something. It will probably never happen, because Paul's a busy guy. He's done Batman in almost every medium known to man and created Harley Quinn.

Buzz has gone on to do a lot of things, not the least of which was creating Realbuzz Studios, which published several comic books—including

Serendipity and *Goofyfoot Gurl*—and someday I hope he finds and resurrects his *Lovecraft and Howard* script.

I was thrilled to see Doug Booth for the first time in years and remet Ron Friedman at TFcon in Burbank, and I've had lunch with him a couple times since then. We worked together to get a giant $600 Unicron figure funded.

Jay Bacal, maybe the most gifted person in this story, never really wanted to pursue any of this stuff again but has been spending his time writing mobile games. They're really cool. Check them out on the iTunes store.

Linda Woolverton went on to write *Beauty and the Beast*, *The Lion King*, the Broadway adaptations of them, and *Maleficent*, among many other things. We keep trying to get together for dinner.

Dave Marconi wrote *Enemy of The State*, *Live Free or Die Hard*, and *The Foreigner*, along with numerous other things that are in various states of development. A couple of years ago, we sold *Agent 13* to Charlize Theron's company at Universal Studios. We watched from the sidelines as a couple of scripts were done, and we're now back trying to figure out what to do with it.

I reconnected with Gary Gygax after the schism created by my sister's acquisition of TSR. Eventually, he figured out that I didn't have anything to do with it and didn't know anything about the coup, and we emailed a lot and spoke on the phone now and again.

Whatever the cause, Gary and I found ourselves on email chains with Joey Thompson and various friends of his. I noticed that Gary had a quote from Matthew on the bottom of his emails.

> *"Let your light so shine before men, that they may see your good works and give glory to your Father who is in heaven."* Matthew 5:16

I asked him about this and, for the first time, found out about his religious beliefs. I'd been utterly unaware of them in the eighties. We started corresponding a lot on all sorts of different topics.

We had to be corresponding again by 2003, because after meeting Vin Diesel while recording the voice track for *Chronicles of Riddick: Escape from Butcher Bay*, Vin went on at great length about his half-elf Drow mage Melkorp, and while I associated Drows with dark elves, I didn't know exactly what they were. I pinged Gary to ask what a Drow was. Gary explained, and that led to me telling him that Vin was as hardcore a D&D player as I'd ever encountered (and after decades of exposure to TSR and gaming, that was saying a lot).

At some point, we were chatting about Roman battle tactics, and Gary mentioned in passing that Scipio used chariots in the battle of Zama, and that was the only time in Roman history that they had ever used chariots in combat. When I was reading that, I had this vision of miniature chariots on the sand table. Roman chariots weren't part of Gary's 3,000+ Elastalon miniatures collection in the shelf at the TSR creative office stable, but I made a note that in some future universe, I wanted to see Roman chariots.

A few weeks later, I was at Phoenix Pictures just off the Sony lot in Culver City. Ultra mogul Mike Medavoy, another guy whom I'd known as far back as USC and Sherwood Oaks Experimental College, was starting up Phoenix Pictures. Stuart Volkow, whom I'd met on the *Dragonstrike* set through Scott Billups, had invited me over to talk about New Media. About two minutes in, it was obvious that Mike couldn't care less about New Media. As he's one of the last standing moguls, there's no reason he should. However, he was scanning my résumé and said, "You were an ancient history major."

"Yeah."

"You know anything about Hannibal?"

"Yeah."

We talked about Hannibal for about twenty minutes, and he said, "Let me get John in here." I figured John was some development guy he was working with.

Minutes later, John Milius, my screenwriting idol, came walking into the room. OMG. It was his job to quiz me on Hannibal. We talked about the Alps and Moloch and Trebbia and Lake Trasimene and, of course, the battle masterpiece of all time, Cannae, and then finally Hannibal's defeat at the hands of Scipio Africanus at Zama.

In the course of this, I slid in: "Yeah…that was the only time that the Romans ever used chariots in combat."

Milius looked at me with something equivalent to profound respect, then turned to Mike Medavoy. "He knows his stuff."

I ended up writing a Hannibal movie for Mike and working with John. But that day, they reminisced for the first time since 1976 about *Apocalypse Now*, and I sat there smoking a cigar with them, in pure fanboy bliss. But that's another story for another time.

In 2007, I was doing a lot of work with Vin Diesel after *Butcher Bay*. I told Vin my memory of Gary telling me how D&D was created. Vin wanted to make a film of it. My story was processed through twenty years of memory and, oddly enough, a TSR video I made in 1994 called *Dragonstrike*, which was kind of my ontology recapitulates phylogeny narrativized memory of Gary's story.

In other words, the story I had was garbled myth of the real origin of D&D, which was far more complex than anything you would be likely to be able to tell in a movie (though I'd love to see a documentary about it, if any of the ones in the works are ever finished), but it boiled down, essentially, to something like the truth.

I contacted Gail Gygax in late February of 2008 and pitched her. She said I should talk to Gary right away. We set up a call for Friday afternoon. That sounded great to me. Not a huge hurry. Movies take a long time. She seemed to feel it was urgent. Gary and I talked. He sounded very weak and hazy, but once we got rolling, he was Gary. He remembered telling me the story, and we both acknowledged that I'd garbled it, but somehow in the garbling, we'd gotten to the truth of it. He was in. We talked a little, and then he said he had to get off.

It probably crossed my mind that this might be the last time I talked to him, but the denier in me figured he'd get through this and a couple more decades. It was the same kind of denied premonition I'd had with Orson Welles twenty-two years earlier. Often as not, people live a lot longer than you think they will.

On Tuesday, March 4, 2008, I got an email from Ernie Gygax saying "The Dungeon Master Had Died." I don't know if that was the last business conversation Gary ever had, but it was probably one of them.

I see Luke and Ernie at Gary Con and see Luke in LA. He taught my kids how to play Dungeon. Oddly enough, despite being a Major in the Army, he still seems like the thirteen-year-old kid I knew at the mansion. If you want to see the old world of D&D, go to Gary Con. Heidi still makes fun of me balking on the diving board at Stone Manor, and Cindy and Elise are great to hang out with.

At one point, there was talk about putting the Sagard "fight-a-path" books on the iPad, because that medium, in my opinion, is the perfect place for pick-a-path adventures. The coding would be simple, and it could trigger a whole new genre heightened by modern tech. We had an interested party, but we needed Gail Gygax's approval to proceed in an orderly way. In the end, we couldn't get a deal made, and everybody moved on.

Frank Miller went on to do *Sin City* and *300*, and as recently as this year, we were sitting in his loft trying to reconstruct a conversation from 1996 for Xerxes. As with any old great friend, decades go by, and we pick up the same conversations we were having in 1987. My daughter, Gwynna, was his PA at Comic-Con in 2014 for the release of *Sin City 2*. She's now at Rhode Island School of Design, and Frank is one of her inspirations. Great friendships do echo down the generations.

My curious relationship with Buck Rogers goes on to this day. There have been various attempts to reboot the franchise as a movie. The most promising was Tom Cruise and Jerry Bruckheimer in the nineties. Currently, I'm working with Don Murphy (producer of many things, including the *Transformers* films), and maybe a film will come from it, and maybe it will be Buck Rogers and maybe it won't.

As I write this, we're involved in an epic and labyrinthine legal battle which has, among other things, re-allied me and my sister. I probably better not say much about it, but suffice to say, I've been working on a piece... nowhere near as long as this...called CONGA LINE OF ANUSES, which is about the Buck Rogers battles.

I'd like to mention about fifty other people. Many of them are still on my Facebook page, and I feel like I'm still in touch with them and we're one phone call away from it being the eighties again. Of course, in the real world, it can't be, but I've discovered while writing this book that certain eras are wormholed or quantumly entangled with each other. All I'm doing is resonating a portal between them. If you play Ingress, you get the reference; if you don't, don't worry about it.

Like people, projects go on to have a life of their own, and many of the things I worked on in that period had a life of their own afterward.

In retrospect, the carnage of *Transformers: The Movie* taught me a lot. The film itself went on to be a real cult classic. Thirty plus years later, I've been to numerous packed screenings of it. At TFcon one year, we had a sound problem and the audience, like at a church responsive reading, filled in the missing lines. They knew it by heart. They knew it much better than I did.

I've said this before, and I'll say it one more time: Killing Optimus Prime martyred him. It made fans realize how much they loved the character. Killing Prime make our new characters look like avenging angels. It gave them purpose. It gave the franchise stakes. It wasn't all about missing rayshots. People could actually die.

At the time, we didn't realize that we were martyring them and they'd be treated like saints. The good news was that, because they're robots, we could bring them back.

In the end, it was more than a marketing strategy. It was a franchise value upgrade strategy. I honestly believe that if we hadn't killed Prime, *Transformers* would be largely forgotten now, like most of its competitors.

G.I. Joe is still going on, but it hasn't had the same post-eighties success as Transformers. It is a far more tricky property than Transformers. Giant robots from a distant planet are a completely different proposition than a real live counterterrorist squad in a world with real terrorists.

There was a moment, I suppose, after 9/11, when a bold, ballsy relaunch of G.I. Joe could have been huge, but it would have been extremely risky, too. If I were head of Hasbro in 2001, I'm not sure what I would have done. Would I have fully embraced the War on Terror and come out full force, knowing it would be controversial as hell, or would I have laid back? I don't know, and as I am not and never have been a Hasbro executive, it doesn't matter. But it is a fascinating question.

There were a couple movie reboots that had a lukewarm result, but, as I said before, to me, the real reboot for G.I. Joe was *The Expendables*. That script would have taken at least a weekend to figure out. The old Joes, played by the real-world actors who were making eighties action movies at the exact same time we were doing *Joe*, come back for one last mission using old Joe tech and defeat the modern and depraved versions of Cobra. Along the way, we get five new Joes, five new Cobras, two new vehicles, and a new playset, and the cycle starts over. And, of course, they would have been led by Marissa Fairborne.

Inhumanoids and *Visionaries* both disappeared without a trace. To me, *Visionaries* was a great self-contained piece, and if you haven't seen it, see it somehow. To many, it was the perfect capper to the eighties toy show era. To me, *Teenage Mutant Ninja Turtles* was the beginning of a new era. But that's a different discussion.

I'd love to see the Earth Corps and the Inhumanoids show up in a crossover with the Joes and/or the Transformers. Who wouldn't want to see Starscream and D'Compose duking it out (with a Chris Latta imitator doing both voices), or see Cobra Commander and Metlar duking it out for control of the Ultimate Cobra Lair at Infernak, with Hector Ramirez (played by Geraldo Rivera) covering the whole thing?

I even, for my own amusement, wrote a scene in which we discover that the Cthulhu-type monster in Lady Jaye's ancestral castle dungeon is an Inhumanoid. But this stuff will probably never happen outside of fan fiction. My suspicion is that there would be too many legal and business issues.

As I write this, Dungeons & Dragons, now owned by, amazingly enough, Hasbro, is making an incredible comeback with a generation raised on video games and extremely high-end superhero movies. D&D games are streamed on shows like *Critical Role*, and the whole category of RPGs has entered an exciting new territory.

In the past year, I've seen Luke Gygax, both at Gary Con, which is populated by the still dynamic first and second generation D&D masters, and at cutting-edge events with whole new generations of DMs hypercharged by cosplay, real staging, and tech advances. He's working with real-world dungeons and immersive actors.

D&D is more alive than ever, and I wish Gary were still around to see it. But some part of me secretly suspects that he's DMing the whole thing from the great beyond.

I've already talked about Buck Rogers, but suffice to say XXVC went on to be commercially questionable in board games, RPGs, and comics. That having been said, nary a season goes by when some fan, writer, or game designer doesn't ask me about reviving it.

Agent 13 was in active development at Universal until about a year ago and might well be in development again. I'm hoping it will be a streaming pulp action show, but that's all I can say right now. Point is, like the other projects, it never seems to go away.

Afterword

SOMETIMES YOU DON'T KNOW what an era is until after it's over. The eighties were an era when all sorts of new things were unleashed on the world. In movies, there was *Raiders of the Lost Ark*, the end of the *Star Wars* trilogy, *Aliens*, *Terminator*, *Back to the Future*, *Goonies*, *Men in Black*, *Ghostbusters*, *Total Recall*, *Top Gun*, and on and on and on.

The eighties were the age of video arcades. Chaotic quarter-eating zones of arguably the best ninety seconds of thrill ever in the entertainment industry. Video games went from *Space Invaders* to interactive text-based games to the first simulations and strategy games. There were home machines, handheld machines, and games on personal computers. They invaded living rooms and offices.

I remember showing Tom Griffin (while I was his employee) a game that came with a pull-down screen that said "boss coming" and replaced the game with a spreadsheet. Not sure if it really worked, but in a few short years, games transformed computers from a dreaded thing to a source of entertainment for loosely supervised employees.

It's not like everything dried up after the eighties, but the energy of our culture went to technology, and with some notable exceptions, we've been living in a world of sequels, spinoffs, and reboots ever since. From my perspective, once *Visionaries* was finished, Hasbro stopped investing in new IP and never did it again. Decades later, they are still benefitting from the golden eighties.

Sooner or later, we'll have assimilated the breathtaking technological advances we've made and a new era of invention will be upon us.

Acknowledgments

I DREAD WRITING ACKNOWLEDGMENTS for the obvious reason—fear of leaving somebody out. And it's impossible not to. For instance, in my first draft, I forgot my family. Very bad move. I was so conscious of remembering everybody on my Facebook page who helped that I forgot my family. So here's the dedication: This is for all of my family members, living and dead. Especially Terrie, Zane, and Gwynna.

My wife, Terrie, gets a second acknowledgment for reading through the galley and pulling out all sorts of things I needed to fix. Saying things that Ace Editor Guy Intocci probably didn't say because he didn't want to hurt my feelings. In any case, the book is a whole lot better for her efforts.

Everybody at Rare Bird: Tyson Cornell, Julia Callahan, Guy Intoci, and Hailie Johnson. And also Stu Miller and Dan Vining who made the connection, and Harriet Beck for making the connection that made the connection. We live in a very complex and connected world.

Richard Thompson gets his own special category.

All of the people who read the book to made sure I wasn't slandering them: Joe Troutman, Tom Griffin, Jay Bacal, Buzz Dixon, Luke Gygax, Ernie Gygax (who gave me thoughts despite having serious eye problems at the time), Frank Miller, Paul Dini, Linda Woolverton, and probably other people. People who let me pick their brains: Carole Weitzman and Hildy Mesnik. Once again, forgive me if I left you off. I'll make it up to you in a follow-up piece.

Of course, Chris Metzen, James Waugh, Mickey Neilson, Cameron Dayton, and the Blizzard guys who convinced me that anybody would want to read this in the first place.

And no "thanks" is ever complete without mentioning John Nee. I don't think anything ever happens anywhere if John Nee isn't involved.

And if you're mentioned in the book, consider that an acknowledgment if I forgot you here.

Then, there's everybody on Facebook who read and commented on various sections of the book as I piloted them there. I'll try to mention you by name in the next section, but forgive me if I blow it.

Some people in particular:

The Hasbro guys: Bob Prupis, Kirk Bozigian, and, most recent, Ben Montano, who I loved working with on getting Unicron kickstarted. Worthy inheritor of the tradition.

AND, of course, all of the ACTORS I love hanging with at various cons and who have great stories: Michael Bell, Gregg Berger, Dan Gilvisan, Peter Cullen, Frank Welker, Morgan Lofting...and the writers. Bryce Malek, Beth Bornstein Dunnington, Christy Marx, Marv Wolfman, Meg McLaughlin. Of course, Doug Booth, bigtime. Other marvel people: The Graz's. Barbara Ferro. Jim Duffy. You know who you are, you're all over the book, and it's been great to get to know Ron Friedman.

The Hollywood Guerrillas: Michael Charles Hill, Scott Buttfield, Tony Cinciripini, Bill Winter.

And desparing of categories because some people cross so many: Carol Monroe, Charles Adam Davis, Charles A. Emanuele, Charles Lippencott, Christopher Joshua Arndt, Cindy Gygax, Cliff Bleszinski, Colin Douglas, Cullen W. Pittman, Dan Arey, Dan Dubno, Dan Durbin, Dan Vining, Deb Newmayer, Derryl DePriest, Dick Melkorp Riddick (who liked hearing these stories), Don Glut, Donna Feldon, Donna Yukavitch, Doug Niles, Elise Goyette, Elise Gygax-Cousino, Frank Mentzer, The Villain in High Noon, Fredda Rose, Gail Carpenter Gygax, Geoff Long, Gregg Berger, Harold Johnson, Heidi Gygax, Howard Victor Chaykin, Jack Morrissey, Jacques Paul Jones (FB), Jason Brown, Jason Rueben, Jean Black, Jeff Butler, Jeff Grubb, Jim and Stephanie Graziano, Jim Atkiss, Jim Geraghty, Joe Troutman, John Barber, John Moschitta, John W. Davis, Kaoru Nishiyama, Kelly Calder-King, Kevin Norman, Kim Mohan, Kirk Bozigian, Larry Bond, Larry Elmore, Larry Hama, Larry Houston, Larry Parr, Lisa Henson,

Lorraine Williams, Margaret Loesch, Margaret Weiss, Mark Henshaw, Marv Wolfman, Mary Kirchoff, Mary Pendergast, Mathew Bradley-Tschirgi, Michael Bell, Michael Charles Hill, Michael Chase Walker, Michael Witwer, Michelle Dykstra Wybenga, Mike Dobson, Morgan Lofting, Naia Haast, Neil Ross, Pat Kilbane, Paul Davids, Paul Eiding, Penny Williams, Penny Yukavitch, Richard Thompson, Rick Giolito, Robert Hacker, Rob Fulop, Robin Enos, Ron Friedman, Rowby Goren, Saad, Keren, and Saaren Ghazi, Scott Buttfield, Scott Mednick, Scott Walker, Sean Daniels, Jason Brown, Shane Hensley, Sheryl Scarborough, Skip Press, Steve Forde, Steven Barnes, Steven Grant, Sue Blu, Sydey Iwanter, Talaria Haast Andimicael, Ted Chase, Terrence C. Briggs, Terri Gruskin-Heller, Tom Wham, Tony Alan Jackson, Tony Furguson, Tyler Bleszinski, Victoria Curtis, Victoria Shellin, Warren Spector, Zahra Dowlatabadi.

In Memoriam

- Steve Gerber
- Gary Gygax
- Roger Slifer
- Candy Montiero
- Gordon Kent
- Keith Boeski (I didn't know until later, but he urged me to actually write this book).
- Joe Bacal
- Wally Burr
- Chris Collins
- Chris Latta
- Dick Robbins
- Jack Enyart
- Lee Gunther
- Len Wein
- Peter Ledger
- Lou Scheimer
- Larry DiTillio
- Mike Cook
- David Wise
- Donna Yukavich
- And everybody else I've lost track of and didn't know they'd died.

The TSR story would have ended about half way, so a word for Lorraine and I'm happy to report that we're fighting side by side against a conga line of anuses.